Rubber Bullets

Michele,
Thank you for
teaching me the art
of real sexy!
Hope you enjoy!
Rori

RUBBER BULLETS

RONI FACIANE

Birds of a Felony Publishing

Colorado Springs

Contents

Title Page

RUBBER BULLETS

WRITTEN BY

RONI FACIANE

BIRDS OF A FELONY PUBLISHING

COLORADO

2020

Copyright Page

Birds of a Felony Publishing

5740 Carefree Circle Colorado Springs, CO 90817

ISBN: 978-1-7348161-4-3

Designed by: Derek Callahan

Editing & Consulting: Kim Palmiero

Dedication

For my children, Faythe, and Andre

My dear, and late, friend Brookie,

But most importantly,

For My Dam Self

Disclaimer

DISCLAIMER

The imagery on the front cover of this book is not meant to slander, defame, threaten, exploit, offend, or piss off anyone in the Supreme Court, U.S. Government, Earth, God, etc. It was designed only with the intent to capture the attention of the audience as it relates to the plot of the authors' story. Nothing more.

The same applies to the imagery of the back cover; the deceased girls' pictures are not meant to slander, defame, threaten, exploit, offend, or piss off any of their families or the public. I intend to honor them to be sure they aren't forgotten.

This book is a memoir. It reflects the author's present recollections of her experiences over time. Most names changed to preserve privacy, some events compressed, and some dialogue recreated. The names of shitty people are changed too. Not for fear of getting beat up but because they may sue for embarrassment long after being forgotten. Nanny nanny.

Memory has its own story to tell, but I have done my best to tell a truthful story. This work depicts actual events in the life of the author, and all persons within are real individuals; there are no composite characters and is the opinion of the author combined with a couple of years of research and a few facts.

You do not have permission, from either author or publisher, to read this book if the following applies to you. We are not responsible for the disproportionate emotions of the reader:

This book details incidents and conversations that include and are not limited to racism and sexism; however, the reader may define them. If either of these pisses you off, DO NOT READ THIS BOOK!

That said, no race, sexual orientation, culture, or ethnicity mentioned in this book has been done so with the intent to be prejudicial.

The stories told here are done so with a shame-free boldness that hopes to spark more inclusive conversations. If this still pisses you off, DO NOT READ THIS BOOK!

In this book, there are controversial topics such as, but not limited to, feminism, patriarchy, religion, sex work, abuses within the judicial system, and shitty parents. If any of these piss you off, DO NOT READ THIS BOOK!

In this book, there are even more topics that may be offensive, and we stand on our First Amendment right and invoke both the freedoms of speech and press to not give a shit how you feel about them. If this pisses you off, DO NOT READ THIS BOOK!

Table of Contents

-CONTENTS-

1.

Bullet 1

BULLET 1 – SURPRISE

GREY AREAS

"Today we are arresting Ben Blass, B-L-A-S-S. He's a little guy, only 5'7," 170 pounds, a little husky, 35-year-old and has a $100,000 case for sales of meth, possession assault with a deadly weapon. So he likes to fight and likes to sell drugs. I called him up and am having him meet us at Arby's here in Huntington Beach, he was kind of hinky at first, but I told him that the agent that met him originally, the old lady, she screwed up and forgot to get his thumbprint and photograph and I needed to have that done before I turn the file in. The agreement is to meet him here at the Arby's, and hopefully, he will show up. The bail bond company hired us to revoke his bond, so actually, technically, he's not a fugitive; his bond has been revoked by the bail bond company for false information, breach of contract, and several other things. They want him in custody right away."—Lipstick Bounty Hunters, 2013, March 18 (title) Retrieved from (link from Vimeo)

It was a standard rundown of how the beginning of a possible bail arrest begins when working as a bounty hunter, and a client has become "wayward," breaching their bail contract. Not all cases are for a failed court appearance. The uneducated assume its impossible to be re-arrested while on bail and not be a fugitive. Many people breach their contracts for late payments, bad-blood with their co-signor, or committing more crimes that create risks for the bondsman and the surety companies forcing them to return their client to jail. Blass was out on four bail bonds, four pending cases (legally creating three additional charges of crime bail crime) with three different bondsmen. It was his last bondsman that hired Staci and Laci to revoke his bond.

Everyone assumed Blass failed to pay his bondsman, but that was not what happened. Blass used a personal check on a closed bank account, not insufficient funds, to bail out and writing a personal check on a closed account—and you know damn well the account is closed—is a felony with intent.

He got out of jail for free and continued to break the law. Many, law enforcement included, do not agree with the "gray areas" bondsmen use as their right to return a person to jail. I get it. It does contribute to unnecessary chaos in the community and overcrowding in the county jails and state prisons.

The cluster fuck is maddening, but in a business where you have thousands of dollars on the line to the court as a bondsman, what would you do?

Bail is a constitutional right and a built-in necessity of our judicial system. Someone has to do the job.

* * * *

Staci notified local police of who we were, where we were, and who we were arresting. Notifying the police is a required practice for bounty hunters who don't want to go to jail, especially if there is no active warrant in the system because the bondsman is revoking the bond for a breach of contractual terms.

Then, we sat waiting for a text from the cameraman or

the decoy bail agent that Blass had arrived. My partners and I reviewed his file and discovered that not only was Blass, a meth dealer but that he also had an assault with a deadly weapon(s) charge. A warning for us to proceed with caution because it was likely there was a weapon on him. At the very least, he was going to resist and fight.

He also was affiliated with local white supremacist gangs. That made me more nervous than the possible deadly weapon. He was going to hate my ass. I worked in a men's prison years prior and understood the risks of possibly being shanked or attacked, but I knew it was a "cage fight" of sorts, and my attacker wouldn't get far. Bounty hunting was a different beast in tactics altogether.

I heard Staci mention that he might be carrying a firearm and to make sure we didn't allow him to pull it. His body language and hands were our primary focal point.

The Arby's that Blass agreed to meet us at was an old-school model that had two entrance doors, each one on opposite sides of the building. We received the text that Blass had arrived and that he didn't come alone. Staci didn't flinch and made one more adjustment adding that Laci covers Blass's wingman. I was to back up both of them, keeping my focus on Blass.

At this time in California, bounty hunters only had the rights of private citizens to make arrests, and anyone could obstruct our justice with no threat of legal consequences.

It's truly a game of "catch me if you can."

We now had our queue to make the arrest. Laci had her pepper blaster, and I had the Tippmann TPX that held seven yellow rubber bullets (training bullets for paintball beginners). Staci was going in empty-handed to be sure she could restrain him and disarm him of any weapons. We hopped out of the unmarked SUV that was parked about 20 feet from the Arby's and entered as planned. Staci would go in first through the main entrance, Laci would cover the same door, and I would cover the second door facing the concrete wall. I went along the backside of the Arby's as Laci and Staci made their way to the front side of the restaurant.

As I approached the glass door, my heart pulsated with both fear and excitement. My hand gripped tightly around the Tippmann, posted at my side. I peered through the door slowly. My timing was perfect. Staci had made contact, and Blass was already resisting. My mind raced, trying to recall every tactic I had ever learned as each millisecond moved by in what seemed like frames of a movie.

Putting his hands up, Blass stepped away from Staci as she tried to apply her cuffs. I quickly assessed his body language and was positive he was willing to hurt her and anyone else who got in his way. I was more concerned at this point if he did have a weapon on him, and I didn't do something, not only could we get our asses kicked but killed.

Blass may have been expecting bounty hunters, but he wasn't expecting women in pink gear and was caught off-guard. Using this to my advantage, I ran in and pointed my Tippmann at him, hoping another woman would distract him long enough for Staci to finish effecting the arrest. He paused for a moment until he realized that my weapon was a paintball air gun and then continued towards me. My partners ordered me to stay and cover my door to keep him from fleeing, but when Blass and my eyes met, I saw a familiar look. It was a look I saw many times working at the prison, a hybrid of desperation and contempt. His threat glared at me, "I am going through that door even if I have to put you through it."

Second-by-millisecond decision-making is no joke people. I am in a restaurant, with patrons trying to eat peacefully, where shooting rubber bullets could bounce off Blass, myself, my partners, the walls, a hot roast beef sandwich, etc., endangering everyone. Not to mention how many civil cases I could stack up with this one case alone.

What the fuck do I do? I had to let him pass by me through the door. I'm 5-foot, 1.5-inches, 128 pounds. Blass would have put me through that glass door with minimal effort.

Laci shot her Taser, but it didn't penetrate him. Staci still had a death grip on his shirt and was not about to let go as he ran out the door onto the outside patio of the restaurant dragging her behind him. Like bull riding but with people. I'm convinced he was so high on narcotics and pumped with adrenaline nothing, but live ammunition was going to stop him.

Allowing him to get outside, I created enough distance to keep anyone from being hurt, and we could get his ass with as much force necessary to effect the arrest. As we ran through the picnic benches, I remembered that our agent and possibly other patrons could be sitting around and still wasn't clear to shoot at him. I could hear Staci screaming for Laci, who I didn't know at the time was fighting off Blass's wingman. Blass is screaming, "bitch get off me!"

Within the same millisecond, I felt my feet hit the asphalt of the parking lot. Blass turned to strike Staci, and while running, I raised my Tippmann aimed center mass and fired all seven shots at him as though I had been doing it for years. Simultaneously, Laci shot both pepper balls from her Kimber pepper blaster at him, hitting him in his face.

Blass flayed around like a bird hit in midair while trying to keep flight. Staci lost her grip and rolled to the ground. I panicked. Even though he was running away, I still had to stop him, but it isn't instinctive, or even logical, to pursue an attacker who hasn't officially attacked you yet. Out of bullets, no pepper spray, no Taser, one of my partners was on the ground, and the other in a fight of her own.

Running after Blass, I had no idea what I was going to do next. I watched him fall towards the ground next to the driver's side of his car while trying to open it at the same time. It must be locked.

Hitting him with my empty Tippmann could be perceived as an assault because I was not in a defensive position. The only difference would be a hearing in criminal court, not a civil one. I could trip and get on top of him, but what if he has a gun? All he has to do is pull it, shoot, and I am dead.

The echo of Alonzo's voice from"Training Day" (Fuqua, Silver & Newmyer, 2001) rang in my head, "you wanna go to jail or go home?"

My only real option was to get close enough to trip or push him up against the car while simultaneously grabbing his arm, not giving him enough time and distance to grab a weapon. As soon as I kicked my leg out to trip him kicking him in his shin, I noticed in my right peripheral there was two men in his car, one in the driver's seat and one in the backseat—FUCKING SHIT!!!

Thankfully, due to my indecisiveness, I hadn't dropped my Tippmann, and because they weren't sure whether it was empty, they stayed in the car.

Blass made his way around to the passenger side with me right behind him, still unsure what the fuck to do. Laci came from behind the car as Blass got in, now frantically slamming the door and forcefully grabbed the handle to pull it open for one last attempt to get him. I saw Blass's face covered in red pepper spray, his eyes bulging in fear and confusion, pleading for us to stop. He grabbed the door like we were violating him, screamed, and slammed it shut.

The driver darted out of the parking lot, fleeing from the scene, and almost ran over Laci. We gathered each other up and saw there was another car parked in front of the restaurant with two women in it that fit the description of Blass's girlfriend and pulling out to leave also. We hurried to the SUV to try and catch up to them, and Laci realized she had pepper spray in her eye. She kept her eyes closed and rocked back and forth.

"Only time makes it go away, I'LL BE FINE!" she reminded me, screaming and annoyed with pain.

Laci was always so laid back, and this was the first time I witnessed her pissed. It would have been worth it if Blass was cuffed in the backseat equally suffering in her pain.

As we exited the restaurant to the main street, another truck came in to stop us, vehicle number three, and help Blass escape. It was successful. We were too far behind once we were on the freeway and eventually lost them in the oncoming 5 p.m. Orange County traffic.

Staci took a detour to meet with the decoy agent to be sure she was safe, finding Blass would have to wait. The phone rang. It was the police dispatch checking on us. Someone called the police and said we were in trouble and needed assistance.

"That's funny. We kicked Blass's ass, and people thought we were the ones that were hurt?" I said as we all chuckled to avoid our current state of hysteria. Staci informed the dispatcher we were safe and no longer at the restaurant but that our wayward client resisted and escaped the arrest even after using force. We may have prevailed by kicking his ass, but it wasn't funny by any means. I'm positive had we been men with live ammunition they would have shot and killed us.

My clothes reeked with pepper spray. I went home to stand in a hot shower and scrub the defeat off me and quickly learned that pepper spray and all of its burn, can be reactivated for another fucking five hours!

* * * *

"You're not going to believe this," Staci said anxiously.

"Probably not," I groaned, still feeling hungover and sore.

We were out every night since looking for Blass, and by this time, he had seen the video. He and his crew had posted many demanding requests along with threats to remove the video. Staci and Laci refused. If they had taken down that video, they would have to take down all of them. They were former LAPD and didn't give a shit about idle threats.

"I just got a call from 'Inside Edition (CBS Television Distribution, 1989)' that Blass has a personal injury attorney now and is filing a lawsuit against all three of us for excessive force and violation of his civil rights. They want an interview for their next show. What's a good day and time for you?" Staci rambled without taking a breath. I couldn't tell if she was upset or not.

My heart skipped two beats. Lawsuit? TV interviews? What the hell!

"Uh, I guess whenever you decide," I said, shocked and now scared out of my mind.

After judging countless others who wound up in these "situations" in the industry and here I was, hypocritically in more shit than any of them had stepped in. Hello, karma!

"Don't be scared, you did your job, Roni. What matters is that you made every attempt to effect the arrest and only fired your weapon when Blass started to swing his arms to strike me. He still managed to get away. That is not excessive force, and we did our job," Staci said with confidence and kindness. There were very few moments she gave genuine praise.

"Here I am holding on for dear life, not knowing if this fucker is going to shoot me, and I fall flat on my ass. But when I looked up and saw you going after him, I was so happy and proud of you, Roni! You were there when I needed you to cover my ass, don't feel bad—fuck them!" she continued.

She finished up her pep talk with instructions to email her my schedule to coordinate the interview. No matter how much we discussed it and I ran it over in my mind detail by detail, I still couldn't shake the idea that I had the media to answer to now and possibly, at some point, a judge in civil court.

The film crew from the network was set to arrive at 4 p.m. but arrived early to set up their equipment and arrange the office for this scandalous story they were about to tell everyone first. My head was spinning. My main focus was not looking fat or guilty. It didn't matter that this wasn't court and that I wasn't going to go to jail, everyone knows a camera carries a system of justice all of its own that can create a jury of millions.

It was the first time I was interrogated, my actions called for questioning, but not by a police officer or detective or even an attorney, but a reporter.

"Why would you ladies be in this line of work?"

"Do you have children?"

"Aren't you scared you will be hurt or killed?"

"How can you risk orphaning your children?"

"What made you want to do such a dangerous job when there are other jobs out there?"

"What do your husbands think of you doing this for a living?"

"Do you think you used excessive force?"

Question after question, I listened to myself answer with confidence and efficiency, but once the interview was over, I obsessed over each one of my answers. The one question I never answered confidently was, why? Why did I choose this profession? Why the hell would I put myself in danger when I had a career and job opportunities? Why would I risk orphaning my children and losing a marriage?

I mean, why the fuck would anyone do this job?

"Perhaps we tend to think that what is kept quiet must be veiled because it is in some way shameful or pitiful, but the secret self I am interested in here probably stays secret for more interesting reasons. We are not very good at finding the right words to convey certain impressions. -—John Armstrong, *Conditions of Love*, 2002.

BE GRATEFUL–YOUR DAUGHTER IS ALIVE

"Oh hell no!" the police woman's voice, now a pitch higher, screeched when I pulled back my daughter's underwear and revealed the layers of bruises that covered her 2-year-old bottom. She touched my daughter's head and saw the bruising on the back of one of her ears. She stood back to get a full view and examine my daughter as both cop and mother. Almost every inch of my little girl's toddler body had been beaten and tortured in some way.

"I'm calling this in and will have an investigator here as soon as possible. They aren't going to get away with this. What exactly happened?"

I started explaining how the father of my child and his wife had been harassing me for two years over custody and visitation. We had had a nasty court case that had gone on for most of my daughter's life, and I had just picked her up from her father's after a six-week court-ordered summer visitation. Completely unaware of the bruises when I picked her up. Her father lived almost an hour away from me, and I drove round trip to pick her up and bring her home.

A couple of days before picking her up, her father and his wife, Toni, told me my daughter had been defiant during visitation, and they had to "discipline" her.

As I explained, I realized they were planting information to start covering their tracks to conceal the abuse. My son and I picked her up, and while driving home, she told us her father had spanked her. She was very articulate for a two-year-old and had just entered the defiant terrible-twos phase before going to visit them. At first, I didn't take her seriously and confused it for toddler tattle-telling. I rarely spanked her and assumed she was trying to get her father, Tyrone, in trouble. That sting will never go away.

When we arrived home, and I watched her trot in the house, I noticed whip marks on her little legs.

Once she was in her room and settled with her favorite cartoon, I called her father and demanded he tells me what happened.

"Where did Faythe get all these bruises?" I screeched.

"She fell," he stuttered.

My hands were shaking. Every part of me was revving up to jump in my car and commit a double homicide.

"Are you sure that's what happened?" I asked as a last-ditch effort to get him to confess before calling the police.

"Yes, I'm sure," he said, again stuttering.

There was nothing left to say; I had to be calm and calculated now. As I hung up the phone, I remembered the somber look on Tyrone's face when I picked my daughter up. I mistook it for his sadness that his daughter was leaving. I never thought it could have been his guilt for hating me so much that he allowed himself and his wife to beat our daughter.

"What race is he? And her?" the policewoman asked.

"Black, they are both black," I told her.

"And you are?" she asked.

"I'm Mexican and white," I answered, sobbing and holding my daughter, who was now sunken into my lap.

If only I could put her back in my womb to comfort her and keep her safe.

"You said you brought her home, do they live locally?" she asked while swiftly making notes for her report.

"No, they live in Moreno Valley, Riverside County," I answered. A strange calmness started to come over me. It felt homicidal without the maniac.

"And you said you have a court order, and you just picked her up before calling us, correct?" her face saddened as she wrote.

"Yes, that is correct," I answered, rocking my daughter.

"OK, I'm going to my car to write a report and make a few calls. This investigation will take a couple of hours, but I am going to have an investigator here shortly. I have a little girl your daughter's age, and I can't imagine what you are going through right now, but hold her tight and push through with as much strength as you can. This case will take time, but they will be held responsible for what they did to your baby. I will be back once I have contacted the investigator." She said, trying to comfort me before leaving.

When she stepped out of the house, I laid on my bed, holding my daughter, resisting the urge to get in my car and drive to kill these two people. But even in my fantasies, I knew the law. There was no way I could justify driving over an hour away, commit a triple murder, his wife was pregnant, and claim temporary insanity.

I wanted to avenge my child, and being present in her life every day to help her heal was the only way to do so. Comforting her and prosecuting her attackers through the court was my only option unless I wanted to go to prison.

The judicial system can only do so much to protect the victims. The "accused" have rights also and, in many cases, it seems, more than the victim. Had I chosen to lash out violently, child protective services would classify my daughter unsafe in my care too. I wasn't going to lose her to his family, or some other family, because I couldn't control my rage.

The policewoman fulfilled her promise. She sat in my parking lot for two hours, awaiting the arrival of CPS. She didn't call the local agency, but the main office in Riverside County located more than an hour away. Since the crime took place in a different city, she wanted to be sure everyone who investigated and collected evidence had jurisdiction to solidify the case.

When the agents arrived from CPS, I could see it in their eyes that they prepared to take my daughter from me if they saw or felt that she was unsafe or uncomfortable. For all they knew, I put those bruises on her.

They took pictures of her bruised body and asked her a

few questions before deciding that she was in a safe environment. They told me they would be filing charges to remove custody from her father.

Shortly after they left, another investigator arrived and interviewed us again and also took pictures. When he finished his interview and started to go, the policewoman came back to give me her card and case report information.

"You stay strong through this. I know you have some law enforcement background and understand it will take time. Your baby is safe now and blessed to have you fighting for her." She patted me on my back and hurried out the door.

I held my daughter sobbing all night and promised myself I wouldn't lose my shit again until I had them in cuffs.

The next day, and every day after, I called every number I had to start the process for filing charges and removing custody. The last investigator who interviewed us told me to keep quiet about the case while the necessary departments collected evidence to file charges against them. They didn't want the two corroborating a story.

Her father, Tyrone, and his wife, Toni, still had no idea what I was doing, but they were starting to become suspicious. Toni called a few days after my daughter returned home.

"Hi Roni," she said with a blatant higher pitch in her voice, trying to disguise the sound of her fear.

My spidey senses told me that they had expected the police to show up the night I picked her up, and since they hadn't, she was fishing for information.

"Yes." My tone sharp and short. She paused, unsure of how to respond. Her being a decade younger, I think she assumed

I'd do what most women her age would do and beat her ass, but she wasn't getting off that easy.

"Tyrone wanted me to call and check on you guys since we haven't heard from you in a few days." Her voice shook like a rookie used car salesman.

"Don't you or Tyrone ever call my house to contact my daughter or me again. You got that?" I said and hung up the phone. If there ever was a time, I missed the old-school phones that left one deaf from a hang-up it was now. My heart raced, and I was proud of myself for not leaking the investigation or using one cuss word.

My daughter heard me from the other room and ran to my chair with a shocked look on her face.

"Mama, who was that?" she asked, concerned.

"That was Toni, baby, and I told her that she and your dad are never to contact us again."

She smiled a big smile as though I had put on a cape right in front of her. I saw a wave of confidence fall over her little face knowing her attackers now feared her mother.

* * * *

"You need to be grateful your daughter is alive, Ms. Faciane. I have two cases where the children died," I could hear the CPS worker holding back her tears while putting me in my place.

Two weeks passed without her returning any of my calls. She could hear and understood my frustration but had to check me. "Eighty-five percent of our child abuse cases are like yours where a step-parent or significant other is the abuser and also the killer. Your daughter is with you and safe; please be patient while we are processing your case. I promise you they will have their day in court." Her final plea for me to control my emotions.

I held back my tears and swallowed my self-pity. The CPS worker then gave me the go-ahead to file the ex-parte hearing, (an emergency 24-hour hearing), to get full custody pending the investigation. I thanked her for her time and hung up.

Holding my daughter was all I could do to ease my pain and accept the CPS worker's words. "Be grateful your daughter is alive, that woman could have killed her."

My rage brewed, knowing that Toni more than likely did try to kill her, and I couldn't use my hands to seek vengeance, giving me no choice but to be rational and tactical.

The next day I filed the ex parte. I couldn't wait for the clerk to stamp the copies making the hearing official so I could finally call and drop the bomb on these two. Tyrone answered as if he had been waiting for my number on his caller ID.

"Tomorrow we have court at 9 a.m." I didn't give him a chance to speak. "And I advise that you be present, but if not, it doesn't matter." Then I hung up on him too.

The next day we all arrived at the courthouse as we had for the last couple of years. They both wore smirks to mock the validity of my case. It took everything I had not to assault them right there.

The court came to order, and the judge called our case. He quickly skimmed over all the documents before addressing us.

This judge knew our case well. I could never read his face before, or even after this hearing, but this time he seemed a little remorseful for granting custody to Tyrone in the first place.

"Are these all the documents? And are the contents true and fact to the best of your knowledge?" the judge asked me.

"Yes, sir," I confirmed.

"The ex-parte request granted," he said, before reading off the conditions of the temporary restraining order now placed on Tyrone. He was not to come near my daughter and me until the next hearing.

Over the next few days, I had to take her to the district attorney's office to give her statement on video as evidence. When the interview was over, the interviewer came and told me, "It was a little difficult because she is so young, but she was articulate enough that I think it will be a success if we need it in court." She thanked me for coming in and walked back to her desk.

The detective who was also part of the interview for the Riverside County Sheriff's Department, came over and introduced himself and handed me his card. He informed me that he had been in contact with Tyrone but that both he and Toni were avoiding giving him their statement.

"How long do you think this will all take?" I asked, frustrated.

"It's hard to answer that ma'am. Do you see all the kids in this waiting area? They are all here for the same reason as your daughter, and me committing to a time-frame would only create more stress for you. But call me anytime, and I will do all that I can." His words intended to comfort me. I respected his honesty.

The Detective shook my hand and proceeded to the next family.

The last crucial piece of evidence was a medical exam from a doctor who specialized in abuse cases for the county. After arriving at his office a week after the first interview, he took us in a room with two couches pushed together in an 'L' shape with toys. It didn't have a window and felt like a room one of the "Ghostbusters" (Reitman, 1989) assembled for research. The doctor sat on one couch and I on the other while my daughter played with the toys. He asked questions, but mostly he observed us.

"The stepmother will abuse her again. She has a hatred for you and your daughter because of your effect on her marriage. I'm recommending the court to remove custody from her father to restricted visitation, and the stepmother is not to have any contact."

Yes! I wanted to high-five him. His report using those specific words were the slam dunk I needed in my case.

"I'm going to have her blood drawn to be sure there are no internal injuries. I'm pretty sure there aren't any, but with the types of bruises she had and the frequency of the abuse, we need to be sure."

More pain my daughter would have to endure to prove that she was a victim. Being hit hard enough to leave marks on her legs, thighs, arms, and even her tiny toddler hands weren't enough.

Toni was vicious and left hand-shaped bruises all over my baby's bottom and injured one ear from hitting her on the side of the head. Now she had to endure needles in her tiny veins. I was living a fucking nightmare.

Fortunately, her tests came back negative for internal injuries.

The next few weeks would be crucial. I would have to appear in my city's local court a few more times to gain full custody. The criminal case was also ongoing but being handled by the district attorney in Riverside County.

THE BOOGEYMAN DID IT

Four months later, we scheduled to meet with the mediator before the hearing finalizing my request for full custody. It was my first opportunity to confront them since this all began. Both of them had successfully avoided their arrest warrants, and I was anxious to get to the courthouse to ask a deputy to arrest them before mediation. My vengeance was to have them cuffed and taken to jail in the very courthouse they mocked us in. It was the only move I had left.

"Ma'am, we dispatched a deputy to the courtroom for you, please go upstairs to meet him." One of the older deputies told me while pointing me towards the upstairs.

Walking up the stairs to the Family Courtroom, I felt like my old self. I had always come to this courthouse as a mom and a defendant, but today I went as the law looking to dispense justice. Rolling my shoulders back, I took each step, confident that this day would be their day of reckoning.

Once I was at the courtroom doors, a deputy approached me—a handsome black man who wore the hell out of his uniform.

"Good morning, ma'am, I'm Deputy Williams. I understand you need to have a warrant checked?" He smiled with his pen and notepad out, ready to assist me.

"Yes, I do. I was told by the detective in Riverside that both warrants for Tyrone and Toni Jones we're now in the warrant bank, which caused the delay in their arrest. They are to appear here today for our last mediation hearing, and I want them arrested."

He wrote all their information down and excused himself to verify the warrants.

A warrant bank is a central cluster-fucked system where all warrants are inputted for law enforcement, in and out of state, to look up and confirm before making an arrest. At this time in 2008, if it wasn't in the bank, law enforcement couldn't confirm it, nor make the arrest.

As the deputy walked towards the courtroom, I saw Tyrone walking up the steps towards the mediation office where I was, and only his parents were with him. He and his father did not make eye contact with me, but his stepmother did. Her eyes were almost pleading with a look torn in emotion. Tyrone knew his arrest was inevitable and brought them to bail him out.

The deputy came out of the courtroom, appearing disappointed.

"Mrs. Faciane, can you come over here for a moment?" he asked, walking me to another corner of the waiting area where no one could hear us.

"It's Ms. Faciane, deputy." I smiled as I followed him. I wasn't flirting, but if a little smile helped push Tyrone's arrest, so be it.

Don't judge me.

"The warrant is still not showing in the bank, and we can't arrest him at this time," he said empathetically.

"What? I called yesterday afternoon, and Riverside County assured me it was in there. This man and his wife are going to get away with abusing and almost killing my daughter. It's such bullshit!" I stomped like a child. It was the only physical response I was allowed.

It wasn't easy, but I resisted the urge to walk over and punch Tyrone right in his fucking face. After months of trying to have these two arrested, this warrant bank had saved them every time.

"I apologize, sir, I'm just pissed," I said, frustrated as I gathered my paperwork.

"Faciane and Wilson," the secretary called us in the office for our appointment.

"I have to go. Thank you for your help." I shook the deputy's hand and left to check in with the mediator's office.

We had the same mediator for two years, and like the rest of the family courtroom staff, he now knew us by name. We all tried to be civil and polite with the appropriate societal greetings regardless of the strangling tension that followed us in the room.

Once we sat down, the mediator began reading the documents in our file, sitting by itself in the middle of his desk. Symbolic of his focus on the new details to our case. He was an attractive black man in his mid-forties and a big supporter of the family unit, which I respected. I could see it in his face that he didn't want to accept what he was reading was true. He too misjudged Tyrone.

It was silent, like sitting in the principal's office waiting for the lecture before calling your parents.

He began to ask me questions about the CPS reports and the steps they took in their investigation.

"It doesn't make any sense why they didn't contact Tyrone?" he said, almost defending Tyrone and not my daughter.

Tyrone shouted, "Exactly! Why wasn't I contacted? They did it wrong, and it's all a lie," his voice started to get louder.

"A lie? All those bruises on our daughter is a fucking lie?" I screamed back at him.

I had held my composure long enough. The mediator dropped his head, realizing he just instigated our possible violence in his office.

"Where did the bruises come from?" the mediator asked, looking at Tyrone trying to regain control of the conversation while giving me a moment to breathe.

"I don't know. Maybe a ghost or the boogeyman gave them to her!" Tyrone demanded without a hint of sarcasm. He was frightfully serious.

The mediator and I both looked at each other, stunned, watching the words floating in a bubble over Tyrone's head.

Seeing him for who and what he was at this moment, it was clear that he could never be trusted to protect any child, let alone mine. He showed no empathy.

This man and I were strangers. We met the weekend before the fourth of July in 2004. Recently heartbroken and on the rebound, some friends took me out to a club to cheer me up. Tyrone was a Will Smith look-a-like underneath the club lights, and though I wasn't looking to meet anyone, he was the perfect cure for my bruised ego.

We exchanged numbers and spent a couple of days talking on the phone, getting to know each other. Tyrone was a couple of years younger than me with no children. After dinner and sex, we didn't see each other again for weeks, and when we did talk, he made his intentions crystal clear.

"I only see myself settling down with a black woman and having black kids," he bluntly told me during a conversation a couple of weeks later. He hadn't called much, and I returned the gesture. I was stunned by his boldness but also respected his honesty.

I'm pretty sure I asked him about our future together, and that's how he answered me. He wasn't the first black man to remind me that I wasn't fit for the race, just the first to admit it to my face.

Less then a month later, I discovered I was pregnant. Not only was I torn whether I should go through with the pregnancy, but if I should say anything to Tyrone at all. I was twenty-nine, beginning a career in real estate with a ten-year-old son and no desire to have more children.

Though I couldn't deny that the thought of having a daughter was tempting, I didn't want to be married no matter how Christian I tried to be. Being a single mother was hard, but juggling a partnership and motherhood required too much sacrifice of myself.

When she was born, I waited about a month before letting him see her. We had no idea how to act towards one another, let alone tackle the task of co-parenting.

We tried to live together and be a family after she turned one year old, but I couldn't forget, or forgive, his comment about wanting a "pureblood" family and play house with him because we had a baby together.

We didn't last six months. When I didn't stalk Tyrone or allow him to use my daughter to hurt me, he decided to take me to court.

Our first hearing was a proud day for me. When the judge

asked the child support attorney appointed to me what type of case she was presenting, she responded, "Your honor this is a non-assistance, non-support case." For those who don't know what that means, I wasn't receiving child support or welfare payments.

The judge looked at us both in with surprise. He looked over at Tyrone with the same look as the detective in "Menace to Society" (Scott & Hughes, 1993), except he was white and wore glasses. If he could, I know he would have asked him, "you know you fucked up, right?" Tyrone had his attention.

"What order would you like for me to set in regards to this case counselor?" The judge smirked now, looking at my attorney and me.

"Your honor, I would like for you to order Ms. Faciane to go directly to the Child Support Office after this hearing and open a case for support and visitation."

She sounded like she was trying to keep from laughing. The judge made his order, as she requested.

"Ms. Faciane, you are ordered to go directly to the Child Support Office and open up a case for support, and set a hearing for visitation." He said sternly. I nodded, and he dismissed us. When leaving to do as the judge ordered, Tyrone chased me through the courthouse, screaming my name, trying to stop me.

His original intentions, with the assistance of Toni, were to take my daughter from me to avoid paying support child support. In the end, he owed me $7,200 in back support.

After fighting for two years in court, the one left with the scars of our war was our daughter.

* * * *

Tyrone stared at me while slumping in his chair as he dismissed the severity of the situation. I was unsure at that moment which one of us was the unfit parent, him for being a neglectful spiteful piece of shit, or me for being the dumb-ass who had a baby by him.

Before I knew it, we were arguing loudly, and the mediator, now to trying to keep us calm, couldn't shut us up. I started to cry and yelled even louder to keep from assaulting both of them.

"Guys, if you don't calm down, the secretary is going to call a Deputy to come in here and end the session!" the mediator's tone now stern.

Just as he ended his sentence, there was a knock at the door. That same handsome Deputy who took my information, now my hero, and his partner, opened the door and came in the office.

"Sir, can you step outside for a moment?" the deputy asked, staring at Tyrone.

The mediators' head dropped in shame.

"Uuuugh," Tyrone groaned as he stomped to the door like a child.

"Turn around and put your hands behind your back. There is a warrant for your arrest, and the judge has asked we take you into custody now."

Still trying to recover from my hysteria, it was almost impossible to downshift fast enough to bask in the glory of my moment.

Once the cuffs were on Tyrone, he had one last ignorant

statement to make before hauled off to be accountable "This is because I'm black, huh?!"

The mediator closed his eyes and couldn't even move to respond. We were both thinking the same thing. The cop was black, the mediator was black, and Obama was our newly elected President.

No baby, this isn't because you're black.

Still sitting in my chair unable to move, I should have been happy. I brought my daughter's assailants to justice, mission accomplished, but it changed nothing. Tears streamed down my face, and I allowed myself to cry finally.

"Are you all right, Ms. Faciane?" The mediator asked, standing against his desk in shock that an arrest had taken place.

"I-I-I had to have him arrested," I stuttered and sobbed. "I tried everything to keep all of this from happening, but I could not let them get away with this," I told him, looking for absolution.

"The reason CPS didn't make contact was to build their case and collect enough evidence first." I frantically explained. He swallowed with the emotion of regret for pushing us to fight because of his misunderstanding.

"We will schedule this mediation for another time to set the final custody hearing. I can't ethically discuss anything further without Tyrone here. I apologize, Ms. Faciane."

He walked me to the front of the office and asked the secretary to schedule me for another appointment a couple of weeks out.

"Did the officer confirm the warrant with the judge to arrest Mr. Jones?" I asked the secretary.

"No, he came in personally and called the Riverside County DA's office. They pulled the physical copy of the court order for his arrest, the deputy confirmed it with the judge and came in to arrest Mr. Jones."

If it wasn't for that deputy going above and beyond, I don't think Tyrone would have ever been arrested and forced to face the consequences of what he had done to our daughter.

I never saw that deputy again to thank him. Whoever you are and are reading this—thank you!

KETCHUP AND EGGS

My daughter was having a play date with a friend of mine while I was busy with the court, and I met them for what was now brunch. We sat and had coffee while I gave her the details of the mediation hearing, and the kids colored their menus.

"I can't believe she didn't show up today of all days," my friend said, also frustrated that justice had only half prevailed. Neither of us could grasp how Toni could hate me to the point of almost killing my child. I hadn't played "baby mama" games with Tyrone, nor did I try to win him back. I didn't break any girl codes or rules, and still, she punished me as if I had.

The waitress made her way over with our plates. I couldn't wait to drown my sorrows in some biscuits and gravy.

"Can I have ketchup for my eggs?" my friend's son asked her. As I watched him slop ketchup all over his eggs, the stench of it made my stomach churn.

* * * *

Growing up on a military base, structure, and discipline was the standard. There were consequences and repercussions if not kept in the highest regard with no room for error or excuses. The wives and children also had to be hard and sometimes even harder than the soldiers. I don't recall my father having many friends who frequented our home, but my mother had various women that she would invite over to hang out with from time to time.

While stationed in Fort Carson, Colorado, in the early 1980s, my mother had two friends who were both German and also military wives. Gretchen's husband, also German, was stationed in Germany, getting their home settled before sending for her. Sunshine and her husband, who was black, were stationed in Fort Carson. Gretchen would sometimes watch me while my parents were at work.

Early one morning, I got ready for school, put on my favorite Winnie the Pooh dress, and sat at the kitchen table eating eggs with ketchup watching cartoons. I was about six years old. It was still dark outside and cold. The living room lights were on, and Gretchen was asleep on our pull-out couch in the living room. I hurried to eat my eggs and get in more TV time before school when there was a knock at the door. When my mom answered, she barely opened it to shield the cold from coming in, but when she saw it was Sunshine, she let her inside. Sunshine stepped halfway in the door and looked at Gretchen, asleep on the couch. Mom hurried her inside to shut the door.

She thought they were all going shopping that day and found it odd Sunshine arrived so early in the morning but was distracted with getting me ready. She told Sunshine she would be a few minutes and to have a seat in the recliner to wait for her. Sunshine had been over enough times that mom felt comfortable leaving her to wait while I finished breakfast. Once she stepped away, Sunshine sat next to Gretchen on the sofa bed.

Being a nosey kid, I curiously watched my mother's friends instead of my cartoons.

Sunshine leaned down to speak with Gretchen, holding papers in her hand. She tapped her arm politely at first to wake her, but quickly escalated to grabbing and shaking Gretchen's shoulders, without caring how rudely she was behaving in our home. The talking turned to full-on screaming in German. Sunshine grabbed Gretchen by her hair and pulled her off the bed, then commenced to beating her ass all over our living room.

My mother didn't jump in to save her. All I remember is my mom's voice shouting at me, "turn around and eat your eggs!!"

How could anyone at any age NOT watch a bloodsport match live and in their living room? As she shouted, I noticed that the babysitter was bleeding, and her blood splattered on the wall.

"I'm not eating these dam eggs, mama!?" was the only rational thought I could have at six years old. And I didn't eat them I kept watching. I don't remember how the fight ended, but Sunshine left, and Gretchen sobbed as she collected her things. Somehow, I made it to school, and when I got back home later that day, Gretchen was gone, and I never saw her again. My mother never shared the gossip of this fight until I was older.

Gretchen was cheating with Sunshine's husband and had written love letters to him expressing her love and wish for them both to leave their spouses and be together. Sunshine found the letters.

I never asked my mother why she didn't stop them because as I grew older, her reason was instinctive. You don't break girl code. You don't play in another woman's kitty box, especially if she is your friend.

I still hate the smell of ketchup.

THE JUST-IS SYSTEM

We finished eating, hugged, and I collected my daughter to go home and get prepared for the next hearing now rescheduled for a couple of weeks out. My life had become consumed with this case forcing me to stay completely focused on my moment-to-moment tasks. Toni had successfully evaded her arrest that day during mediation, but within a couple of weeks, she too was booked and bailed out on charges for corporate injury on a child. Her arrest didn't relieve me of my anger or pain either.

Keeping my daughter distracted with a fuller life, I enrolled her in preschool. We stayed as busy as we could to keep us both from becoming depressed. Left to deal with our post-traumatic damage alone, I had become their victim too. Some nights my daughter wouldn't get off the bed because her Toni told her alligators were hiding underneath it. She woke up screaming, petrified several times. All I could do was swallow my fury and comfort her in hopes enough time would pass for her to heal and forget most of what happened.

At our last hearing, the judge awarded me full custody. Tyrone was ordered three hours of visitation every other Saturday and was not allowed to take our daughter around his wife and could not leave the city we lived in while she was in his care. The criminal case was also wrapping up. Their initial "not guilty" plea fell apart with the irrefutable evidence the district attorney had stacked against them.

"They were both found guilty," the District Attorney told me proudly.

They initially had felony charges for 'corporal injury on a child' and 'child endangerment,' but when they pled guilty, both charges dropped to a misdemeanor. Their sentence was 30 days of house arrest and probation.

I was livid.

"They are guilty, and all they got was house arrest? What kind of punishment is that?" I felt my tongue turn scalding hot as if I was breathing fire at him.

"I understand your disappointment Ms. Faciane but, I assure you this is..."

I cut him off.

"I'm not disappointed. I'm pissed! For months I did everything you asked, and all they get is a time out in the luxury of their own home after they traumatized my child?" The flame of my tongue took over, and I have no idea what else I said.

"Trust me, Ms. Faciane, we strongly feel that this was the best punishment for them. It is on their record, and they will have five years of probation assigned to them. This was the best deal we could get."

I hung the phone up on him. The verdict was an example of the "just-is" system for my daughter in surround sound. A system that gives house arrest to child abusers but would have given me five-plus years for battery or longer for attempted murder, if I had beaten them the same way.

All I could do was smile like a good girl, eat their betrayal, and accept their lack of punishment for the crime.

Tyrone kept only a couple of his visitation dates. Once Toni had their baby, he stopped coming to visit. No courtesy call to let me know he was no longer going to visit, just disappeared. All the fighting, drama, and trauma he inflicted on us to end up a fart in the wind. My daughter, now 4, was heartbroken, and as much as I wanted to brainwash both of us into hating him for it, I couldn't.

I had to accept it was a shitty situation, moving on with our lives was all we could do.

* * * *

It was 2009 now, the financial crisis still plagued the economy, and my real estate career had become almost non-existent. Fortunately, I was willing to take various jobs to pay the bills, part-time housekeeper on a ranch, literally shoveling horse shit, as well as a full-time assistant to a publisher. Horses are more fun to work with than people. Money was tight, and eventually, these sources of income dwindled too.

Searching and applying for work for months and still nothing. Anything over a minimum wage in a tourist city like Palm Springs, California, had dried up. I hadn't paid my rent in four months. Eventually, I had no choice but to apply for welfare assistance. We qualified for food stamps for two months with one lump sum payment to pay a few bills, and by the third month, we were disqualified for me not having check stubs. I was too poor to be poor.

Fortunately, Tyrone honored paying his child support, and we lived on less than $500 a month for almost six months. Unsure how but we always had enough, and thankfully none of the utilities got turned off, but I couldn't keep living in an apartment without paying my rent. I had no idea where to go other than to my mother's house, who was living on the north side of Long Beach, California, at the time.

I didn't just fear the danger of living in a big city or the hype of it's "drive-bys" but more the possibility of running into a prisoner I may have pissed off over a decade prior. Regardless of my fears, I wasn't going to be homeless with my baby because of my pride.

* * * *

It was challenging to wrap my head around, moving away from the only place I lived as an adult and built a community of supportive friends, church family, and business contacts. Spending so many years in a small pond, I was unsure I could survive in the big city. My skills were still limited, but the stain of one woman's words on my ego forced me to set fire to my fears.

Amelia, a white woman in her early fifties, had been a manager of mine at an escrow company before the crisis and opened her own office shortly after. She observed my work ethic and hired me to work for her. Though I was loyal and had the potential to become a great asset in the real estate industry, having a toddler during a financial crisis was not the brightest career move, and Amelia made sure to remind me of it. Times got hard fast, and she was on the verge of having to decide whether to lay me off or keep me. Before deciding who to let go, she chose to share her assessment of me.

"You don't read much, do you?" she told me while refusing to look me in the face.

Almost intentionally being dismissive as she flipped through a pile of paperwork on her desk.

"Huh? Yes, I re.."

"Well, I mean, you didn't go to college, right?" her tone sharply interrupted me.

"I didn't graduate, but I have atten.."

"You don't speak educated or read books," she interrupted me again, now agitated.

"You need to get an education and start reading books on your own, or you will never be more than an hourly wage earner who struggles to support her family. And you will not be speaking with my clients on the phone until you do."

She looked back down at her paperwork to dismiss me. I know my exact words to her because I said none of them, only composed myself and walked out the door—shocked, humiliated, and confused. Only a small part of me wanted to kick her ass. After all, she was right, and I couldn't get mad at her, let alone offended.

Amelia was like a mentor, and because I admired her, her words meant something to me. As much as I wanted to ignore what she said, I forced myself to embrace it instead. Being around strong women like her who gave me opportunities at real success was not to be taken for granted. She was pissed at me for settling for such mediocrity, and because she cared about my children and me, she wouldn't spare me her opinion on it.

Not long after she said those words to me, I landed in court with an abused child. Her lesson had nothing to do with my race, but about surviving

a race. My "race" for economic stability as a woman and a mother during the "Great Recession."

Month five was creeping in, and I still had no way to pay the rent, I packed a few small boxes just in case we had to move.

SPITTING IMAGES

The phone rang one afternoon, and in my desperation, I was sure it was the answer to my prayers.

"Roni?" I could hear my stepmothers, Mary, scratchy smoker's voice on the other end.

"Hey, Mary, how are you?" I asked, now concerned to hear her voice.

"Roni, your dad is ill and in the hospital. It's his breathing and heart. I called you to come to see him if possible." She sounded a little panicked and now had my full attention. Neglecting my parent's problems was unavoidable while dealing with my own parental life. I hadn't been in contact with my father for some time.

"Yes, Mary, I will be there in the next 48 hours."

When I hung up the phone and started scrambling to get ready to drive to Las Vegas, Nevada, it dawned on me that I would have to ignore the toxic relationship we had.

Dad had grown bitter in his older years and attached himself to a new family, and I was jealous of having to share him. Regardless, he was my dad, and it was my job to show up for him even if I had to play fake in front of everyone to do so.

He was shocked to see me when I walked into his hospital room while waiting to be discharged. We started talking about what happened, and while he explained, I tried to ask more questions. He quickly became agitated and irritated with me. I sounded like a mother, and maybe I was acting a bit overbearing, but I needed to be sure there was nothing more he needed from the doctors before taking him home. Mary didn't accompany him to the hospital during prior visits, and my step-brother wasn't confrontational enough.

"Quit asking me all these questions, you sound like your mother!" he yelled.

My mother? Talk about the mighty falling. Even 22 years later, I'm stuck in between his anger towards her and their divorce.

Once upon a time, he was proud to claim me as the "spitting image" of himself, but somewhere and without warning, he had demoted me.

I stayed a couple of days to be sure he was healthy enough for me to leave. He lived with his wife, her two kids who were older than me, and her daughter's three kids. Whom he adopted legally, making them my siblings.

It was absolute chaos in their house. My father stayed in his room watching TV while blocking everyone out and disengaging as part of the family, much like he did when I lived with him and throughout my childhood.

One of my new siblings was a toddler and left most of the day in her crib in full diapers of urine. Quite a few times, I changed this baby's diaper out of pity because my hints on her behalf her did not appeal to anyone's good nature. It may have been the wrong decision to move to Vegas, but I felt there would be a mutual benefit for all of us as a family.

"What do you think about me moving here?" I asked my dad and stepmother while we were at the table, watching TV and eating.

"It's up to you," my dad said, displaying no emotion.

"It's hard to get jobs here," Mary quickly chimed in. "Robert and Leslie (her two kids) haven't been able to find work at all," she said, discouraging.

"I'm sure I can find something and have my place in two months at the most, and this way, I would be close by to help with my dad and the kids," I said, waiting for one of them to approve.

My dad shrugged his shoulders as if he could care less either way.

My stepmother reluctantly said, "Sure, that would be nice."

Had I been paying attention, I would have caught her haughty tone. I should have given more thought to my decision to move, but I couldn't leave my dad's health in the hands of this family.

Also, I was jealous that these children had a part of him that my children didn't. Twenty-four hours later, I was applying for work and planning my move.

* * * *

I don't know much about my dad. The first 30 years of his life are just as much of a mystery as the life of Jesus. He was born in New Mexico in 1943, and after graduating high school in Montclair, California, he joined the air force. He was 5-foot 4-inches and weighed two pounds less than the required weight to enter the military at the time. Determined to be a soldier no matter what, he sat in the chow hall for as long as it took eating tray after tray until he gained the two pounds.

Whenever I asked about his race or nationality, he never claimed to be "white" but a "Heinz 57" with Scottish and German.

When he met my mother at thirty-one years old, he was living with his parents and working at a car wash. They were a decade apart in age and as opposite as two people could get. She was a young Mexican woman starting her life, and he was a square white man looking to start a family. They were captivated by their differences and shared a similar quest to rebel against a racial system. "West Side Story (Wise & Robbins, 1961)" shattered the taboo drawing whites and non-whites together.

They were married in less than two months, and I arrived

approximately ten months after. Pressed to provide, dad joined a different branch of military, Army, Infantry Division.

Military life was much like a single parent life for mom. We moved several times throughout my life and spent many months without my dad around, but when I was a young girl, he and I were close.

At seven years old, he started taking me out, running like one of his troops. The goal was to run a mile eventually. It didn't matter how many times it took me, he made me go with him until I ran the entire mile. My grandmother mentioned years later how much it bothered her that he treated me like a boy.

His philosophy was that every thought should enact a willingness and desire to improvise, adapt, and overcome no matter the situation, and if it didn't, you lacked common sense. Because he was a proud military man who took pride in being an American, he never discussed religion or politics, nor do I ever recall him voting. Whoever his commander-in-chief was none of his business and reserved for civilians.

Somewhere he decided to rebel against his race and family, and I'm positive he married my mother to piss his mother off. His parents saw Mexicans as 'dirty' and 'inferior' to them as white people. I never really knew them growing up because of their indifference towards my mother, and moving around in the military made it easier for my father to pretend they didn't exist. Rarely did he mention that side of our family.

After 13 years, they divorced. Dad became even more bitter towards women, and once he was forced to retire, bitter towards other races. When I started dating in my older teen years is when he began to change towards me, and I began my rebellion against him. He wanted me independent but provided for, insisting a minority man, any minority, wasn't good enough for me. I became determined to prove him wrong.

When my son came along, my father moved to another state, and we saw him sporadically over the years. He showed little interest in my son, his first grandson, but I didn't dare show any emotions over it. My father was the champ at stonewalling, and the more you wanted his attention, the more he reveled in ignoring you. Showing him, I didn't give two shits would soon become my only defense. As the years past from my twenties into my thirties, we still couldn't repair our relationship. Moving towards my forties now, I was determined to change to that.

Not one bite for months in Cali, but in less than a week, I had two interviews in another state. It was confirmation that the operation "rescue dad" was my next move. I drove back to Vegas to give my interviews and was offered a job during the first one.

"Are you sure you're comfortable with me staying with you until I find my place?" I asked to confirm it was safe to finalize the move.

"S-sure, I don't mind at all," my dad said with little enthusiasm.

"If he says it's OK," Mary said, almost reluctant to reply.

I saw her hesitation, but didn't care and chose against my better judgment to ignore her. For the first time in my adult life, I needed my dad and Mary's insecurities weren't going to stand in my way.

The next day I drove another 4 hrs back home to finish packing and give up my apartment.

Military kids grow to learn there is no better way to get

over a shitty situation than to leave and start over. I was excited and terrified all at once.

Now that Tyrone was no longer coming to visit my daughter, and I had full custody, I didn't need his permission to leave either.

When I got back to his house and went to hug him, the games began.

"We need to talk," dad said as he motioned for me to sit down at the table. "We aren't able to help you very much with money, but we can help with babysitting while you work." His words were stern as if waiting for Mary's nod of approval from behind me. We were barely in the door, and they were unwelcoming us.

"I understand, and I came here to help you guys. I will have my place very soon and will buy food and give you money for rent and bills," I responded confidently, looking at Mary, who had moved by his side.

"No, Roni!" she interrupted. "You don't have to give us any money, just pay for your snacks, stuff for your baby and save to get your place. We don't mind." She smiled through her contempt to assure my father she meant what she said and ease his apparent nervousness of me being there. I watched him cringe to his wife, an act I had never seen before.

My first step-monster Helga tried to have power over me as a mother figure in my teenage years. She failed to prove fit, and he separated from her within nine months. He stood more ground with my mother, not that she allowed him to, but he didn't cower to her.

He and Mary were married for some time now, and he had adopted her grandkids at sixty-seven years old. Perhaps the responsibility of this new family made him feel submissive towards her, or he got seriously screwed with a financial obligation to a new set of kids.

That small voice started to chant in my head "red flag," but I dismissed it. I just got there.

2.

Bullet 2

BULLET 2-DISGUST

STEP-MONSTER HOUSE

My new job, a real estate company in Las Vegas about 10 minutes from the strip, was a relaxed environment with a staff of six women, including myself. We were of various ages and backgrounds. Our manager was a laid back, patient guy. He respected women, no matter how frustrated he appeared to get.

Sin City life was a culture shock for me. A couple of my co-workers openly passed out anti-depressants to one another to take with their morning coffee. The owner of the company was a good-looking Jewish man, in his early 30s, and built like a Ninja Turtle.

He was making a lot of money with a thriving business in a failed economy with an office full of women. You couldn't tell him he wasn't big pimpin'. It was the first morning I had seen him in the office after starting with the company just a week prior.

The last time I saw him was during my interview, and

though he appeared impressed with my experience, he unsuccessfully tried to intimidate me. I knew his type all too well.

"Good morning, sluts," he shouted, standing in the door facing our desks.

No one flinched.

Everyone, minus me, said "good morning" almost in harmony back to him. I just stared at his face. He turned bright red and started to smirk, like a spoiled brat who knows his parents are watching him but doesn't care. As far as I was concerned, he had just put on a prisoner's uniform, and I'd politely treat him as such.

"I know you aren't referring to me, I'm from California," I sassed at him as I sat down at my desk, dismissing him.

An immature response, I know, but I had hoped it sounded "gangsta bitch" enough that he would shut the hell up. It was too tempting to humiliate him in front of his vulnerable and submissive staff. Judging by the lack of response, I was pretty sure this was a regular occurrence, and these women were too afraid to say anything. Or this was another Vegas, "what happens here stays here" formality.

I wasn't sure if he was waiting for me to put him in check or not, but once he realized none of us had time to entertain his immaturity, he left. We didn't see him for the rest of the day. After I got home, I filled with frustration that I had to deal with another farm animal for a paycheck. My hope was in keeping my big feminist mouth shut long enough to earn a couple more paychecks, get my place and find a new job. STAT!

The real shitty part was having to go back to my dad's house with no space of my own after working in this environment all day. My stepmother was always at the table with her cigarette in one hand and an oxygen tube up her nose watching TV. How I missed the dangerous and obvious risk of us exploding while staying here, I will never know.

Dad spent most of the day in his room, eyes glued to the TV or napping. Every day I had to give myself a pep talk to stay patient and be a good daughter while also trying to fit in with a new family full of strangers. Although he never really had much to say to me, whenever I mentioned my childhood or any memory associated, he became irate.

"How the hell was your childhood so bad?" he screeched with a look of disgust.

None of the memories I shared with him were in judgment for his performance as a parent, but, when reminding him he wasn't present for most of my childhood, he would quickly defend himself with "that's your mother's fault."

Almost a month had passed, and one more payday was all I needed to put a deposit down on my place. Dad still hadn't opened much to me and seemed to lump my daughter in with the other kids in the home. The honeymoon that never began was officially over.

Soon, no matter what the topic of conversation, he seemed to distance himself further and further away from me. His face was either fixed in a blank stare or scrunched up in disgust in front of the television. Somewhere his retirement broke him.

* * * *

Dad wasn't my physical disciplinarian growing up, but when he did want to be abusive, psychological warfare was his weapon of choice. Rarely did he need to use physical violence because my mother wore heavy hands.

In fact, as a kid, I would start laughing when he yelled at

me. Not because I didn't respect him but because I didn't fear him like my mother. Up until this moment in my life, I denied he was capable of abusing little children. Had I been more honest with myself than fearful of my life situation, my decision to relocate near him would have been different.

The youngest of his now adopted children, my legal little sister, was an adorable, spunky, energetic two-year-old girl who adored our dad. She had been whining in their room for a few minutes when I heard him snap at her in a familiar military tone so loud that even I froze sitting on the couch.

She came running out of their room with my dad on her heels. He kicked her like a dog, and she fell to the ground. He stood over her like a madman and paused, daring her to get back up only to knock her down again.

"Dad!" I screamed to get his attention before moving in front of her to protect her from him. "That's enough! What the hell is wrong with you?" I yelled, trying to snap him out of whatever hallucination he was having.

Emotionless, he turned around, squared his soldiers, and marched away like his mission was complete.

I picked her up, hugged her, and gave her what she had been asking for, juice I believe it was. The other people in the house were silent like this abuse happened often.

I was beyond mortified. Who the hell was that guy?

Once I realized the predicament I put us both in, I had no idea what to do, and calling the police to press charges on my sixty-seven-year-old father for child abuse was not it either. Not that I don't regret that decision, but at the time, there was no fight in me for someones else child. Especially when her mother also watched and did nothing.

An unfortunate moment where there was no denying I put my daughter in another dangerous home, not any safer than her own father's house.

I fucked up.

Dad's only response to the details of his granddaughter's abuse case was, "that's what happens when you deal with those people."

"Those" referring to black men. Not a hug of comfort or a few kind words for either of us.

The fact that he was now terrorizing his own adopted white kids, as a white man, in his own home, was morbidly poetic.

Once everyone had calmed down, I sat at the table with Mary to find out how typical this behavior of his was.

"Your father has been mean to me since you've been here," she said, shifting the blame towards me.

"Mean to you? Why? How?" I asked.

Immediately I knew she was trying to manipulate me into believing, somehow, I had triggered my father's current state of anger and frustration. She jumped from one topic to the next, like a black widow webbing from one side of her desperation to the other. Listening intently to her, I waited for an opportunity to oppose her argument, but then she brought up their sex life.

They hadn't had sex in more than a decade, and she was complaining to me out of pure distraction. My disgust for her stooping so low pushed me over the edge.

Sitting up in my chair, I looked her square in the face and told her, "Well, you did ask him to help raise a bunch of little kids in his sixties. I don't think my dick could get hard if I were him either,"

She was speechless, but if her looks could kill.

Perhaps showing off my accomplishments and the little success I had attained in my career to gain his approval was a bit excessive but, it didn't keep me from being generous and kind towards his adopted family.

I might have been the only contributing factor in his rage, but I doubted it.

FIGHT LIKE A MAN

A few days later, I got a promotion to a new position at work with a bump in pay. It wasn't enough incentive to stay with the company but enough to take the pressure off me until I found something else. The owner's harassment still concerned me, not because I feared him dishing some at me but that it may escalate to a verbal altercation between the two of us.

However, not even twenty-four hours later and before I had a chance to celebrate, it escalated.

One of my coworkers, not much bigger than myself, and he was playfully yelling back and forth to one another. When I glanced back at them, I saw him make a fist and punch her so hard in her arm that her body went limp, barely able to hold her up.

Her face flushed bright red, trying to hold back her expression of agony and sounds of pain. That muscle-bound coward hit her like she was a man.

His face was now glowing with satisfaction as though he had won. No one moved. No one said shit, and no one stopped him. Even I sat there waiting for this woman to stand up for herself. As much as I wanted to get in his face and risk my job to protect her, I didn't have a backup plan. It would have been irresponsible as a single mother in my current situation to make that kind of bet at that moment.

She, too, was a single mother of three children, all under the ages of 10 and couldn't risk losing her job either.

It was so quiet you could hear a pin drop, but we all knew what the other was thinking. Maybe we would have felt we had more power in numbers to say something if she had spoken up, but she didn't. She only cradled her arm, sunk in her seat, and went back to work.

He glared at her like she was a "good dog" retreating to her cage.

We only had another hour of work left. No one said anything, not even "good night" when leaving the office.

Driving home, I grew angrier at myself for not defending a woman who was too afraid to defend herself. It wasn't like me to cringe over the fear of money, but in 2010, the desperation to suck a dick for a paycheck became surreal enough that throwing a perfectly good job away for a simple assault on someone else would have been considered ludicrous.

Mastering how to beat his breed of a bully was something I, unfortunately, didn't get a chance to show her.

I, too, had already had my turn with this kind of supervisor.

* * * *

During my orientation to work for the prison, the human

resources rep, Louis, warned me that the male staff members would harass me more than the prisoners in this job.

"You won't have to worry about the prisoners as much as you will the male staff. You are attractive, and many of them will want to date you." Louis said with a parental tone.

It was my first week and Sgt. Beecher, one of my many supervisors, an attractive, half-black, and half-Filipino man, maybe 5-feet, 7-inches tall, held the standard puffed up masculinity in a badge attitude.

"Faciane, are you from around here?" the sergeant asked with a flirtatious grin.

We met once before when I waitressed at a restaurant in a local town months prior. He kept taking my disinterest as a challenge.

"No, I am a military brat, from all over," with a polite and quick smirk, I answered him. Hoping he would ask someone else the same question to keep from making it completely obvious, he was flirting with me. Being the swing shift supervisor for the night, it was his job to take our newbie group around the yard and provide us necessary training. There were six of us. Only two, including myself, were women. I noticed the confused look on my co-worker's faces, unsure if the sergeant's question to me was leading to a training lesson for the group.

One of the other trainees interrupted to ask Beecher a question allowing me to escape further questioning.

Prisoners were watching our group, and I could hear the many voices moving about behind us. It was about six p.m., already dark, and the prison was full of the evening commotion of its resident's routines. When I turned to look back at Beecher is when I felt the impact of his fist hitting my shoulder. Fortunately, he was nowhere near the size or strength of the ninja turtle, but it was painful nonetheless.

"What was that for?" I demanded still unsure this was happening. Still so young and inexperienced with men—especially in this type of male-dominated environment that I had no idea how to react or how to fight back. Boys are supposed to outgrow hitting girls they like, they said.

He smirked, ignored my question, and hit me again. Before I could get any more words out, he struck me again, and this time, he landed his punch on my right breast. Making it three assaults in total. Grabbing my shoulder and cradling my own body, I dropped down and accepted defeat. He chuckled with satisfaction.

When I looked up at him, I saw in his eyes that he had every intention of making my life hell, and I would have a hard time stopping him. It was no secret that I dated black men, but when I showed no interest in him and started to date one of his white subordinates, he quickly needed to establish some sort of penis power over me.

Something split in me forever defining this as my "Hulk" moment. It felt like controlled rage, but none like I had ever felt before.

Whatever it was, was cold and calculated and would become my super suit.

He wasn't going to see me cry. None of them would see me cry. I gave in to my fears of striking him back to avoid any creative retaliation towards me in the future. We were in prison for fuck's sake. Anything could happen here.

Excusing myself, I went to the watch office and grabbed some coffee. My shift was almost over, and the graveyard sergeant was walking in for the shift change.

"Evening, Faciane, you OK?" she asked, concerned.

Upset and humiliated for not defending myself, I avoided finding Beecher and the group by stalling even after I drank my coffee. Beecher was just a couple of inches bigger than me, and because of the chain of command and the notoriety of his position, I had to let him punk me.

My only vengeance was to treat him like someone he didn't respect, a prisoner.

"No, I'm not OK, Sgt. Hanson. Can I speak to you for a moment?" I asked, trying to control my breathing and stay calm.

After explaining to her what happened, she was pissed. She gave me the impression Beecher had a few priors of this kind of behavior and was having to bite her lip not to expose his, and the institutions, dirt. Even as an employee, prison is no place to make enemies over personal bullshit. You must depend on these people to help keep you safe.

If you are going to throw the gauntlet, it better be for a damn good reason.

She sat me down and told me how to write him up for misconduct, just like I would any other prisoner who assaulted me. I had no idea I could do that, and her passing on that kind of power to a fellow inexperienced woman was real feminism. Hanson was a white woman, in her mid-twenties, no kids, and a work ethic I respected. She must have had some respect for mine too.

Hanson was the first woman to tell me I was a victim of an assault, and because of her, I learned to fight with my pen.

My complaint had no malicious intent, only to bring my assailant to justice through the proper channels.

After approving my report, she submitted it to the graveyard shift lieutenant, her supervisor, for approval and disciplinary action.

Before our shift ended, the lieutenant called me in his office to get my verbal side of the story. He listened intently, kept quiet, thanked me, and then dismissed me. When Hanson saw me walking out of his office, she asked me to wait and went into his office, closing the door behind her.

She wasn't in there long before she came out with a confused look on her face and put her head down.

"Let me walk you to the control building to turn in your gear," she said, almost mumbling.

Grabbing my things, we walked out of the watch office together.

"The lieutenant has decided that the best solution would be for Sgt. Beecher to give you a written letter of apology for his actions." Hanson was about 5-feet, 10-inches tall, and was walking with her hand on my shoulder. Initially, I mistook this for her trying to console me, but as she began to speak, I realized she was trying to keep herself calm.

Her hand tightened as she continued.

"What? An apology? Aren't there men in here who have minor domestic abuse charges?" I gasped, now even more confused. What just happened to me wasn't about racism but sexism and the abuses of power.

"He's a sergeant," she mumbled, trying to stay professional. As we reached the gate to get off the yard, she stopped me.

"Look, the truth is, he has clout with the supervisors.

Beecher has been here for some time, and he's dating the captain's daughter. There is only so much I can do because he and I hold the same rank, and most of the lieutenants are his friends. Reporting him wasn't wasted. You let them all know they can't fuck with you without consequences. The prisoners will hear about it too. I'm sorry, Faciane, but I'm proud of you. You will make a great officer. Go home, have a drink, and start a new day tomorrow. Good night." She patted me on my back like a big sister. That's who she was trying to be for me, a sister in arms. She turned to walk back to the watch office to start her shift, and I buzzed the gate to get the hell out of there and go home.

I felt numb, walking up the stairs to leave. Beecher was signing paperwork before going home himself. Our eyes met through the glass, and I looked at him as to turn him to stone. Nodding my head at him, I let him know the game was afoot, turned in my keys, and went home. It wasn't until I reached the parking lot that I felt my anger waiting for me. I vowed to learn the rules of this new game and beat them at it.

Regardless of the outcome, I had won. Beecher learned I was capable of threatening his livelihood and for bullies like him that scares them more than physical violence.

Of course, I couldn't let him walk away from his assault that easily. I got to dispense my justice months later.

He transferred to another facility, and I attended his going away party.

Long story short, the last time I saw Sgt. Beecher, he was naked, rubbing one of his nipples with one hand while holding his very limp dick from performance anxiety in the other, begging me not to leave his house.

Fair exchange, no robbery.

Once I stopped reacting like a victim and more as an overcomer, men became much more intimidated of me.

YOU CRY LIKE A GIRL

As much as I wanted to help this woman as Hanson had for me, the logistics of this company would not allow me to do so. We were at the mercy of a sole proprietor and in the middle of recovering from a national economic collapse. None of us felt we were able to stand up for ourselves and risk losing our ability to provide for our families.

Being a single mother puts a person at the mercy of having to "eat shit with a rusty spoon" for their children—my grandmother's philosophy on the sacrifice of motherhood.

Now, all I wanted was to get to the house, wash off my day, and be with my daughter. We were days from our sanctuary.

Since my dad and I never spoke about workplace drama before, I figured this was as good a time as any to get his opinion on my situation. Curious how he would have handled it had he been there. He made it clear when I was growing up that he didn't support women in the military. However, he never gave his opinion as a supervisor about proper workplace etiquette between sexes.

Everything was so classified.

Dad was sitting outside when I got home. An unusual place to find him, but for the past couple of days, he had been sitting out in the same chair. It didn't matter that he had emphysema to Mary and her kids, who still subjected him to their cigarette smoke inside the house. The fresh air was good for him.

"Hey, want to take the baby to the park, just you and I?" he asked after I had changed out of my work clothes.

I was thrilled and quickly felt like his little girl again. It was the first time he had asked to do anything with his estranged granddaughter and me since we had moved in.

"I'd love too. Let me get our shoes on," I said. Then like a family, we walked to the park together.

We finally were able to get some alone time with him and all of his attention. It was the first time in many years, and I decided I wasn't going to ruin it with work bullshit. As we walked together, he also held my baby's hand for the first time. My heart was full. It was too good to be true. So good, I had forgotten all about the red flags given since arriving on his doorstep.

We started some small talk and watched my daughter run about chasing after bugs happy as can be.

"Look," his tone turned serious as he grabbed my hand, turning to face me. "Mary and I aren't going to be able to watch the baby, after all, you're going to have to find a babysitter." He said, turning away from me after completing his sentence.

It took a few seconds to process we were about to be homeless after living in a constant state of fear of that very thing for the past few months.

"WHAT?" I screamed at him.

His betrayal was sweet like a kiss. Diverting me from the house to protect his wife was deceitful and strategic. None of his words proved he was unwelcoming us from his home, but it was clear that's what he meant. Gently grabbing my daughter's hand, I marched us back to the house, babbling obscenities like a madwoman trying to control her manic insanity. Hearing myself repeat over and over again, "I have nowhere else to go—if you can't babysit, I can't stay here."

My daughter was almost running to keep up with my stride while looking up at me with her frightened eyes. At five-years-old, she was already familiar with rejection from those supposed to love her, now having to watch me endure the same. Trying to hold in my emotions to keep from upsetting her made me want to hurt my dad even more physically. Eventually, I lost my shit.

I tried to pack my car as quickly as I could, while dad stood within feet of me to be sure I got all my things to leave. Like a well-trained soldier, he didn't flinch, watching me make a complete spectacle of myself. When he would yell at me as a young girl, I would cry, and he would say, "you always cry how are you going to defend yourself if you always cry like a girl?".

Calling him a racist and a shitty father was my only defense to keep from crying and showing him my frailty.

It wasn't until I yelled something rude about his adopted white kids that he flinched, exposing his weakness. He came towards me like he might get physical and muttered, "keep them out of this." Unfortunately, he was putting me in a survivalist position, and I couldn't stop my horns from coming out.

Stepping towards him, I got as close as I could to his face and regrettably, threatened the man I called dad before being banished from his home.

"What are you going to do, old man? I will throw your ass on the ground!" I told him in my most disrespectful tone.

My only weapon left was to emasculate him. The words came out like fire, and I didn't care how much damage they would eventually cause. Dad said nothing. In his eyes, I watched him disconnect his parental chord from me.

Once I had all my things packed and started my drive back to California, I called to tell my mama.

I'M MEXICAN?

Driving away covered in tears and mascara, my little girl was confused and scared to speak. Even the cat didn't make a peep for more than two hours.

It felt like a nightmare I couldn't escape from having to call and quit my job under these circumstances. Hearing the disappointment in the voice of the only woman in the office, I could trust was the cherry on top. Fleeing like a thief in the night from a job I searched for months to find made me sob from Vegas to Primm.

"Of course you can come to stay with me as long as you need it. Call me when you get off the freeway, and I'll wait for you outside," my mom's voice filled with excitement.

For years I childishly resented my mother, but even when I took my dad's side, she graciously pretended not to care. She knew who my father was but allowed him to be my hero because she wanted her daughter to have a family unit—even if meant hiding her pain.

Mom was born in Orange County, California, in 1953. Mexican families like hers still were fighting for equal rights and their own space in a very racist America.

What I do know about her side of the family is also very limited. My grandmother has more Yaqui Indian blood, and her parents were from California. No one is sure about my grandfather because his grandparents raised him.

Rumor has it his parents were in a taboo interracial relationship, his birth father being from the middle east. But I'm not too sure about that. He is still the only Mexican man I know who had an afro. In the neighborhood he and my grandmother grew up, he was nicknamed "Borrego" for his coarse hair, blatantly shaming him for it.

The only real culture I ever knew was a military one. Respect and manners were expected and demanded. Only the occasional reference to a white racial superiority existed. I can still hear my grandmother saying, "sit up and eat like good white folk" in her faint Mexican accent. She spoke Spanish fluently, but my mother didn't.

My dad wouldn't allow her to teach us Spanish either.

"They are American kids, and they will speak American," he would ignorantly say.

My mother, preserving his ego, never corrected him to say our language was English. We had to be American, not necessarily smart.

Until we moved to Blythe, California, from Colorado Springs, Colorado, I had only been around civilian families and unaware of what a Mexican was until I was about eight years old. This new small home town of ours was an agricultural town. We moved into a house behind my grandmother and her husband, who had a farm. My 'never-missed-a-step' grandfather was a kind white man who treated me like his own and taught me the ropes of being a country girl.

There was a group of kids that rode the bus home with me, who were labeled "awkward." Being the new kid, I didn't have any friends and kept quiet to avoid a label of my own. The group of awkward kids was made up of dark-skinned boys, not black but brown, and they didn't smile, nor did I ever hear them speak. Not even to defend themselves. They didn't act like typical kids.

One afternoon the bus driver assigned me to sit next to one of these boys, and I was uncomfortable. There stop was after mine, which meant I had to ride the whole way home next to him. When I got inside, and my mother asked about my day, I told her the bus driver made me sit next to a 'creepy' boy.

"Creepy boy?" she repeated curiously for more details.

"The kids call them Mexican," I said innocently.

My mother's face twisted up in a fury, and she couldn't control her momentary anger.

"Roni, you're fucking Mexican!" she screamed as she stormed into her room to avoid yelling more obscenities at her dumbfounded eight-year-old.

Standing there, I thought to myself. "I'm Mexican?"

Later I learned those young men were the sons of migrant workers who worked in the fields before and after school, which explained why they never smiled. They had to help provide for their families while the rest of us little spoiled bastards got to go home and complain about who they had to sit by on the bus home from school.

Nothing in our home gave the impression we were Mexican except my mother's 'Cheech and Chongs' record album that I wasn't allowed to listen to because of its adult content. My dad added "Up in Smoke (Chong-Adler & Lombardo, 1978)" to the movie collection when I was a few years older, giving me a warped image of what being a Mexican was.

All I learned was smoking weed could get you deported, and if you go to Mexico, don't eat burritos from a truck.

My grandmother's home also didn't have anything that

stood out as Mexican. She had a lot of art and pictures of native Americans but nothing that shouted, "Hey, we're Mexican" at you.

With all her "act like good white folk" talk, I didn't even realize my grandmother was Indian, and not just a collector of beautiful Indian paintings and art until I was a little older.

The food we ate was also accommodating more of my dad's taste. Mom made fried tacos, but we always put ketchup on them. What real Mexican puts ketchup on their tacos? None. I know because everyone who I have told this story to has confirmed that.

It wasn't until my parents divorced that I noticed their racial and cultural differences. They tried to remain friends, but my father could never get over my mother, a Mexican, leaving him to pursue a bigger and better life than he could provide her.

* * * *

It felt like I had been driving forever and on autopilot. It was now after midnight when I looked up and saw the 710 freeway exit to Long Beach, California. Pulling up to my mother's apartment building, I could see her standing outside, waiting for us. I was happy to see her and worried that we might get jumped in the alley on the north side of town. We hugged and cried.

"Thanks, mom, for letting us come over on such short notice," I hugged her tighter.

"You're my baby, and I didn't want you over there with those fuckers anyway," she chuckled. She was happy to have us with her. For the first time in months, we were somewhere safe.

LIFE IN THE LBC

I was devastated to leave my dad's house on such bad terms, but forced to move back to the sunshine state, this time near the beach, wasn't even close to a punishment. Granted, we lived in a part of Long Beach that was known by the rap gods as "drive-by" territory, but it was nothing like I had imagined. The Popeyes restaurant down the street with the bulletproof glass had the most courteous employees, even the addicts who stood out front were polite.

Unsure I could handle living in this city made it difficult to relax. Everything moved so fast in comparison to the small valley I had known for so many years.

It wasn't long before I learned how to get around. Well, I was still too afraid to drive on the freeway, but I had mastered the side streets. After landing a job at a lending company, I moved into the apartment upstairs from my mother, a one-bedroom, one-bath tiny apartment. Not my top choice of where I wanted to live, but I was close to my mother and as safe as I was going to get.

I enrolled my daughter in a private school, and before long, she too felt our lives had stabilized. Each day I grew more confident living in the city, but like a prison, I didn't feel fearless in it. It wasn't easy to ignore the police frequently were called, and those "could be" gunshots were fired by real guns.

"California Corrections policy states that if an inmate takes you hostage, they will not authorize any negotiations on your behalf. You will have to wait for the CERT (prison tactical team) to come in and get you. The prisoners will hide you, exchange your uniform for prison clothing to camouflage you, cut all your hair off, and may do other horrible and vile things to you. Please be sure to remember this when you are out there doing your job because no matter how nice these prisoners are to you, they will harm you when deemed necessary." —Some fucking guy whose name I can't remember paid to tell Corporate correctional officers this information in February of 1998.

One of the department directors gave me this speech on my first day of work. I never saw him again after that day, but I won't ever forget him or how I felt hearing those words.

It was February of 1998, months shy of my twenty-third birthday, and this was my orientation speech as a newly employed guard at a corporate men's prison facility. Not only could I be harmed, but they just made it clear they would NOT negotiate for my life if I ever was taken hostage, and neither would the State of California. They paid pennies for the risk, but I had a four-year-old son to support.

Putting on a badge made me cringe, but I had no real viable skills, and this was an opportunity to build a career, get real benefits, and set a positively deranged example for my son. If I could have made the same amount of money doing something else, I would have.

The sound of the gates closing behind me walking through every Sally Port (gates that open up for vendors and employees to enter the prison) to get to the yard were deafening, and I can still hear it ringing in my ears.

In theory, I was free to leave the prison, but, in reality, I was only allowed to leave whenever someone decided to let me out.

In my first month there, my training officer drilled continuously in me to keep a 'non-routine' routine. He stressed how being unpredictable was necessary for working in a prison setting, and one escape route to the main gate could save my life.

"Always change which dorm you go in first and which one you come out of last. Never do your perimeter (fence) checks at the same time. You have over four-hundred sets of eyes watching you, and that's not including staff members. The same goes for their ears. They can hear you over the radio report your every move to the others on duty and the control tower. Keep busy and keep moving."

Just like the prisoners, my new life was now plotting how to be inconsistent consistently. Those bastards gave me hell, and I dished it back with as much sarcasm, wit, and wet ink as I possibly could. Whether I had realized it or not, I had joined a gang where respect, for a woman, was worth more than money.

Six months later, I met Barnes, a young black man in his late twenties, about six-feet, two-inches, three-hundred pounds, and a shot caller from Oakland, California. I'm pretty sure he was gang-affiliated, but he never verbally confirmed it. If he had, I would have had to classify him as such, and he knew that.

One afternoon while supervising the cleaning crew, I noticed taking inventory before shift change that someone didn't return a squirt bottle. After giving the guys on my cleaning crew several chances to give it up, they wouldn't budge, and I had to report it missing. The missing bottle forced the lieutenant to recall and shut down the yard. Better known as "everyone gets back to their rooms for a time out." They had to stay that way until someone returned the squirt bottle. You can do some severe damage with hard plastic, a lighter, and an idle mind.

Shenanigans like this were the most annoying part of the job. Why they would take something so stupid was beyond me until I realized they were probably up to something. If I had to guess, someone wanted the yard shut down to keep the cops out of certain dorms or areas to transact business. Or beat the shit out of someone.

I crept by every window I could, listening for anyone hurt, now my only concern at this point.

It grew closer to dinner time, and I was starving now sitting next to one of my coworkers, making small talk waiting for the call to unlock the yard. The prisoners were only allowed out to use the bathroom one at a time, and the front door to the dorm closest to me opened up.

"HEY!! You know the rules. Whatcha doin?" I shouted like a mama towards the door.

Barnes comes out of the dorm, pretending he didn't hear me and walked towards us. Trying to make myself appear taller than five-feet, two-inches, I stood up to repeat myself louder. Improvise-Adapt-Overcome. It's almost surprising how often that works well for us vertically challenged people.

"Are you Faciane?" he asked, now close enough for me to see his face and hear his voice.

"Yes, I am, and you are?" I asked curiously that he specifically asked for me.

"My name is Barnes, heard you're looking for this," he smiled, pulling that dam squirt bottle from behind his back!

I had heard about moments like these from older guards. They only happened in either a setup or if you had earned some respect.

Pausing for a moment before taking the bottle from him, I studied his body language, looking for signs of a setup.

"Why are you giving this to me?" I asked ungratefully before taking it from him. I knew every prisoner who could see us was watching.

He chuckled, knowing I wanted that damn bottle so I could go home, but we both knew I wasn't going to show him any desperation for it.

"I heard you were looking for it. I'm hungry and would like

to get some dinner, and the faster you open the yard, the faster that can happen. Go ahead and take this to the lieutenant and be the hero."

He put the bottle out towards me for me to take it. Even I couldn't deny he had a charm about him and a great smile. Bastard.

I took the squirt bottle and called the lieutenant on the radio to meet me at the watch office, but I didn't feel like a hero. I felt stupid as hell for parading it in my hands as if I found gold. Only in this world did this kind of nonsense make sense. After handing it over to the lieutenant, I asked to write my report after I ate. I was approaching cranky.

"Who gave this to you?" the lieutenant demanded angrily.

"A prisoner," I answered, dismissing him.

"Faciane, I need to know who gave you this squirt bottle!" he was almost yelling at me now.

Never had I seen a superior take an incident like this so personal before. But I had spent enough time on that yard to know that even though we both wore green, we were not equals. Whether he liked it or not, I had more pull than he did. He would have to fire me before I betrayed that over a squirt bottle.

"I can't tell you that sir, all I can tell you is that a prisoner gave me the bottle" I stood firm unaware of the vendetta this would birth against me.

The lieutenant was redneck white, and Barnes was gangster black, I didn't dare give in on those two principles alone. Not because I feared a racial war, but I knew that Barnes' race and the situation would play a more significant role than taking the bottle, risking them wrongfully accusing him. The lieutenant wanted someone's ass for having to lock the yard down and pay over time.

Whoever had the stupid bottle last was the guilty party, whether they took it or not. I know Barnes wasn't the one to take the bottle. Some other douchebags took it to be stupid. Barnes was able to both retrieve and turn it in because he had enough clout to do so. And for him, giving it to the cute female corrections officer might earn him a favor in return in the future. It was part of the game. They hide it, and we have to find it.

After letting the lieutenant bully me for a few more moments, I reminded him I had to get to my post for the chow hall. He couldn't argue with that, but he made it his mission to mess with me every time I worked his shift.

To pay him back, because nothing is free in prison for anyone, and to piss off the lieutenant and all like him, whenever Barnes was on the write-up list for violating the new shaving rule, I'd warn him to stay out of sight. I couldn't let him slide with the other codes, but that shaving rule was ludicrous to me, especially for minorities.

Barnes taught me a lesson to staying safe no matter where I roamed, prison, city, life, etc., but the lieutenant in his narcissistic need to be a bully could have gotten me killed.

HUNTING FOR BEGINNERS

My real estate career was still unstable, and I had already gone through two dishonest employers. "Dog the Bounty Hunter (Hybrid Films, 2004-2012)," was my favorite show at the time, corny and cliché I know, but it was one of my guilty pleasures and made me miss the hunt. I hadn't chased a prisoner in years, but after my case with Tyrone, I had become obsessed with learning more about the process of warrants and bail. The show was the perfect outlet for my rage.

Duane "Dog" Chapman appeared genuine when he spoke to people about helping them change their lives, and I admired his passion for soul hunting while conducting his arrests. His perception was from the perspective of the prisoner, whereas mine was from the perspective of a former guard.

One night I was especially intrigued by the show and looking for a career change, I googled 'how to become a bounty hunter.' After reading more about the bail industry, I grew an even greater interest. Mostly because it wasn't just a skill I could learn but a business I could eventually build on my own. That interested me the most.

But this wasn't a regular job or business that you could go out and get hired that easy. One has to have a network of bail agents and bond companies that can trust them with their cases and keep them from getting into legal trouble. Not all cases require making arrests. Some hire for help to file bail motions for extensions with the court. These take a lot more finesse, knowledge, and courage, having to stand in front of a courtroom like a professional and not a gun-toting badass.

After looking at exclusive online groups, messaging several people introducing myself with not one response, I finally got a bite.

Ken was very private about his identity, but what he did disclose was that he was an experienced bounty hunter who was also former military, 34yrs of age, and also, Latin and white. He had extensive experience in bail law and was eager to answer all of my questions, which was precisely the kind of business associate I needed.

In less than a week, he began sharing all the information he had acquired in his years of hunting with me. He helped me enroll in the required classes so that I could legally join his team.

It had been a while since I had attended any use-of-force training, and I missed the thrill, except being hit with non-lethal weapons, such as tasers. I'm still unable to equate how getting electrocuted effectively teaches someone how to use a taser, but that's me. While I watched them each roll around on the floor convulsing, it reminded me how stern I would have to be with the men this time around.

In this business as of 2012, our authority as bounty hunters in California stood on a couple of penal codes, and no former law enforcement or military training was required. The only background check performed to prove the "no felony" requirement was when applying for a bail license. All that was needed was a 20-hour training class with an accredited, licensed bail school and 40 hours of laws and arrests with the Sheriff's department. These were only certifications, unverifiable through any local, county, or state licensing system.

If my lingering rage hadn't left me in such denial, I would have paid more attention to the yards of unprotected political tape I was about to wrap myself in.

"Want to go to Sacramento to work an immigration bond this weekend?" My heart raced as I read Ken's text. "HELL YES I DO!" I eagerly responded. "Wait, what is an immigration bond? LOL." I added.

I hadn't heard of this type of bond before, nor was it mentioned in any of my research.

The way Ken and an ICE agent explained it to me is (as of 2012) if someone is here illegally and caught, they are arrested and bonded out with an immigration bond posted with the federal government, not the county or state. After years on bail, if the immigrant turns fugitive by missing court Immigration and Customs Enforcement will not arrest or assist in an arrest until

AFTER the bondsman pays the full bond amount to the court. This type of bond could drag on for years. A complicated process and probably why I didn't hear much about them, they weren't ideal cases.

But Ken was willing to take any case he could to build his network, and I too was willing to invest in a new client. We spent the few dollars we had between us, drove all night, eight hours, and stopped at the first Denny's for food, coffee, and to go over our paperwork.

We made notes of the fugitive's name, location, and description to give the police when it was time to make notification and confirm the warrant. We only had one address on the bail application, but when I entered the phone number in whitepages.com, it gave us a second address. We decided to door knock both locations.

The first address there was no answer, but the second address, a woman who matched our fugitive's description, was walking in front of the building towards the laundromat when we pulled up.

When we knocked on the door, a large Latin man in his early twenties aggressively opened it. He was about six-feet, four-inches tall, at least 350 lbs and already hostile before we had a chance to identify ourselves.

"No one lives here by that fucking name," he shouted as he stomped out of the doorway, trying to intimidate us with his size. I could see right through his tantrum.

"We are going to make some calls. If we have any further questions, we will be back. Thanks again." Ken told him before turning towards me, signaling that we needed to get back to the car and call the bondsman.

"That's her," I told Ken when we got back to the car.

Except for her hair color, which was lighter in her booking photo, the woman we just saw had freshly-dyed hair, her height and weight was the same. It wasn't difficult for her to get a fake ID off the Internet and deny her identity to keep evading the bondsman and ICE.

Ken shrugged his shoulders and took a drag off his cigarette,

"Doesn't mean shit if we can't get ICE or the police department to come and confirm her identity. We can't arrest her with an ID that says a different name because if we are wrong, that is a false arrest, false imprisonment, and a few other criminal charges I don't even want to think of right now." He reminded me while looking through his phone for the bondsman's number.

We both called and left several messages with ICE. Ken told the bondsman we had to stand down and wait to speak with the immigration to get their assistance to confirm this woman's identity. We had to leave left empty-handed.

We made no money, and the case was given to another team because the bondsman didn't care about following the rules, he didn't want to pay the court.

The case was bothersome on all fronts. How an "illegal" can get detained, bailed out, stay in this country another five to seven years, then get deported if the court deems to do so is absurd.

I told Ken I wasn't willing to do another immigration bond, no matter how much it paid.

* * * *

"I got a new case and recruited a couple of new guys to go with us to door knock the house, do you want to go?" My mentor sounded eager on the other end of the phone as if he had caught a big fish and couldn't wait for me to see it.

"Of course I want to go, what time?" excited to work a real case, I agreed.

He explained the plan that he and his new trusted allies had constructed. As much as I trusted Ken to know more than me when it came to tactics, I should have asked more questions about his new teammates. You should know as much as you can about the people you are going to kick in a door with carrying fully loaded firearms because you could end up in jail with them. Not only was I going to be accountable for my shit, but all the shit these fuckers did too.

The bond was almost due for payment to the court by the bondsman, making this case not only a priority but frustrating. When this close to the deadline, a bail bond agent can get desperate and hire every bounty hunter they can to make the arrest, but only the one that makes the arrest gets paid.

The fugitive was known to live at this house with a woman and her kids in Santa Ana, California. He was Latin, in his early forties and had warrants for drug charges. That was all the information we had. Ken had confirmed the arrest warrant with the sheriff's department and scheduled us all to meet at 11 p.m. that night to do a door knock on the house. We were sure the fugitive would be home by then, and it would be dark enough for us to remain unseen covering the doors and windows of the house.

We all met in a parking lot a couple of blocks over, and I recognized a few of the men from social media posts. We did our introductions while everyone geared up with their firearms, and I only had pepper spray. Quite confident, I wouldn't need any more weapons than that since I was only going for backup and to intervene if a woman ended up involved in the arrest.

"You still need to carry a firearm just in case we all get separated," one of the guys said.

They all looked like former military or military relatives. They were funny guys, but they scared the shit out of me. I felt like I was in a redneck comedy, and all we needed were horses. Somehow, I ended up with the shotgun. All I could do was pray I wouldn't have to use it. Having fired enough live ammo a few times before, I knew I could handle the weapon, but I didn't feel as badass as I thought I would.

The plan was Ken, and I would knock on the front door to gain entry while the others would cover the windows and back doors. The only problem with coming through the back door of the house was there were two mini trailers in the backyard where our fugitive could also be hiding.

The guys were supposed to quickly check the trailers while we knocked and gained entry through the front door. Once we were in, we would signal them and let them in through the back door.

We had been knocking for what felt like at least five minutes before a petite Latin woman maybe in her late twenties, who was about to pop pregnant, answered the door.

"Letty?" Ken asked. "I'm Ken. I spoke with you earlier today about Robert, a fugitive who used this address to bail out some time ago?" He said, reminding her who he was.

Ken stepped in the door and walked towards her, making her aware she didn't have a choice to say no. The house was extremely dark. I walked slow, trying to use my other senses since I couldn't see who or what was in front of me.

My heart raced as it might jump out of my chest. Almost immediately, I understood why men loved this job. If I had a dick, it would have been hard. The rush of fight-or-flight adrenaline is better than anything you can get by prescription. It makes you feel invincible and that what you are doing is heroic even if what you are doing is fucking stupid.

"Yes, I remember," she said as she tried to create distance between us. "As I told you, that guy has never lived here while I have been here, but my parents used to live here, and they may know him. I will get you their telephone number, and turn on the lights. It's dark in here. I apologize for taking so long. I was sleeping." Her tone was surprisingly calm.

I could only hope that her footsteps were walking towards a light switch like she promised and not for a weapon. In the same instant, I could see a shadow of a man moving towards her, one of our guys. This prick put his 9-millimeter to this pregnant woman's face. In complete shock, I was still able to react.

"HEY! Don't put that in her face. She's complying!" I screeched, trying to add bass to my voice like a mama about to whoop his ass.

To be sure he knew I was dead serious, I moved towards him with the shotgun until he lowered his weapon. I'd deal with his ass later.

She quickly made her way to the light. We started to look through the house. I realized, by the number of men that were coming out of the trailers and the way the rooms set up, this woman's house was full of possible illegal immigrants.

There were kids in a bedroom that the woman claimed to be her children, but one of the rooms had a locked door. When a man finally opened it, he was shirtless, and there were also two, possibly under-aged teenagers, in there. My lack of knowledge in sex trafficking left me unsure of my authority to react. I looked at the man who was now looking at the shotgun in my hands, and he was extremely nervous.

Looking at the mother, who didn't flinch, it was clear this was normal behavior.

"My uncle shares that room with my older daughters," she said.

It haunts me to this day that all I could do at that moment was stand there, watch and ask a few questions. How could I prove she was lying? I didn't speak Spanish, and if they were illegal, they had a strict script of exactly what to say to the authorities. The anxiety showed on their faces, frightened to death of the armed white men now storming through their home.

If I had called the police, they would have to prove there was abuse going on, and if they weren't citizens, they would be detained and possibly deported. Now I was torn between two devils. If I called the police, they would take them to a temporary foster home if they were citizens. If they weren't citizens, I have no clue where they'd go, but I was sure it wasn't a better option. Neither of these agencies can prevent cruel abuse to children while in their custody.

When the girls came out of the room, I lowered my weapon.

"Thank you," the mother said to me with a look of appreciation of my efforts not to scare her kids.

She started speaking Spanish to the girls who ran to her frightened. When the uncle came out of the room, I tried to look for an expression of guilt or shame, but he avoided looking at me. The guys searched that room for the fugitive and still didn't' find him. Once they finished, I took a peek to see if there was any evidence of inappropriate behavior with the girls, but there was nothing visible in my short assessment. As I knew there wouldn't be.

"Your uncle lives in this room with your daughters?" I asked.

As I said before, I lacked adequate training for this situation, and proof of a felony wasn't blatantly in my face. A lot of impoverished families share rooms and sometimes beds, with their kids, and that's no evidence of anything.

"We are adding another room for him to the house since he pays rent, the girls know it's temporary," she said stroking one of the girl's face lovingly. Either this chic was one hell of an actress or just a naive mother.

It would be another year before I learned about sex trafficking, and this case haunts me every time I think about it knowing what I know now.

Ken reviewed everyone's ID, took their information for the bondsman's paperwork, and we left, once again empty-handed.

Unsure whether I wanted to be in this business, after all, I went home that night unwilling to work with this group of men again. So far, this was not hero shit.

THEY SMELL FLESH

"I can't believe he put his gun in that woman's face!" I screeched at Ken on the phone the next afternoon after having time to absorb our outing the night before entirely. "She could have gone into labor and sued us for it, not to mention the unthinkable that he could have made a fatal mistake with his weapon!"

Ken knew I was right, but he held his tongue while I vented my fears and frustrations at him.

"I know, I'm going to talk to him about that," he said calmly.

Ken understood the risks, but he also knew that in this business, there was strength in numbers, and that included getting paid.

For me, I had a career in real estate and didn't want to watch a bunch of yahoos play cops and robbers. I was looking to be part of an elite team that did their jobs well and gave it some purpose, not more dysfunctional men wearing badges.

There was no denying how scared I was that night watching one of my team members put his gun in a pregnant woman's face. It's something you don't forget. And something I know she will never forget. No one knows how they will react when surrounded by a group of people who could harm or kill them.

Everyone has an opinion and a plan on how to handle them until faced with it in real-time.

* * * *

My encounter was one night while on duty at the prison after walking in dorm eight during swing shift with at least 25 inmates talking, laughing, undressing, and unwinding from their day. Swing shift was known as the "cop shift" because of its early afternoon to late evening chaos. Everyone is off work, eating, showering, watching TV, and getting into shit like you would expect mischievous teenagers to be. They are out of their dorms, wide awake, and looking to fuck with the cops out of sheer boredom.

I opened the door and immediately greeted with the

stench of man cave prison hell. The aroma of sweat, unauthorized food, and a 115 report (disciplinary report) was in the air.

Stepping in as I usually did, with my left hand at my side ready to engage and my right hand on my microphone clipped to my belt prepared to call for backup.

"Good evening Faciane," I heard inmate Sandoval say as he smiled with a wicked flirtation. His body jerked, trying to keep its composure. Sandoval was the MAC Rep for the 'others' and was himself, I believe, Cherokee Indian in his late forties.

Directly facing me, he was next to the only other door on the opposite side of the dorm. Passing each set of bunk beds slowly, I took a mental note of how many prisoners were in the dorm and who I could identify by name later if needed.

Sandoval watched me move like stalking his prey, our eyes locked on one another, being we were both alphas. I knew they could smell my flesh and all my smooshy places like wild and hungry animals. I kept my stare cold and calm, hoping he saw that he was going to have to commit to my death if he decided to engage me. They all would. My hand was now wrapping around my microphone as I inconspicuously unclipped it from my belt. I made it halfway through the dorm when Sandoval and three other inmates moved to block the door in front of me.

I stopped and smiled at them. At this moment, I should have been pissing on myself, but instead, my blood started to cool, and my heart stopped racing. A calm but fucking crazy came over me. Every woman worries about this moment.

I sat many nights staring at my TV, replaying various scenarios from my workday, and wondered how I would react if something like this were to happen to me.

In one of dad's movies I wasn't supposed to watch as a kid,

Flesh & Blood (Verhhoeven &Versylus, 1985) there was a scene where a group of men kidnapped a woman to assault, but when the ring leader began to rape her, she enjoyed it and reciprocated the sex. It was his kryptonite. He couldn't continue the rape and fell in love with her.

As twisted as it sounds, all I could think of at that moment was who I had to fuck to avoid a gang rape? At least until someone realized I was missing and the CERT team arrived in time to save me.

A prisoner moved in my peripheral, and when I turned, I saw four other prisoners move to cover the door behind me. Fuck!

"What are you going to do, Faciane?" Sandoval asked, still flirtatiously.

His face was red with arousal, and I'm positive that had I looked, his dick was fully erect, anticipating my response.

Taking one last look around to assess everyone in the room, I went back to staring at Sandoval.

I pulled my microphone to my mouth, rested my finger over the button, and told him, "Let's see who goes first," and stood there waiting.

It felt like the longest five seconds of my life, but they all started laughing, and the men moved from the doors. Sandoval chuckled at me like a child.

"We are just playing with you, Faciane," he said. "Have a good night."

My fear was frozen at the bottom of my shoes. As much as I wanted to run out of there in relief, I had to play it cool. Making my way to the door, I looked around the room at each one of them to let them know they weren't going to scare me out of doing my job.

They knew I was scared, but they wanted to see what I would do about it.

There were few guards the prisoners couldn't bully, and with such a turnover in the prison population, I had to prove myself almost every time I stepped on that yard. They were consistently testing my strength as a female guard in a man's cage.

Holding my composure, I pretended I didn't almost become a local headline and walked out the door. Because I knew the prisoners would be watching me, I didn't dare give them the satisfaction of seeing me frazzled or crying. I waited to get home to do that shit.

The protocol required that I write up every prisoner who was in that dorm and have them moved to a different prison. But I wouldn't and didn't. Not because they didn't break the law, not because they didn't scare the shit out of me but because they too were training me. They were teaching me to be better at my job. To make me test myself and question my abilities in not just the job, but life, as a woman, mother, and human being. Every moment of every single day.

* * * *

Ken contacted me two weeks later.

"We have another address for Robert we are going to try, would you like to come with us?" he asked in a hopeful tone. He knew I didn't feel safe with his new team, but he wasn't going to deny me the opportunity to hunt with them. Ken was a great partner like that.

"Sorry Ken, I don't have a sitter, but keep me posted if you need me to do anything on the computer or make calls for you." I politely and dishonestly declined.

I'm pretty sure he understood I was traumatized and unwilling to work another case with him and his chosen ones again. I hadn't confessed my uncertainty about whether to continue pursuing this business with him yet.

Not that I was naive to the idea that this job was as easy as a twenty-five minute TV show portrayed it to be but partially to its reality of dealing with real-life people in these scenarios. It started to feel like an overwhelming intimacy I had no desire to share with the people I was going to arrest.

Another month passed, and Ken had no new cases but contacted me to tell me he had landed a job with a team of all women. He would book the client in the jail after they made the arrests. They were also looking for a female bounty hunter to work with them.

"Are you interested?" he asked, excited for me.

All women? I wasn't sure that was what I wanted, either. Forgive me if I wasn't thrilled at the idea at first. Male dominating professions are stressful enough with the men, but the women are no picnic either. I had invested too much not to meet their team at least and see if we had the chemistry to work successfully together.

"Yes I am interested, how do I contact them?" I asked him hesitantly.

"They said to meet them at BJ's Restaurant tonight." He instructed confidently.

Sitting there nervously waiting for them, I had no idea

what they looked like and feared they were going to be "girly" girls that want to carry weapons and be cute.

Two blond women, twins, in pink shirts and black tactical pants, came in the door.

"Hi, I'm Staci, and this is my sister Laci," Staci introduced herself.

Standing up to greet them, I put out my hand for a proper handshake, and Staci had a firm grip. They were far from girly girls and both former LAPD, who had a successful bail and private investigation business over the years. They proudly boasted their success in using less-than-lethal weapons for all their arrests.

As we sat and continued talking, they both took turns asking questions, mostly about my experience while sharing theirs. They cussed and cracked jokes the whole time, and though there were two of them, both reminded me of Hanson.

I knew we'd make the perfect team.

3.

Bullet 3

BULLET 3-HAPPINESS

FATAL BEAUTY

I was a sheltered kid except for dad's collection of Hollywood "sin-ema" movies that he illegally copied onto VHS tapes. He was a movie junkie, and traveling both nationally and internationally in the military gave us a broad genre of movies, many unknown and unpopular to most.

You wouldn't be a true Keanu fan if you didn't "Dream to Believe (Lynch & Kramreither, 1986)" and aspire to be a gymnast dating a cute hybrid Asian guy who serves burnt toast in bed.

Many of these movies reflected his misogynistic views regarding women, but there were a few with strong female leads. Of course, they were women he found to be attractive and with sex appeal. One of my favorites was "Fatal Beauty (Goldwyn, Jr. & Holland, 1987)," starring Whoopi Goldberg, who plays a narcotics detective pursuing personal redemption.

Not only did this movie tastefully portray a strong woman

in law enforcement, but it also tried to depict the diversity in the 1980s crime world.

She was a former addict whose daughter, a toddler, overdosed after getting into her stash of drugs. Her character's risk-taking courage wasn't fueled by some cosmic force to be "good" at her job, but in taking responsibility for the consequences of her addiction and the death of her child.

She dedicated her life to ridding every parent of their stash without judgment.

Who knew I would see my reflection in this plot as an adult. Many times during this season of my life, I asked myself, what would Rita Rizzoli do?

The desire to work with an all-male group had diminished because I didn't feel safe working with them. Most of the men Ken recruited that night had no law enforcement or military training, which didn't make them deficient in skill only in their experience. My fear wasn't so much that I, myself, would cause someone to shoot me, but that I would get hit because of some fucker on my team who pissed off someone else. I had no desire to drown in piss every night to make an arrest.

The first time I heard of this team of women, I refused the idea of applying with their company. Yes, Sgt. Hanson was superior in her job—but she was a rare breed. It didn't take long to see that Staci and Laci were different. They were well trained and had over a decade of experience with a successful bail business, and regular clients who supplied them bounty hunting cases. Plus, they were very humble. We had chemistry from the moment we sat down. They, too, were military kids and found sanity in the chaos of the law.

They hired me that night part-time to start with just one catch; they posted videos of their arrests online.

The one thing I always said I wouldn't ever be part of was to tape and post videos of the arrests. Many times since starting in this business, I saw other teams post pictures or videos of their arrests, and I judged them, even had the nerve to lecture someone about the legal ramifications for exploiting their clients. Now, I had to classify myself as the biggest hypocrite.

* * * *

Ken taught me to keep my face hidden to be the most effective huntress, and I agreed with this strategy because I favored being in the shadows more than in front of the camera. Still, I was too excited about the opportunity to work with a well-known team to decline their offer.

Though I was very camera shy, the idea of being a hero for my daughter and myself mutated my confidence.

Pondering their offer for a few minutes while they explained their marketing events, I heard my self blurt out, "I'm in."

"Awesome, we'll text you later this week when we will be going out on our next case. Be sure to wear dark pants and a pink shirt. As you can see, we love pink." Laci instructed.

Pink? I fucking hated pink.

They had it on everything. All of the company cars, logos, and marketing swag drenched in color pink stamped with pink and red lips on them. Even their dam handcuffs were pink.

But, there was no denying that Staci and Laci were on to something by wearing such a non-threatening color. When I started working with them, I noticed how people responded to us as opposed to the other uniforms I had worn in the past that were all darker tones. Wearing pink did make it easier to de-escalate most situations.

Staci and Laci were not only bounty hunters but also had their own bail bond company. I obtained my bail license to add to my credentials in the event my non-existent criminal background ever came in to question.

The first few weeks out together, we didn't get to do much, but some recon (reconnaissance) and surveillance. Eighty percent of the job is sitting in a car, watching for the wayward client, and eating snacks.

Our first arrest was for a white man in his mid to late forties, who lived in an upper-class neighborhood, which was odd to me because he had a warrant for not showing to court for unpaid traffic tickets. It didn't make sense for people with money to get arrested for something so minor and in their control.

Do parking tickets get bounty hunters sent after you? Yes, in 2012, it did. If someone had unpaid parking tickets, a warrant was issued for their arrest and once arrested, given the choice of bail. While out on bail, they're still in the custody of the bondsman. If they missed their court hearing, the judge reinstated the warrant.

Most bond companies work with their clients any way they can, but some leave their bondsman no choice but to call in the cavalry. At this point, it turns to what I like to call "mob-shit," and it's either give up the money or the body.

In the majority of cases, the defendants can't afford to take care of the tickets, but this guy just had "better things" to do.

We had been by his house a few times the previous nights I worked with them, plus Staci and Laci had been looking for him on their own time with no luck, but this night we came around the corner and saw that all the lights were on and the garage was wide open.

"Oh yeah, they're home, time for Roni to get her first arrest," Staci said, excited to see how I handled myself.

If I couldn't handle an arrest like this, I wasn't cut out for the job in backing them up. The best way to learn what a person can do is to put their feet to the fire.

Staci took the lead as we approached the house, then Laci and I followed, covering the back. Staci knocked on the door, shouting "Hello, Hello." and then turned the doorknob to open the door. She made entry, and we both followed her inside.

If a person puts their address on a bail application and breaches the contract with their bondsman, yes, they are legally allowed to send bounty hunters to not only walk into the house but kick in the door if not permitted entry.

"Hello, Hello! Anyone home?" Staci repeated. We walked into the living room.

"We're in the garage!" we heard a woman faintly shout.

When we made our way back out, and to the garage, we saw the man who fit our fugitive's description. Staci quickly approached him.

"Put your hands behind your back," she commanded as she grabbed his wrist and started to wrap it around his back to cuff him.

"What the hell is this? You guys can't do this!" the man shouted and started to resist.

Staci had to wrestle him to the ground. Laci jumped in to assist, and I tried to stand over his legs to keep him from squirming as they cuffed him. As he screamed obscenities and threats, a woman, presumably his wife, came from the front of the house.

"I need you to stand right there, ma'am until we have him handcuffed," I told her in my most firm tone.

I didn't feel she was a threat, but no one wants to go to jail, and some people will do almost anything not to—including murdering you. Fortunately, she had no desire to engage us, only to check on her husband and be sure we did not scare her kids.

"Once we get him in the car and comfortable ma'am, we will explain everything to you," Laci hollered at her as we walked the now shamed man to the SUV.

I helped him climb up into the backseat and buckled his seatbelt. The man complained about us and the system the entire drive to the jail.

"Roni, since it's your first arrest, you also get to book our fugitive. It's a waiting process, but you can learn the paperwork and how to do it for our future cases," Laci instructed me as she pulled in the parking lot of Twin Towers Correctional Facility.

Wait—what?

"I have to sit at the jail and wait to book him in?" I asked, confused.

"Oh yeah, this is the L.A. County Sheriff Department, and it's almost midnight you will have to wait for a little while. It should be no more than an hour. Text us when the booking is complete, and we'll be back to get you," Laci said, confident I wouldn't fuck it up or lose our fugitive.

They called Ken to come and assist me since he was their official booking agent.

He and I sat with this guy for almost two hours before they booked him in.

Staci and Laci picked me up then took us out for food and drinks to celebrate our first arrest together. I felt high.

"I liked the way you handled yourself during the arrest, Roni," Staci said, sipping her glass of red wine.

"Yes, me too, you stayed out of our way and made sure no one stepped in. That is the kind of partner we need for this team," Laci added.

I blushed like a schoolgirl but didn't have the heart to tell them I wasn't that badass. The confusion of what to do when they tackled the guy to the ground left me with no other choice but to wing it.

"To a capture well-done and many more," Laci raised her glass to invite us to toast with her. I felt accomplished smiling at them both as our glasses touched.

CRAZY BITCHES AND CLEVER ADDICTS

After a few weeks of training, we landed a case where the fugitive resided in one of the largest methamphetamine user compounds in Garden Grove, California. It was on a three-acre lot in a residential area, and even the local police knew the location well.

The property was registered to the city as a licensed drug and alcohol recovery home, but known to be the home to many felons and fugitives. When we pulled up to do a door knock, it was already dark. I looked through the cracks of the wooden fence as we made our way to the front and saw the place was fucking creepy. If it weren't for the city lights that surrounded it, I would have thought I was about to enter an abandoned rural town reserved for horror movies.

We knocked on the front door, and three people answered while a group of six, or so, others peeked over the side gate and started with their "hellos" and "who are you looking for."

"We are Bounty Hunters, and we are looking for Shannon Dennis," Staci said to them.

"She isn't here anymore," one woman said as she came out the door.

We all took a defensive step back. More people came out of the door, and we quickly became outnumbered by an unpredictable group of people.

I slipped my hand in my pocket and put my index finger around the trigger of my Timber pepper gun, preparing myself for any possible altercations.

They were way too eager to invite us inside to search for our fugitive. No one had voluntarily invited us in.

Eventually, the boyfriend and co-signor of our fugitive made his way out of the house to us and swore he would let us know when Shannon came back to the compound. But he also claimed, confidently, that she wasn't coming back to the property.

We left for King Taco to eat and strategize a new plan, letting them think we had given up. We decided on going back to scope out the outer acres of the compound after midnight.

Staci and Laci never asked to search the house but had every intention of exploring the property. We didn't need their permission since the address was on the bail application.

We parked behind the property, and I climbed onto the ledge of the brick wall. There were several trailers parked with piles of junk spread out between them. Below the wall I was standing on, someone dug a ditch and deliberately stacked junk in it. It looked like a booby-trap to me, ensuring no one could hop over the gate and sneak-up on them. This game was a battle of wits.

I quickly climbed down to relay our newest obstacle to Staci and Laci.

"What did you see?" Laci eagerly asked.

I explained the ditch the clever recovering addicts had set up.

"So, what should we do?" Staci asked, hoping for a better suggestion than the obvious.

It wasn't so much that we weren't up for searching this three-acre compound but understood the reality of what we were up against. This place wasn't the average home, anything and everything illegal could be happening inside, and we needed to be prepared to handle it and still make it out safely.

I knew I wasn't ready, but this wasn't the time to chicken out.

"I say we go back to the front and act like crazy bitches," I chuckled, zipping up my jacket and pushing up my sleeves as if my lunatic switch was activated.

"I agree, we aren't going to pull her out any other way at this point. This place is too large to search with just the three of us, and even if we do, they already know we are here and have time and space to move her around," Laci sighed, moving back towards the SUV. She was right and had a point. That's what I would do if they were looking for me.

"At the very least, we will get someone to come out and tell us something," she added.

"Ok, so Roni, you have your pepper blaster, right?" Staci asked.

"Yes, I do," I said, both nervous and excited I would possibly have to use it.

"I'm going to bring the shotgun. Once I chamber a rubber bullet round, they will take us seriously," Laci said, chuckling.

I loved that idea. It's a 'shit-your-pants' kind of noise.

"Ok, I'm going to carry the taser," Staci said.

"Let's pull up close to the front door honking with the bright lights on," Staci said, laughing like a schoolgirl pulling a prank.

"Blasting country music," Laci added with the same giggle.

"Hell yeah!" I agreed, unable to control my chuckle at their plan.

We drove back and pulled up to the front door in the big ass black Suburban with the brights on, honking, and blasting country kick-ass music. I knew we were fucking up someone's high, and hopefully, they would be pissed off enough to push our fugitive right out the front door.

The same group of people poured out of the front door, and Laci slammed on the breaks. We hopped out of the truck, making it clear we weren't playing this time.

"S-H-A-N-N-O-N!!" we all started to shout.

"What the hell is this shit," one of the guys standing in front of the house yelled. The others grunted, groaned, and shouted 'fuck you' from behind the fence.

"Where is Shannon? We know she's here, and we aren't leaving until she comes out," I said sternly.

We continued our banter back and forth, but when the group tried to dominate us, Laci racked a round in the shotgun to get their attention. It makes such a distinctive sound that rattles through all of your vulnerable parts. Watching the front door, I saw a man coming at us, fast, and from the inside of the house. He was holding a bottle behind his back, and I could see it in his eyes he was unsure whether he should throw it at us.

"Do you have your taser ready?" I asked Staci. "This guy is coming towards this front door fast."

She tapped her pocket to assure me she was ready. The man and I locked eyes again as I stepped towards him prepared to engage with as much force necessary. He quickly realized he didn't want to exchange any violence and pulled his arm from around his back to take a swig out of the bottle in his hand; it was soda.

Another dramatic twenty minutes later, the boyfriend and cosigner of our fugitive came out the door again. Staci asked her standard questions, which only added to his frustration. I'm sure his high was gone, and being interrogated by three bitches wearing pink in front of these friends for a second time made him combative.

There was no way to prove it, but he appeared to be stalling us with his tantrum while our fugitive continued to hide or make her way off of the property.

He eventually clammed up and walked back into the house. We had to come up with a better plan.

Before we left to go home for the night, Staci gave the company number and reward information to a few of the residents in hopes someone would give Shannon up soon.

* * * *

"Meet us at the office early today!" Staci shouted in the phone before I could say hello. "We got a call from someone at the compound to help us locate and arrest Shannon. She is with her now."

It was hard to believe how effective offering a reward was when they first told me, but rarely is their loyalty amongst thieves.

We met at the office to gear up, then headed towards the compound. Shannon must have pissed this gal off for her to not only give up her location but to do so without trying to hide her own identity. As we waited for her to meet with us, we contacted the local police to let them know we were back at the compound. I could hear the police officer on the other end of the phone line giving a stern warning to Staci.

"You know when we search that compound, we go in with no less than thirty men fully armed. You ladies better be careful out there,"

Laci gave him the perfect response. "Good thing we're women, we only need three." I can still hear her say it. We chuckled. Well, they did. I fake chuckled. The police only went in this place with thirty men heavily armed? And all I have on me is pepper spray? Hearing that made it difficult not to be petrified.

We met with the informant in a strip mall a few blocks down from the compound. She was looking to get some vengeance while making some extra cash. I don't recall the exact amount of the cash reward, but it was large enough to make it worthy of her time if we made the arrest.

The plan was for her to wait at the strip mall until we made the arrest, and we would come back for her after. She gave us a rundown and a generic drawing with the layout of the compound, including all the trailers and connected rooms for us to pinpoint Shannon's exact location.

We parked around the corner and approached the compound from the front door, which was already open. Staci started shouting for, while Laci racked a rubber bullet round in the shotgun to announce that our mini Calvary was coming on through.

We moved quickly through the adjoined shacks and trailers. A few of them were off the ground and had holes dug underneath for people to hide or store drugs, weapons, and any damn thing else. Once we made our way to the room where Shannon was supposed to be, she wasn't in there. Of course.

I was so focused on covering the rear and where we were going that I missed the audience that had gathered to watch us. Staci noticed the crowd too and motioned for us to follow her back out the way we came. The residents started to talk shit and brought out their dogs, signaling it was time to get the hell out of there.

Once we made it out the door, Staci sent a text to the informant. Laci guarded Staci, and I watched the front door to be sure no one came out after us.

Staci's phone rang. She took the call while walking away from the compound towards the corner of the street and then shouted, "She's right there down the street!" and took off running.

Laci and I took off running behind her, and I still couldn't see who the hell we were chasing after. I faintly heard Staci describe her while running, but I couldn't see anyone that fit the description ahead of us. I can now confirm Craig's wisdom from the movie "Friday (Gray & Charbonnet, 1995)," you aren't catching a crack or meth addict on foot.

We split up through an apartment complex. I had to stop to catch my breath and realized I had no idea if I was running in the right direction. I couldn't breathe.

We made our way back around and met each other a few streets over. The informant was standing on the corner, waiting for us. She saw Shannon was picked up by a guy riding a beach cruiser bike and was more than likely at a house a few streets over. It was another house Shannon was known to hang out at it.

The house appeared to be empty until we walked up to the door and saw a couple of women leaving. They said they hadn't seen Shannon in over a week and were mere employees of the homeowner, not personal associates.

I was tired and highly annoyed by this time. After being out-ran by an addict, my partners, who were both older than me, I was now feeling not only my age but how out of shape I was. And hungry.

Tired of getting nowhere, I decided to stop asking where Shannon was and started looking for clues that she was somewhere inside one of the rooms on the property.

She had to have shown up either on a bike or on foot. Once I started to search towards the back of the house, I noticed a second portion of the house lit-up with a group of people hanging out inside. This part of the house wasn't visible from the street.

I called Staci and Laci over to help search it. The owner of the home came out of the back door once he saw my flashlight. He was reluctant to let us search it, but I could tell he didn't want the cops doing it and gave in. We went through both sections of the house. The front was mostly full of storage and the back set up as a living space with rooms and a bathroom. We searched all the rooms except one. This particular room belonged to the owner, and he had it suspiciously locked from the inside.

He had been cooperative with our search until we wanted in his room, which only made it more suspicious that she could be hiding there. Staci went out front to contact our informant to find out if she had any updates, and Laci guarded the locked door. I spoke with a woman visiting the house about her relationship with Shannon.

Staci came back in and told me to go out front and check the neighbor's yard for the bikes.

"If they are outside, she is in this house somewhere," she whispered.

I did as she asked and did not see the bikes.

Going back to the house to tell her that the bikes weren't out front, and I heard her screaming, "She's in here, she's in here!" I ran as fast as I could through the house to the now unlocked room, pushed the door open, and saw Staci struggling with a woman who looked like a zombie. Staci found her hiding under a pile of clothes in the closet.

It wasn't apparent she was Shannon at first because she looked nothing like her last booking photo. I ran towards them, jumping on top of Shannon's legs to help restrain her while Staci put the cuffs on. I, too, struggled with the strength this tiny woman had.

Staci was trying to hold her down as she bucked her body. She was high as a kite and fully loaded with adrenaline.

Laci heard the commotion and came to the door. When she saw Shannon resist us while we struggled to contain her, she shouted for her to stop, and then shot her in the back of the leg with a rubber bullet.

I felt the bullet vibrate through my pants, almost grazing

my calf, and her body stiffen in shock as the ball made its impact. Staci managed to get the cuffs on her and stand up. Shannon accepted defeat and stopped flailing around. I pushed her towards Staci while moving off the bed to also stand up.

We each held one of her elbows while quickly moving her out of the house and to the SUV. Laci followed with the shotgun in hand to shield us from anyone who may try and interfere with the arrest.

Never had I seen anyone this strung out on drugs before, to the point that they looked like a subhuman zombie.

Her hair was dyed half black and white like Cruella De Vil, in the 101 Dalmations movie (Herek, Hughes & Mestres, 1996). She was about five feet, seven inches tall, and couldn't have weighed more than 90 pounds. She had hardly any clothes and was now crying, screaming and spitting like a rabid animal. She was bleeding from the rubber bullet and an open scab from the scuffle I tried to clean her up without getting her blood on me. The moment I regretted not putting a set of gloves in my pocket.

Staci called the police to let them know we were code four (everything is under control) and made our arrest. It had been more than two hours since we had made our original notification. Shannon appeared to be delirious while rambling about her mean boyfriend. All I could think to do in calming her was to ask about her kids. Within ten minutes, three police cars showed up and offered to take her in and book her for us.

They were all polite, professional, and a little impressed with us.

All I wanted to do was go home and shower. Also, remember to buy gloves and a damn treadmill.

A few days later, Staci found out from the bondsman that

Shannon was released back to the compound under the guise of rehabilitation because it still registered as a licensed rehabilitation facility. It was this ludicrous part of the system I hadn't witnessed before. Not only her bullshit release and the fraud taking place in the name of rehabilitation, but all that work and risk for her to be right back out there? This nonsense had to be a fluke.

But it wasn't. Shannon's case was not unique in both the bail business and in real life. A perfect example of what recycling criminals for-profit looks like and how it has plagued society.

No one wants that life, they end up there, and it could have easily been my life with just a couple of different choices. It was hard not to empathize with her.

And then, we got a new case.

AN UNFORGETTABLE PERFORMANCE

The co-signer on our new case was the wife of the defendant, who insisted on being taken off the bond because, as she put it, "he is going to flee the country."

She was about to include all of us in the most dramatic and betraying performance of her life.

This client, Arturo, wasn't yet a fugitive and had a prior bond with the bondsman that hired us but fled the country before the bondsman could arrest him. After Arturo completed his sentence for that case, the bondsman again trusted to bail him out for this current case because he had a credible co-signor. He had another week before having to turn himself in to do two years in prison.

When we arrived at bondsman's office to go over the paperwork, the co-signor and her friend were with him. Layla, the co-signor and wife, began explaining that she was an adult entertainer for a dance club and that Arturo was jealous and had been threatening to hurt her. She already planned the arrest.

Her plan was to fake like she was having a miscarriage, giving us the perfect opportunity to arrest him in front of the hospital emergency room.

Layla added that she "was" pregnant, had had an abortion without him knowing, and he still believed her to be pregnant. She continued her scandalous story, chuckling and boasting that she had already conspired with her doctor to lie for her. She had convinced the doctor that Arturo was violent and threatening her. He, too, continued to lie and confirm her pregnancy to Arturo.

The contemptuous look on her face as she told her story and plotted her husband's capture with us was revolting. I wanted to get as far away from her as possible before I said something I couldn't take back and upset my partners and the bondsman. I hated this case already.

Unfortunately, it didn't matter that she was trifling. She wanted off the bond, and the bondsman didn't want to risk Arturo fleeing the country again.

Yes, she had the legal right to have him arrested and returned to jail, but because of her approach, helping her felt like selling my soul to the devil.

It was hard for me to believe this woman was a victim, and I became pissed that we had to indulge her and make the arrest. But I turned off my emotions and did my fucking job.

The next evening went almost just as planned. We hid on the side of the hospital facing the emergency room so we could see Layla and Arturo pull in the parking lot and walk up to the front entrance of the emergency room. She dressed for her part entirely.

She held a look of pain on her face as Arturo helped her out of the car. Wrapped in a blanket with her hair tied back, waddling while hunched over, she kept her stride slow towards the entrance. I could see he was genuinely concerned for his wife and the baby he thought she was carrying for him.

I wanted to arrest her for abusing the system and creating a cluster fuck of a situation for someone she claimed to love. At the same time, concerned about the violence this man might unleash upon us once he realized we were arresting him in the middle of him attending to his distressed wife and baby.

As they approached the emergency room door, we quickly ran towards them, screaming at Arturo to put his hands up. Immediately he looked pissed enough to fight.

Layla quickly got into character and began to cry uncontrollably. Pleading and screaming, "don't arrest him, PLEASE" while slipping Arturo's ID in my left hand behind my back as I pointed the taser to his chest with my right. When he started to resist, he caused Staci to struggle to get the cuffs on. I demanded him to comply.

"Get in the car, or you're going to get tased!" I shouted at him.

I hurried to get him closer to the SUV before having to use any force. He continued to curse and yell at us.

Laci was so close to Arturo that she was worried I would accidentally tase her too. Staci got the cuffs on him, and he got in the truck though pissed and confused why we were arresting him.

"I'm turning myself in in ten days," he said a few silent moments later. Calmer, almost pleading.

He began explaining his side of the story as we all came off of the intense adrenaline we had racing through our veins.

"Yes, but we were told you were going to run to Mexico and not turn yourself in," Staci said in her lecture tone.

He was a young Latin man raised on the streets of Los Angeles, California, and had tattoos on every area of his body that was exposed, including his face.

The tattoos were mostly pictures of a woman and children, presumably Layla. Others were names, romantic sayings, and maybe a handful of smaller ones that could have been gang-affiliated.

I was stunned that he turned his body and face to a shrine for his wife. The same woman who just had him arrested while taking her to the hospital, for miscarrying the baby, his baby, she had already aborted.

It was a mortifying experience as a mother knowing her son could face the same betrayal with a woman as a man one day.

* * * *

In Arturo's current case, he tried to slice another man's neck with a box-cutter during a fit of rage for disrespect between the two at work. Once he returned to jail for this case, he decided a life change was long overdue. Arturo wasn't ashamed of who used to be, only proud of who he had become. His brown pride shined bright through his smile.

Did I mention he pulled up to the hospital in a new Range Rover?

Layla called Staci's phone to speak with Arturo, Staci put her on the speaker to allow him the call. Still, in character, she cried and begged to know why we arrested her husband. Staci told her to call the bondsman and meet us at the jail.

A few minutes went by, and she called again, and this time she wasn't in character.

"There are things you need to explain to me, Arturo. I looked on your computer, what's this stuff on your computer Arturo!" she demanded.

"I don't know what you're talking about being on my computer?" He responded, shocked and confused.

I looked at Staci, and we both wanted to laugh, but the confusion of Layla switching characters in the middle of her fucking script left us all unsure how to react. Layla screamed more questions about other women at him, and every time he tried to answer her, she interrupted with more accusations and threats. I had to intervene.

"Sorry, Layla, but you will need to talk to him about this later we need to get our paperwork done to finalize the arrest. Staci will call you later," I explained, then hung up on her.

She continued to call both Staci and my phones, to scold her husband.

"What the hell did you do?" I asked him, now even more flustered with his wife. Did she have us arrest him just to snoop through his shit?

"I have no idea what she is talking about," he answered with that lost child look on his face, scrambling to figure out what he had done wrong.

"Were you talking to someone on social media, and she saw it?" I asked him.

"No, I don't have those kinds of accounts," he said, growing frustrated.

We sat there in silence for a few seconds, and then he exclaimed "OOHHHHHH!!!!" with a massive grin on his face and started to chuckle.

"I play dominoes on the net and have people I play and talk to, that must be it. But I didn't say anything out of line. She's trippin." He said, straightening himself up as his confidence had returned.

As I suspected, as soon as we arrest her husband, she went through his computer and analyzed his conversations to confirm her suspicions that he was cheating.

Now that she showed her hand, and some of ours, he started to tell us about prior incidents where Layla used his trust to betray him.

There are three sides to every story: yours, theirs, and the truth.

His story goes;

When he caught this case, he voluntarily took anger management classes and started a legit business he enjoyed to change his life and break away from the prison cycle.

He had dedicated his life to Layla and her children and even started attending church. Not only did she criticize him for going to church but refused to attend services with him.

Her jealousy of other women created a rift between the mother of his biological children and him, disallowing him visitation for over two years. She controlled every part of him.

"The last time bounty hunters arrested me, she called

them on me, but when I tried to get away, she put sugar in the tank of my car so that I couldn't leave," he told us, oddly amused.

We pulled into the jail parking lot, walked him inside, and I stayed to book him while Staci and Laci returned to the car to contact the bondsman.

He was at ease while waiting for the Sheriff's deputy to take him, and I was a mess. It didn't seem fair.

"I only have two years to do, and this will all be over. All I care about is getting back to my business," he said confidently.

"As dedicated as you are, I know you will. Make your contacts and stay focused," was all I could off.

It can be complicated in these situations as a woman. I have to avoid appearing weak or attracted by not showing emotion and still give positive and affirming words to take with him inside those cold walls.

Granted, he was a violent offender who had done enough time to be classified as dangerous, but he was also the husband to and victim of a possible sociopath.

We chatted another twenty minutes before the booking deputy came out to the waiting area to take him inside the jail. I took my cuffs from the deputy once he exchanged them for his own, wished Arturo luck, and left.

Hurrying, I ran back to the car to find out what Layla's damage was.

"She is crazy and keeps calling," Staci said, irritated.

"Did you know that she criticized him for going to church and did this to him before his last anger management class? That he voluntarily took?" I told them now able to express my disgust with his predicament fully.

"What?" Laci asked in shock.

"According to Arturo, not only had he volunteered for the anger management program on his own, but Layla tried to sabotage his efforts as often as she could. He built a network of support with the staff in the program to shrink his time and get his record cleaned up to move forward with a different life." I sighed, slumping in my seat, looking for the package of starbursts I had brought from home.

"That's fucked up," Staci said.

We sat there and had a few minutes of silence before driving off to get dinner and discuss our new case.

After this arrest, I assisted with many cases where the cosigner wanted off the bond, and we had to return the defendant to jail. A large percentage of them were women who were manipulating the rules of the contract to seek revenge on their partners only to bail them out again later.

Laci and Staci, and soon myself, despised these types of cases. It was a power play that wasted time and money. Not to mention a fucked-up game to play with someone's freedom for them, not "behaving."

FORGIVENESS COSTS

"Roni?" I heard a woman's voice on the other end, pretending to be unsure whether it was me on the phone.

"Who's this?" I asked with as much attitude as possible.

I wasn't sure if it was her, but when her phone number

flashed on the caller ID, I recognized the area code and immediately became defensive.

"It's Toni," she stuttered fearfully of the fire I might spit at her.

That same rage, as though more than four years hadn't passed, began to rise in me. The image of choking this woman to death once more danced around in my head. I sat there, quiet, with the phone to my ear. Speechless for the obvious reasons, I kept silent and waited.

"I know this is crazy of me to call you like this, but I told Tyrone I was going to. I want to ask you for your forgiveness. Tyrone misses Faith, and we want her to have a relationship with our son."

I wish I could tell you what she said after that and for the next few minutes, but I haven't a clue. I sat in a mini-state of shock while every emotion ran through me. I wanted to laugh, cry, and scream.

My daughter saw me slumped on the floor next to my bed, phone to my ear, and asked who it was. Once I whispered her step monster's name, her eyes widened with a look of horror than quickly, surprise. I motioned for her to sit in the other room so I could keep focused.

The only words I could calmly get out were, "My daughter was traumatized for more than a year after you beat her. Many nights she awoke from a deep sleep screaming that you were going to come to after again. It took her months to feel safe to get off her bed because you told her there were alligators underneath it. Do you realize what you have done to her? Not to mention me?"

To keep from showing too much emotion and breaking down, I stopped myself. Toni wasn't going to get that from me. It didn't matter her intentions because she made it clear this gesture to gain my forgiveness was to appease her family, not mine.

As I charged up to spit more venom at her, she suddenly began to sob uncontrollably and loudly.

"Oh my God, what have I done?" she screamed into the phone.

I remained quiet, allowing her a moment to express her humiliation. It had been over four years, enough time for me to mature. Well, some, anyway.

As she sobbed, I tried to listen to her with understanding. I, too, came from a long line of abusers and heard the familiar shame in her voice that mom had after attacking me as a kid.

I felt forced to choose between my hate for her and her vulnerability.

"I don't know what to say," I said after she paused to calm down.

"I want to work things out with you, Roni, so we can heal and work on being a blended family," Toni pleaded convincingly.

She explained that it was hard for her husband, Tyrone, to deal with emotions. As if I gave a fuck about his feelings.

That bastard wasn't calling us, Toni was. Her step-parent hands may have bruised our daughter, but he was the biological parent who knew it was happening and did nothing to stop it.

My emotions continued to pull me in every direction. I soon saw my daughter's shadow as she crept her way closer to the door to hear the conversation. When she saw me, I tapped my hip, motioning for her to sit down and listen to me confront her tormentor.

Toni started explaining her side of the story, one she had probably rehearsed several times.

"I was jealous of you. You're beautiful, Latin, and have a big booty. No woman wants the baby mama to be cute," she chuckled while trying to mask her uneasiness with such a brave confession.

"What? I never treated you like I was better than you," I responded like the former mean high school girl I never was.

Well, what the hell do you say to something like that? What she said to me was that real ugly truth most women deny, play games, and even beat your kid to avoid admitting. And here it was thrown right in front of me like shit I had to pick up and do something with it.

Tyrone inserted Toni in both of our lives, and she played the part as best as she knew how. I couldn't deny that I understood her. Her confession of jealousy echoed in my ears.

I had been there myself, comparing myself to an ex or the kid's mom to "out-do" her to gain points with the man. The danger in this is becoming so desperate that women end up treating each other like enemies.

There is no denying the power of this kind of jealousy, not to mention the race factor. Toni made sure to add "Latin" to her list of envious reasoning.

She felt she couldn't compete with Tyrone's attraction for women of other races, just as I couldn't compete with him wanting to marry only a black woman.

I respected her honesty, even if having to swallow it was like drinking glass. If only I could confess my jealousy of her ability to love a black man and bear his children free from prejudice and judgment. Black love is an acceptable societal measurement of success for her culture while bleaching my Latin roots, is a societal measurement of success for mine. But I didn't dare share my vulnerabilities with her.

Toni explained her mother abused her as a child too, and as I listened to her describe her childhood as a young black girl, I realized the parallel of our lives.

In the 1960s, Malcolm X tells his story in *The Autobiography of Malcolm X* (Alex Haley, 1965) how racial circumstances forced his mother to lie about her race and say she was Latin to gain employment. When her employer discovered her dishonesty, they fired her.

In the book, *How Race is made in America* (Natalina Molina, 2014) in the 1930s in San Diego, California, Mexicans also were segregated and separate from whites in schools. Which forced many Mexicans not to shop in black-owned establishments or socialize with their black neighbors out of fear of being classified as "black."

Natalia describes these racial scripts or common themes that shape racism, as strategic agendas amongst the black and brown communities

Both our mothers were successful women of color who worked hard and ate a lot of shit from white feminism and affirmative actions that came after their mothers, our grandmothers, generation. They were a generation of women who wanted their daughters to be financially independent, married to good men, and bear children who could change the world. Still, and silently, setting a standard that required abuse towards their children.

Most of us make jokes about getting our asses whooped and believe none of it affected us, but it did. It didn't make our mothers cruel, just recyclers of antiquated rules and principles their parents gave them. Both Toni and I had cultures that taught us to raise our children with violence, humiliation, and shame.

As the colonist said, it should be.

In *A People's History of the United States*, Howard Zinn writes that a priest with the pilgrim colony, John Robinson, believed that "children were stubborn with a mind that arises from pride and that it must be 'broken and beaten down.' Their foundation of education being 'laid in humility and tractableness (easily led) and other virtues, if permitted, will come later."

A surprising philosophy considering we all grew up watching white people treat their kids so kindly on television. Many minorities were and still are, encouraged to abuse their children, but we won't admit it.

Mom came from an abusive family, as did her parents. My great-grandmother, Yaqui Indian, took my grandmother and put her feet in fire to keep her from running out of the house. She was six yrs old.

My grandmother unaware of her abuse until noticing the neighbor cry watching her scoot across the sidewalk on her butt because her feet had burns on them.

As a preteen, my grandmother struck my mother hard enough in the face to lock her jaw. They had to go to the emergency room to close it.

My mother left marks on me a few times and wouldn't allow me to go to school for fear of being reported to authorities.

It's a learned behavior that I had vowed never to inflict on my children, but Toni had, and the only way to set it straight was for her and me to become allies in motherhood to ensure if we moved forward, it would never happen again.

There was no making it right.

* * * *

In memory of Yanika Denee Daniels.

A little more than a year before Toni's call, the daughter of a dear friend was shot and killed while hanging out with friends at a local dance club celebrating her birthday and Mothers Day weekend.

She was a young black woman in her late twenties and a mother of two. The person who killed her was a young Mexican man who carelessly pulled a gun to show off, and it went off, firing a bullet that hit her neck and killed her before anyone could get help.

Her family would be justified to seek vengeance, but they didn't. Instead, her parents forgave and asked that everyone else also forgive. The foolish young man didn't mean to kill their daughter. He was inexperienced handling a firearm and trying to look badass in front of his friends. It was a stupid mistake he'll pay with the rest of his life for.

They inspired forgiveness in all of us that knew them. If those parents could forgive, I should be able to too.

The only way it would work was if I communicated with only Toni and kept my dealings with Tyrone to a minimum, if any, at all.

Toni and I were on the phone for quite some before my daughter asked to speak with her. Bravely, she stood up to confront the monster who haunted her dreams. I handed her the phone, and she slowly took it and placed it on her ear. I watched her courage sprout before my eyes.

"Hi Toni, how's my brother doing?"

She had been waiting all these years to meet the sibling who witnessed her abuse from the womb. Toni answered her question and began making amends while pleading for my daughter's forgiveness.

"I forgive you. When can I come to see my brother?" my daughter eagerly asked.

I sat on the floor next to my bed as if glued to it. Having no idea what to say or what my daughter should say, and I certainly did not want to influence her emotions either way. Soon I heard her say goodbye and handed me the phone.

"My dad is going to call me in a few minutes," she said, with a bright and happy smile I hadn't seen for some time. I chose to make our truce about her healing and not my vengeance, so I pretended to be happy for her. It was a matter of minutes before an almost identical number called my phone. I knew it was Tyrone. Speaking with him would ruin the last hour of hard work his wife and I had done to save his family. Fuck that and fuck him.

My daughter joyously answered the phone and began to speak to him as though no time between them had passed. I could tell by her answers and questions he was working his way to an opportunity to visit her.

As much as I wanted to oppose it, I couldn't. Toni asked for forgiveness, and at this time in my life, I was still a die-hard Jesus freak and believed I had no other choice but to forgive her. In my logic, the only way to keep Toni from being the ghost in my baby's nightmares was to forgive her.

"My mom's a bounty hunter now," I watched my daughter boast to her dad with pride and confidence.

"Oh. Really?" I could hear her Tyrone respond with a curious tone.

"Yeah, she has handcuffs and pepper spray and can arrest people," she sounded so grown up, letting her father know she had security now.

As she continued the conversation, I could see that for her me becoming a bounty hunter was crucial in her ability to feel safe with her dad again. She knew I could arrest them if they got out of line this time, and that made her fearless. She stood there, daring and bold as I had never seen her. Being that hero for her made her feel protected, and I couldn't take that from her, no matter the regrettable risks that awaited me.

Of course, I wasn't completely delusional. No matter how sincere the apology, there was no guarantee that my daughter was safe with those two.

My grandmother once told me that the only way to guarantee a babysitter would give your baby the best care was to pay them well.

Tyrone owed me seven-thousand-dollars in back child support, and I agreed to release the entire debt from our account with the Division of Child Support Services. All Tyrone would have to pay was the current monthly charges and the medical expenses ordered by the court.

I hoped, for a season at least, that money would buy their loyalty.

VIDEO INFECTIONS

Less than a week and numerous threats later, Blass hired Todd Greene, a personal injury attorney from San Diego, California. He was most known for winning a $17 million lawsuit in a battery case where a black man was beaten outside of a bar by a white man, and the beating crippled him.

Greene saw the perfect opportunity to create a cash cow out of the bail industry, beginning with our fight at Arby's trying to arrest Blass, now evidenced on the video uploaded by us to Youtube. As much as I wanted to believe Greene's aggression towards us was racially motivated by my "alleged" assault on Blass, I'm more inclined to think he was defending the pride of every male ego.

Jim Moret with "Inside Edition (Lachman, 1988-present)" was our first interview, and he was so laid back that immediately I felt at ease. Most of the conversation focused on Staci and Laci's experience and success in the bail business, but towards the end, he turned to me.

I explained my side of the story with as many details as I could remember. My words still lingered over my lips when I heard Mr. Moret ask, "A taser, pepper spray, and rubber bullets—do you think you used excessive force?"

I responded as though he was a judge about to convict me.

"No," I answered him with conviction. Blass was dangerous, and I wasn't going to allow the media, my partners, or anyone else to plant doubt in my mind.

I was amused by watching the aired version of the interview that included Greene and Blass's interviews. After accusing me of blinding him with a rubber bullet, the camera zoomed in on Blass's eye, and it looked like he rubbed Neosporin inside of it to appear infected. Prison shenanigans 101.

I almost choked from laughing. Prisoners find craft ways to get to the medical ward for whatever reason. Blass, I'm sure, was no exception.

After this first interview, it seemed like every news and gossip network wanted to talk to us, as well as many journalists for newspapers. It didn't take long to learn that no matter how much I explained my side of the story, the media was determined to create their narrative about who I was. With or without my permission.

We were just one of the many stories, in public opinion, where law enforcement, private or government, did their jobs poorly. The secret sauce in ours was its level of sexy. Three women, wearing pink with pink handcuffs, shooting white guys at fast-food eateries, apparently boost ratings, especially when a Latina pulls the trigger.

The public and Blass wanted us arrested for excessive force, but since we didn't make the arrest, the elements required to charge us weren't there.

The law allows as much force "necessary" to effect the arrest—this includes physically restraining someone or having to use, preferably, a less than lethal weapon on them. In California, bounty hunters are private persons or citizens, and in 2013, The California Penal Code 843 (PC843) defines a citizen's arrest as:

"An arrest is taking a person into custody, in a case and the manner authorized by law." An arrest may be made by a peace officer or by a private person (citizen).

Blass violated not only his bail contract but also Penal Code 843A:

"If a person has the knowledge, or by the exercise of reasonable care, should have knowledge, that he is being arrested by a peace officer, it is the duty of such person to refrain from using force or any weapon to resist such arrest."

Many people like to debate this code because the language

does not specify "or private person" as it does in Penal Code 834, but it applies.

Blass did not have the authority to resist us, and because he did, and the arrest was legit, we committed no crime.

Soon, it seemed like we were giving more interviews than working on cases.

Everyone wanted their side of our story to tell; Good Morning America, Geraldo, NBC, ABC, Fox, local newspapers, and a few international news networks. Most were rude and appeared to be creating a narrative that only supported Blass and Greene. One journalist dared to apologize on our behalf.

Fuck that and fuck her, I still don't apologize.

My interview with Telemundo was refreshing, and I felt justified for the first time during this entire experience. Staci and Laci worked all through the night, and with the interview being first thing in the morning, they asked that I do it by myself. It was the only interview I had done alone.

I quickly grew a healthy fear of getting disgraced in another language, one in which my mother could translate. When I arrived at the office, the crew was setting up, and the host, an attractive Latin man, starts speaking to me in an Antonio Banderas accent. He complimented me on my beauty and expressed his and the network's gratitude for agreeing to interview on such short notice.

I shyly apologized for not being fluent in Spanish.

"No problem beautiful, we will have it translated. Don't worry," the journalist assured me with a charming smile.

The bright lights turned on, and the camera started to

roll, as the stunningly handsome reporter began commentating his segment. Most of what he said I cannot recall now, but I do remember his excitement.

"Tell us about this exciting and amazing event!" He asked with a cheesy grin as if I had done something historic. It dawned on me at that moment that perhaps I had.

I legally shot a white supremacist with rubber bullets, in a public place, as a Latin woman and didn't go to jail or get deported for it.

The Latin community viewed my actions as heroic, vindicating me. This network was not interviewing me to judge or exploit us like the others.

As I floated through his questions, I tried to sound as confident and professional as possible, and within minutes it was over.

The reporter and his crew seemed pleased with how the interview went and began to pack up to leave. I stood there, smiling, unable to remember what the hell I had just said.

The handsome reporter came over to say his good-byes and shook my hand.

"How did I do?" I asked, hoping he would be honest if I bombed the interview.

"You did just fine, Bonita," he said, brushing his hand over my cheek.

His gentle gesture of comfort sent chills down my nether region. We call them Latin lovers for a reason.

I kept my composure and changed the subject before overstepping my boundaries and adding another scandal to my resume.

"How did you hear about our story? Did you see us on other networks?" I asked him curiously.

His response still makes me blush.

"No, actually, it was one of our fans who called in and asked us if we had seen that 'badass Latina' shooting the white guy with rubber bullets on TV. We knew we had to come for an interview," he blushed like he got a little starstruck answering me.

It felt good to get "blooded" by the Latin community finally. I'd endured many incidents where Latin people shamed me for not speaking Spanish or treated me like a guera (white girl), but this day, they wanted to hear what I had to say.

Most of our cases were for Latin clients, which always bothered me, and still does.

Now that they too were backing me up, I was determined to finish the job.

Blass' ass was mine.

* * * *

Greene made sure to keep Blass out of our reach by moving him around between cities for interviews and medical treatment for the eye I allegedly blinded.

It was Easter weekend, and we decided to spend the holiday looking for him. As licensed private investigators, Staci and Lace were given the gift of phone pings from the tech gods and were able to track his phone to San Diego.

We also suspected him there because most of the networks interviewing him, and Greene's office, were also located there.

We spent most of the night driving in circles looking for him near Denny's restaurant in a business section with a couple of corporate hotels just off Interstate 8. After about four hours, we stopped at Denny's to use the restroom and grab a coffee. When I came out, Staci and Laci were having a conversation with a police patrol unit, which had also stopped to get coffee and parked across the parking lot.

As I headed towards them, I noticed a black older model, four-door sedan, parked in the shadow of the building across from the restaurant and adjacent to where Staci and Laci were. It was a closed gas station, with a covering over it that gave a dark enough shadow to hide most of the car, including the identity of the driver. I couldn't recall seeing it when I went inside to use the restroom.

Whoever it was didn't conceal themselves very well.

Standing there for a moment, almost delirious with exhaustion from being up all day and night, I stared at the car, trying to see who was in it.

Nervous the lights were going to turn on, and the car would come charging at me like the classic eighties thriller movie "Christine (Kobritz, Franco & Carpenter, 1983)". The person in the vehicle must have noticed me because they quickly sat up, started the car, and began to pull away.

When the car pulled out of the night shadow and into the light of the Denny's, I had almost a perfect view of the driver and saw he was a white man with slicked-back, brown hair. While lighting his cigarette, the guy drove by me slow intentionally for me to see him. It was fucking Blass!

I ignored my exhaustion and ran as fast as I could to Staci and Laci to tell them I was positive I spotted Blass while pointing at his car now getting on the freeway. The police officers assured us before we pulled away from that if we needed anything to give them a call and they would back us up.

Staci quickly checked the location of his phone, and it continued to send us in circles. Phone pings were excellent at providing a general area, maybe a one-mile radius, but not for an exact location.

Blass or someone with him must have spotted us sometime after our fiftieth circle around the hotel and started watching us too. We finally had to give up and call it a night.

The next day we learned that Greene had a court hearing that combined all three of Blass's bonds under one separate, bondsman to protect him from our arrest. A legal and crafty course of action that kept us from going after him again.

"We can't touch him now," I heard Staci sigh.

I felt defeated, and not because we couldn't arrest him, but because he had everyone convinced, he was the victim.

A SECOND CHANCE

What neither of these guys planned for was the karma of their arrogance.

Laci called me that same night to tell me that Greene made the error of only combining Blass's last three bonds but forgot about the first bondsman. Leaving a fourth bail bond, and in the first lien position, unattended.

Greene was clever but still pulled a rookie move. He wasn't

as well-versed in bail law like personal injury law, but he was about to get a crash course. He was no match for Staci and Laci.

"The bondsman watched Blass on the news and called the girlfriend, also the cosigner on the bond, to find out what was going on, and she told the bondsman that 'he (the bondsman) would never find him (Blass),'" Laci said almost laughing.

"No fucking shit?!" I started to laugh too.

The minute Blass's girlfriend told the bondsman that he "wouldn't be found" while also unwilling to disclose Blass' current location as the co-signor of the bond, breached their bail bond contract with both bondsman and the surety company.

In her ignorant and arrogant determination to protect her man, she gave us the legal second chance we needed to return Blass to custody.

This time, we weren't taking any chances in him escaping us. Staci and Laci planned to have back up with us too.

With all the media attention, I knew we still faced the possibility of retaliation from Blass's friends. The odds of being shot at or assaulted were growing by the day.

Within hours of taking the assignment from the bondsman, Staci and Laci contacted a fellow bounty hunter, Chase, to request his team and him back us up. He informed them his team was also hired, before us, to find Blass and they had searched his residence once before. It was the perfect storm because they already knew the lay of the land and how to get us in and out safely.

Blass still had no idea his first bondsman revoked his bond and that we were coming to arrest him again and most likely was sitting at home comfortably without a care in the world.

The plan was for us to go in first, and Chase and his team would cover us while we made the arrest. Blass wasn't going to be arrested by anyone else, Staci and Laci made sure of that.

When we met with Chase's team a few blocks down the street, they confirmed it Blass's vehicle parked in front of the house.

"Hey, you should have kicked that guy in the nuts instead of trying to be nice to him," Chase shouted in my direction at me.

Over the years, I learned that aggressive sarcasm, or shit-talking, is how most alpha males build a rapport with women in male-dominated industries. They do so with no intention to harass or harm, just not well versed in she-speak.

It's usually the older guy in the group who used to be hot, still wants to be seen as such, and has the Zen master wisdom of the group.

I knew that taunting me was Chase's polite way of saying, "Hey, cute girl, don't be afraid to kick some ass around here," in man-speak.

Still, for fun, I had to show him I didn't need a dick to know my job.

"I wasn't in a defensive position. You're right, I guess I could have, but that would have helped prove Blass's accusations that I used excessive force. I didn't want to go to jail; I wanted to go home." I sassed back at him.

He smiled admiring my brains and booty, I mean beauty, then quickly moved on.

Chase began to explain that there were a couple of older people also living at the residence, and no one resisted them when they searched the entire home. Because Blass wasn't home at the time, they did a thorough search of his room and found an antique firearm, an archery weapon, and a Border Patrol jacket. All of them were parole violations, plus a few new charges.

Chase outlined the house for us on a piece of paper, explaining how to get in and out quick and whole, and then assigned us our positions.

All I could think about was the Border Patrol jacket. It was a cruel vision of Blass and his white power group using it to rob and harass immigrants who couldn't call or go to the police.

Over the years, I met and worked with many immigrants and their families, and I highly respected them all for working hard jobs while struggling with learning a new language.

The thought of Blass tormenting any of them infuriated the shit out of me. I couldn't help but make it personal.

Some years prior, I had locked my keys in my car while pumping gas, and when I asked the clerk if he could help me, he looked at me like I had shit on my face and was not helping me with a damn thing.

The pump over from mine had a Mexican family in a van, and the man asked me something in Spanish when I came back to my car. He must have noticed I was in distress.

He looked inside my driver window and saw my keys were still in the ignition. He said, "llaves?" (I remembered that meant keys) and pointed with a chuckle. We didn't have to speak the same language to share a comical moment. It was such a foolish error that I, too, had to find some humor in it.

Looking around, I picked up a rock to suggest breaking

the back window to get in the car. Again he chuckled at me, even louder this time, and quickly took the stone from my hand.

"No-no-no," he said, continuing his conversation in Spanish.

The determined man went back to his van to find something to help get the window down far enough to reach his hand in to open the lock. When he returned, his wife was with him smiling empathetically.

I think he asked her to retrieve something from their van to wedge in my car window, and instead, she grabbed the gas nozzle and handed it to him.

He wasn't looking and had his hand behind him, and when he felt it was the gas nozzle, he turned around and screeched at her. She cracked up laughing, assigning herself as our comic relief, pranking him while he helped the pinche guera. I greatly admired not only their generosity but their fun spirit. It was past dinner time, they had children with them, and they were taking the time to help me. Their determination and unconditional kindness corrected my image of what being Mexican looked like.

When the man finally got my door open, he picked up the rock I had given him early on and chuckled at me. His way of reminding me that I wanted to break the window while he was confident, he could get the door open. His lesson was patience before panic.

* * * *

Staci and Laci planned to report all Blass' weapons violations to his parole officer once he was in custody, but we all knew that wasn't going to do shit. If this fucking guy was on his fourth bond, the state could care less about what he had hiding in his house.

I would have to use my rage to walk fearlessly in a home where known Nazi folks, with weaponry, wanted my head on a platter. Reminding myself of the death and rape threats given to my children and me for weeks, I prepared myself to engage them.

We all geared up, and Staci made notification with local law enforcement. Then, we all jumped back in our vehicles and headed over to Blass's house.

Trying to visualize and predict any possible situation we could encounter, I became stoic. Having the men's team with us was comforting for the power in numbers, but they were full-metal-jacket armed, and adding that to this unpredictable situation was unnerving.

We parked about half a block down the street, just enough distance if we had to run back to leave but not too far to escort Blass if the arrest was successful. My heart began to race, and I quietly took deep breathes to calm it down.

We got out and quickly made our way to Chase and his guys, who were parked closer to the house to cover us when we were ready to come back out. Staci and I went in weapon-free using only our hands while Laci held the taser.

Before I knew it, we were in the house, and I heard Blass yelling, "YOU CAN'T ARREST ME!" at us.

Holding up what was probably court papers and NOT wearing a fucking eye patch over either of his eyes!

See? I knew it.

Blass's girlfriend and another man started screaming for us also to leave while they threatened to have us arrested for false arrest and trespassing. Chase and his men held Blass' family back with their firearms drawn on them ready to use deadly force if necessary, making it crystal clear there would be no interference by any of them this time.

Staci slapped the cuffs on Blass's ass while he continued to scream "FUCKING CUNTS" and that we were going to jail.

Neither one of us flinched at his attempt to distract us. Staci and I and moved him quickly out of the house while Laci covered us.

The men were right behind her, making sure no one shot at us on our way out the door. I heard his girlfriend screaming, "YOU FUCKING NIGGER, RONI! I'M GOING TO GET YOU, YOU FUCKING NIGGER RONI!", over and over. It took everything I had not to turn around, go back and pound her teeth down her throat.

Chase quickly caught up to cover us at the SUV and chuckled at me, "Damn Roni, that crazy bitch is pissed at you. She picked up a brick to throw at you when you were leaving the house."

Blass also chuckled, "Oh yeah, she's no joke and can take all of you, bitches."

I was almost amused. Blass overestimated his woman. In my experience, bitches who pick up bricks can't fight.

Staci opened the door and started pushing him to get in the truck. I climbed in on the other side to pull him to the middle seat and buckled his ass in his seatbelt.

"I'd like to see her fucking try. I noticed she waited until we were pretty far away before she started selling her wolf tickets," I mocked once buckled in my sit and able to calm down.

"You're a bunch of fucking cunt niggers," he said over and over as we pulled away to head towards the police station.

WE'RE ALL NIGGERS

Here it was, the moment we spent weeks to get to, sitting in the back of the SUV with a handcuffed Ben Blass. I could have overdosed on the adrenaline pumping through my veins. It was the rush of a huntress who had caught her first real wild game.

Staci had him fully engaged in a conversation about his charges, while he continued to call us "niggers and cunts" between giving her the details and moving his body around in the seat.

When I started to talk to him, he became even more agitated, causing me to instantly look for the stun gun I kept in the back seat in case he tried something. Blass proved he was a pro at evading situations of accountability, and being cuffed didn't make him any less dangerous. That's when he threatened to head-butt me.

Our eyes met, and I saw right through this scared man who was not the "supreme" leader he wanted us to think he was. I hoped he saw looking back at him, me fully prepared to elbow his fucking face or gauge out his eye, blinding him for real, if he dared to touch me.

He continued to rant about his charges with Staci for another 15 minutes while I watched and listened. Laci drove and also listened to him intently. Once we got closer to the jail and the hype of the arrest had faded away, Blass began to speak in a normal tone. I could hear the fear creep in his voice. No one wants to go to jail.

I took full advantage of the opportunity to dig deeper into

the mind of this stranger who I allowed to put me in so much danger.

"What makes you think I'm black, Ben?" I asked him, curious. "Is it my curly hair and a big butt?" we all giggled at my question.

"Yeah, Ben, Roni isn't black; she's Mexican," Laci added as she drove glancing at us from the rear-view mirror.

"My dad looks just like you, Ben, white with brown hair and green eyes. So why do you think I'm black? Not that it bothers me, you think I'm black. I'm just curious why you assume so."

He sat there, annoyed, and quickly blurted out as his only and last defense to my interrogation.

"You're all niggers, you're a nigger, they're niggers, you're all niggers," he yelled as he moved his head back and forth to affirm his words. Staci and I looked at each other in agreement.

Yep, Ben, we're all niggers.

* * * *

We pulled up to the front of the Orange County Jail, on the intake side, and Staci's phone rang. It was the on-duty Orange County Sheriff notifying us that Greene was trying to have us arrested for false arrest, false imprisonment, kidnapping, and any other charge he could stack on us.

Laci and Staci got out of the truck to deal with the phone call to ensure we didn't go to jail. I stayed with Blass and the camera girls. Staci and Laci brought two for this arrest to get as much video as possible in the event it was needed as evidence.

"You guys are going to jail I'm telling you, you fucked up

big time. You guys kidnapped me," Blass chuckled confidently at his words.

"Blass, you do know one of your bonds was not addressed in the court hearing with Greene, right?"

He continued to chuckle.

"Oh yes, they were, and you guys are in so much trouble, and I can't wait to see you go to jail," he taunted me like a child.

But as quickly as the words left his lips, his cocky expression changed as he started to put together what I had just said to him.

His first bondsman was the only contract he appeared to honor and had the best rapport with but probably hadn't a clue that his girlfriend fucked that up in her attempt to help him hide from us. I sat there for what seemed like an hour waiting on Staci and Laci to tell me we were clear to book him in the jail.

I got out of the car to find out what was taking so long and found out they had to call the bondsman to come and assist with the booking. Greene, being positive we made a false arrest, made a scene with the Sheriff to have us arrested.

It didn't matter that he didn't like us, getting Staci and Laci, and anyone with them, arrested wouldn't be that easy. They had over decades of law enforcement experience and knew the law, especially bail law, well.

"As soon as the bondsman gets here were leaving to go celebrate," Laci said as I walked back to the car. Seeing the look on Blass's face after he realized his Attorney didn't help him avoid us after all tasted as sweet as candy.

Spending this short time with him allowed me to assess

that he wasn't a hardened criminal, after all, but another wannabe gangster addict. It was easy to forget that it was his request and our refusal to remove a video that started this.

We discovered shortly after posting the video that Blass' was humiliated because his son saw it. His initial intention for hiring Greene was to pursue justice for both him and his child.

I hadn't expected there to six degrees of separation between us.

Out of guilt, I asked Staci and Laci if we could book him with a phone card so he could contact his son. They bought him one.

"Is there anything I can get for you? Water? We bought you a phone card to call your son when they allow you phone time." I asked him.

Blass said nothing and leaned away from me like he feared my kindness.

"You can give me my eyesight back," he said with deceitful sarcasm.

"I'll keep praying for you," I told him sincerely.

Now, did I sit down and ask God to protect this man while we were hunting him? No, but I did ask that we all make it out alive and well, and that included him too.

My confession made him scoot even farther from me, almost lying his head down on the opposite seat.

"God let me down, I don't talk to him anymore," he sounded like a sad child.

He felt vulnerable for a brief moment with me, and I saw

what he was hiding. Like many other men who go in and out of prison, he felt undeserving of love and acceptance. I was unarmed and couldn't think of what else to say, but I did feel an exchange of energy between us and an overwhelming amount of empathy for him.

"It's time to book him in, his bondsman is here and going to do it. Blass, let's go," Laci said, quickly opening the door.

I pushed my emotions aside and helped her get him out of the SUV. We both walked him to the cement block by the jail where Chase and his team were standing, and Staci was still talking with the Sheriff.

"Want a cigarette now?" I asked him, trying not to draw too much attention to us. I kept a pack of cigarettes in my bag for people who needed one or two before going inside. Smoking wasn't allowed in California jails.

He nervously nodded. Sitting him down where Laci and Staci could watch him, I ran back to the SUV to get him a cigarette and some water. Can you dig it? Homie threatens my life, and I'm fetching him shit.

No one wants to go to jail, and I respected not making it any harder than it had to be on any of them; Blass' included. Karma is real.

When I got back to him, I poured some water in his mouth, then lit and gave him a cigarette.

"Ben Blass, I can't believe you made me go through all this for you," I heard a man's voice approaching from behind me. Turning around to meet him, I saw an attractive light-skinned black man in a suit wearing an excited smile on his face.

"Roni, this is Blass' first bondsman, Cedric, who hired us to revoke his bond," Staci said, introducing us.

I was in shock. Are you fucking kidding me? His bondsman is black?!

"Hi, nice to meet you," I said, trying to keep my composure and not state the obvious. Cedric quickly shook my hand, opened his folder to pull out his paperwork, and started talking to Blass.

Blass stuttered, trying to explain himself.

"Your girlfriend said I was never going to find you and you were leaving the state, what was I supposed to do? And then I hear you're calling this beautiful woman of color here a nigger? And I'm your bondsman and also black? No, Ben, you're too much of a risk and need to find a new bondsman," he sternly lectured his wayward client.

Watching Blass's body slump over like a child who just realized why he was in time out, and could no longer blame anyone else, was almost sad—almost.

We left shortly after the bondsman arrived and celebrated our small victory.

The case was over, but the publicity of it all wasn't, and neither was the lawsuit. Greene threatened to make us pay Blass fifty-two million and would continue to plot how to get it from us.

We just took out his knight and awaited his next move.

Greene kept his word and filed the lawsuit a few days later.

The same day we were all served, Staci and Laci decided our best recourse was to counter-sue him and have him served during our interview with ABC News.

Greene, along with his publicist, stood less than fifty feet away from us while we did our interview in front of the same restaurant our fight trying to arrest Blass took place. Staci and Laci had one of their process servers approach him and announce, "Excuse me, Mr. Greene, you have been served" and handed him the lawsuit while he gave his interview to the reporter.

Even the news reporters weren't sure how to broadcast the story at this point. When they aired the clip, the reporter described it as "something strange and unusual" and giggled with surprise.

We were all so proud of ourselves for another small victory.

We felt Greene's actions to pursue a lawsuit against us violated a few of our civil liberties also, and the best vengeance was for him to lose the fight he started.

But the reality, as I would soon learn, is courts aren't supportive of civilians suing Attorneys. We would have to dump thousands of dollars in an attorney of our own to facilitate a counter case.

Ignorantly, we went for it anyway and lost because, as a public business Greene had every right to report misconduct or unethical business practices, whether true or false, to the public on behalf of his client. It didn't matter to anyone of authority the scandalous shit he did to do so.

After he paraded us around on various TV networks, Greene was sought out by a few bail clients looking to avoid the consequences of breaching their bail contracts. It gave Greene a false sense of security that he could take down the bail industry by going after the surety companies who were the only entities to afford his fifty-two million dollar plan.

Like a snake in the ground, he waited and watched to make his next move.

4.

Bullet 4

BULLET 4-CONTEMPT

THE CLEVER SETUP

Approximately a month after our 15 minutes of fame, Sean, a bounty hunter who mostly worked alone, contacted Staci and Laci to assist with a new case. The small bond company had already hired a couple of teams, out of desperation, to find their client, now fugitive, Jimmy Watkins. They were months shy from the deadline, and if Watkins weren't found, they would be on the hook to pay the full fifty-thousand dollars to the court.

He was a young black man, late twenties who had established trust with the bond company over the years with his prior cases. The state charged him with first-degree burglary for his current case, and because he faced prison time, he was a no-show in court.

The bail agent was sure Watkins still resided in Hawthorne, California, but could have made his way upstate to Oakland, California, or interstate with relatives.

One of the contacts listed on the bail application was

Watkins' girlfriend, Cheryl Davis. Her address, along with his stepmother who co-signed the bond, was on the bail application.

Sean explained that Davis had filed a lawsuit for one of the other bounty teams hired to find Watkins for harassment already. The bail agent was suspicious that Davis had seen all the commotion from Blass's case on TV and contacted Greene to help Watkins avoid arrest.

Immediately, I didn't like this case.

Davis' stood by her story that Watkins no longer resided or visited her residence, but the bail agent had a credible source who confirmed the two were still in contact.

Staci and Laci decided to make contact with Davis and get her side of the story before risking another lawsuit.

We made our way to Hawthorne to do a door knock at Davis' apartment.

It was a two-story design, and the buildings arranged with Davis' apartment building facing the street. There was a clear view of every resident's front door and that none had back doors.

Perfect for keeping Watkins from escaping us, but shitty for a tactical and discreet approach. The gate to enter the complex required a code we didn't have and had to wait until someone came by to let us in.

After about fifteen minutes, we lucked out, and someone arrived and opened the gate. Entering the complex, I noticed two tall black men were leaning over the rail of the second floor watching us.

These neighborhoods are monitored closely by its residents, and they need to know, and will know, who is who or there will be a major misunderstanding.

They saw who we were and kept watch as we made our way closer to Davis' unit. I'm positive both Watkins and Davis were already informed that we were there.

We made our way to the door of her apartment, and Sean knocked first. No answer.

Staci knocked, and we waited. Still nothing.

After ten minutes of nothing, Staci placed some marketing souvenirs and a business card for Davis to contact them, and we left.

They wanted to give Davis ample time to respond before kicking in her door.

It wasn't until we left Davis's apartment that Sean decided to disclose that the prior team had already kicked in Davis door. She and Greene were suing them and the police department.

Shit! I smelled, and feared, a set up for another lawsuit coming.

We all went to dinner to go over the information attached to the case from the bail agent. I knew there was something more appealing for Greene in this case other than just suing bounty hunters or us.

Combing through the entire file, I found all the penal codes and looked them up to find out precisely what charges Watkins was facing, in this case, to try and figure out why he decided to run.

Penal codes can be hard to interpret, but from what Staci could decipher, Watkins had broken into someone's house to rob them, and the person was home. Watkins fled immediately, but his act still carried the elements to a "home invasion" charge.

Then I found a notice on one of the court documents that read:

"Notice: A Suspected Child Abuse Report (SCAR) may have been generated within the meaning of Penal Code 11166 and 11168 involving the charges alleged in this complaint. Dissemination of a SCAR is limited by Penal Code 11167 and 11167.5, and a court order is required for full disclosure of the contents of SCAR."

"What the hell does this mean?" I screeched at Staci and Laci, feeling my body heat up with a familiar rage.

"Could mean there was another case that had to do with a child, Davis has a little girl, maybe that's why she's saying she hasn't seen him and they are no longer together," Laci said, taking the paper to read it herself.

"It's hard to tell on these forms, but I haven't seen that on any other case printout before, so it must have some significance," Staci added, also curious.

No, not a child abuse case with a little girl.

My determination to find Watkins had just been put in overdrive, if for nothing else to find out what the hell that notice meant.

The bail agent believed that Watkins was sneaking into Davis's apartment late at night and leaving early in the morning, making it difficult to catch him any time during the day. She urged us to do a thorough search of the apartment as late or as early as possible.

We all agreed that the lookouts ruined the element of surprise, and we would have to be a lot more crafty in catching him.

They gave Davis another day to call them, and after twenty-four hours passed, we were on our way back to Davis' apartment. This time Sean made it clear that if there was no answer, he was kicking in the door.

We were to back him up.

I don't recall how we got back in the complex this time, but once we were in, we immediately spotted Davis's car parked in a space close to her unit. Presumably, she was now home. Both Sean and Staci knocked on the door, and after a few seconds, the blinds moved, confirming that someone was inside.

Still, no answer. Sean knocked again

"Cheryl, it's Sean. I'm a bounty hunter hired by the bond company to locate Jimmy Watkins."

No answer.

"Cheryl, we want to search the house to tell the bail agent he isn't here, and we will leave. Please open the door," Staci said, facing the door.

No answer.

Staci and Sean continued to knock for about five more minutes until Laci intervened and suggested we call the police to let them know we were going to have to kick the door open.

It was wise to cover our asses with an extra layer of protection by police at this point.

Staci contacted the supervisor on duty at the station, and

he agreed to back us up if we needed, which made me feel a little better but not much.

We were on the second floor of the two-story apartment complex that had only a thin metal railing in front that didn't look secure enough to hold much weight pressed up against it.

"How many kicks do you think it will take me to get in?" Sean mocked, almost excited as he leaned up against the unsteady rail.

He was not a petite man and watching him put so much confidence in the rail to support him and his weight while kicking in the door made me even more nervous.

"Cheryl, we're going to kick in the door unless you open up. The police are also on their way!" Staci and Laci started to scream while Sean braced himself.

Standing there, watching him take his first kick, I tried to control my adrenaline and prepare for what was about to happen.

Kicking in a door may look like a cool scene in a movie and give the appearance of being badass, but in reality, its some scary shit unable to foresee what's on the other side of that door.

There was a little girl in this apartment, and pepper spray or rubber bullets could cause her harm. Not to mention if Watkins decided to ride out in a blaze of glory with his weapon of choice.

My rookie opinions didn't matter, only the arrest to avoid the fifty-thousand-dollar payout. Being that there is a casual lack of empathy in this business, my mind could only visualize a biased scenario based on the information given.

What I "knew" was that there was a mother in this apartment, possibly protecting a man over her daughter, and I wasn't going to let her get away with that without saying something.

* * * *

It took Sean about eight kicks before the door gave and opened up. We quickly rushed inside.

Sean went in first, then Staci, Laci, myself, and the camera girl. I felt like I was moving in slow motion.

The first thing I saw was Davis's phone pointed right at us to record everything. The minute I saw it, I knew we got set up.

Sean steadily moved to the bedroom door to search, and Davis jumped in front of him, smacked him in the face then swung on Staci.

Staci and Laci were impressive when dodging an assault. They trained as boxers for the LAPD; bobbing and weaving was muscle memory. Davis missed.

She continued to swing at Sean before he rushed towards her and then pinned her against her dresser, restraining her, while we searched the room.

Her apartment was small, with only one bedroom. Once we entered the room, I saw her little girl sitting on the bed watching everything.

I became enraged at Davis for making us kick in her door only to play a game with Greene and protect her fugitive boyfriend, who may have abused her little girl. Or another small child.

Watkins and Davis had been together for a few years, and allegedly, he didn't have children of his own.

Staci started checking the closet, Laci, the kitchen and living room, and I checked under the bed.

Scared shitless, I could get my head blown off, I quickly perused what I could see with the lack of light and got back up.

The little girl didn't dare move, almost calm, and I felt like shit looking at her sit there. I was unable to control the words that were coming out of my mouth.

They sounded something like:

"What the fuck is wrong with you" while adding something about her allowing us to kick in her door and traumatize her daughter.

She said nothing but continued to videotape us. I wanted to snatch that phone out of her hand, but because I feared a charge of robbery, I chose to get ethnic instead.

I remember ending my speech with something along the lines of "don't allow some sorry ass nigga to put you through this shit" and stormed out to help search the living room.

The police had arrived and quickly moved toward the bedroom.

"Sean had to restrain her while we searched because she assaulted him. She videotaped the whole thing, and we're sure it's for Greene." Laci informed them.

Yep! Greene used Davis to set us up, and I said "nigga" on video. Fucking shit!

Not that I was worried about people calling me a racist, but Staci and Laci may not appreciate the backlash my choice of words would bring on them and their company.

I was curious to see how he would spin this one. Greene could try to label me a racist, but after being called a nigger just a couple of weeks earlier by Blass and his girlfriend, it would be difficult to prove.

Still, it wasn't my most shining moment on camera.

We stayed for another thirty minutes to give the cops our statements on what happened for their reports and left.

As we drove home, it hit me. Watkins was only five feet, six inches, and could have fit in the corner of that bed between the mattress.

I replayed my search under the bed and remembered a bunch of clothes and plastic bags stuffed towards the corner closest to the wall, possibly put there deliberately. Then I remembered how the little girl was positioned on the bed, near the same corner by the wall. Motionless and non-reactive to what should have traumatized her. She wasn't scared, not crying, and not even trying to move as if someone told her to stay there and not move.

Damn! He was in between the fucking mattress!

Letting my emotions get the best of me distracted me from my investigation. Not only the probability of dealing with an abused child with a neglectful mother but the fear of getting shot looking under the bed.

We went through all of that to come up empty-handed and gave Greene another case to have a field day over.

LEARNING FROM A LEGEND

And there it was, the next day, Staci and Laci forward me the email with the link of Davis video already on Youtube.

Greene posted the few minutes of us going in the apartment and some of us searching Davis room before the police arrived, where Sean rushes her to the dresser, and then I go on my rant and end with the dramatic "don't put up with this shit for no nigga" statement.

Greene even added written words over the video "bounty hunter makes a racist comment at," to provide the exact time for the audience.

He intended to discredit us, primarily me, further and file another civil case against us for violation of Davis' civil rights.

Now let me first explain before you jump to judge me. My motive in what I said was personal, and by default, I didn't filter my speech.

I intended to converse as mothers to get her to see how she endangered both their lives because of Watkin's behavior. Not judge her actions based on her or her man's skin color.

And frankly, at that moment, I didn't give a fuck about being politically correct about it. Camera or no camera.

"Guess what?" I could hear Laci smirking on the other end of the phone.

Afraid to answer her, I responded with a very reluctant "What?"

"'Inside Edition' wants another interview, this time for Davis because Greene is going to sue us along with the Hawthorne Police Department. Like he did with the other team hired to find Watkins." She laughed it off as though it sounded ridiculous, but I was not amused.

"The good news is..." Laci started, but before she could continue, Staci snatched the phone out of her hand and almost yelled, "Yea, Roni, we decided we aren't going to take this shit lying down. They fucked with the wrong women."

She was pissed. Yes! Fucking finally! I needed someone other than me to be upset. Laci was the sweet and rational one, which I needed, but not this day.

"We called a few attorney friends and other people we know, and they told us to contact Bernard Perez. Do you know who that is?" Staci asked.

He was a legendary bounty hunter featured several times on television shows, also known for locating missing persons, and surprisingly, I had never heard of him. Now in his seventies, he ran his own bail bond company and assisted local authorities with unsolved murders and missing persons cases. He'd been a bounty hunter for more than forty-five years, and rumor had it he'd also trained Dog the Bounty Hunter and other successful teams.

"He is said to be the best. We called him to explain our situation, and he asked that we visit him in Sacramento. We decided to do the 'Inside Edition' interview up there with him and are driving up there tonight. Can you fly out tomorrow morning after you file the restraining order? We will book you a flight and email you the ticket information." Staci became winded, talking so fast. They were packing to leave for the airport.

My head spun to absorb every word she said while trying to formulate some form of response that wouldn't sound like me lashing out in defiance.

I wanted to run and hide under my covers and pretend I had never started this damn job, but then my ego kicked in to remind me that I had never backed down from a fight before, and I sure as hell wasn't going to now.

"Yeah I'll be there, I'll look for the email. You guys drive safely." I told her before hanging up.

To be clear, I didn't give a shit about being judged for kicking in the door because we contacted the police beforehand, and that covered our asses legally. My concern was getting labeled a racist and how it would affect my daughter, who was still healing from her stepmonster's race war. I didn't want her to think a comment I made, one I would have made, and had made, to anyone of any race, defined me the same.

I also had to face the fact that this was possibly another smokescreen so that Davis could continue to hide Watkins. Like the Blass case.

Searching for him now at her house was going to be impossible to do without it looking like harassment.

Greene used process servers, who paid the homeless and drug-addicted in my low-income neighborhood, to lurk about in the alley behind us and harass my mom. Public records still showed her address as my current residence.

No one had a clue I lived upstairs, and mom wouldn't tell anyone where I was.

To keep from committing an act of violence, I filed a restraining order for Greene to stop harassing my residence. He wasn't sending process servers to Staci and Laci's home, only mine. I requested that the court order his office to have all legal documents served to me at their office too.

Unsurprisingly, the judge denied my request for a restraining order, and I learned that an attorney could legally harass you with a process server all they want. Even if they endanger you, your home, and family to do so.

* * * *

I arrived at the Sacramento airport the next afternoon, and Staci and Laci picked me up with a full itinerary.

"We can't wait for you to meet Bernard. He totally has our backs and is going to appear on 'Inside Edition' with us and tell everyone that we did nothing wrong." They had both excitement and relief in their voices as they described their time with the legendary hunter.

We all tried to conceal our emotions, but I could tell having someone respectable in the industry siding with them meant a lot. They'd never show it, but I think they had become frightened over the lawsuits too.

We pulled up to Bernard's bail bonds office located in a cute little downtown area, on the famous H Street surrounded by several other bondsmen, law offices, and close to the state Senate's building. Nervously, I followed my partners through the building and up the stairs.

The structure was old and smelled like history, with several articles framed on the walls that featured some form of praise to Bernard.

"Look at this picture, Roni," Laci said as she motioned me over to her.

It was Bernard in various pictures as a young man with famous and official people. He was handsome, charming, well known, and as Staci and Laci described him, "a big mouth who likes to start trouble."

"Maybe he isn't up yet; I'm going to try calling him," Staci said as she stepped closer to the stairway while Laci showed me more articles.

My anxiety subsided, and I grew excited to meet the successful and well-respected Mexican man. No matter how the trip went, I knew I was going to learn something from him.

"He wasn't up yet but will be here shortly. Let's get some coffee." Staci said, hanging up her phone.

Walking back to his office, coffee in hand, and caffeine fueling my veins, I felt high being in Sacramento by the state Senate getting ready to meet a bounty hunting legend.

When we got back up the stairs, Bernard's office door was wide open, and I could hear the screeching of a big ass bird.

"That's his parrot, be careful because he will bite you," Laci whispered and nudged her elbow at me with a smile.

"You woke up late, huh? We thought you would be here already," Staci greeted Bernard.

"Oh, yeah, I was up just didn't remember what time we said we would meet," Bernard said with a country drawl.

I was behind Laci and couldn't see him yet, only his dusty black cowboy hat.

His office looked like a set of a movie, staged for scenes of old-time private detectives. Huge stuffed animal heads mounted on the walls, newspapers, papers, and books were stacked and piled in various places. In between the front door and his desk was a large white parrot in a human-sized birdcage.

Looking up from his desk as I stepped in his view, he took a quick assessment of me through his tinted glasses.

"This is Roni, Roni this is Bernard Perez, the famous bounty hunter," Staci said as if he had been waiting to meet me, making me nervous all over again.

I didn't let him see me flinch. Marching quickly towards his desk, I put my hand out to give him the most solid handshake I possibly could.

Regardless of what he already thought of me, I was going to show him I wasn't a dumb woman and would demand his respect like anyone else—legend or not.

But I was still starstruck.

"It's nice to meet you, Mr. Perez," I said with a smile.

"Well, hello there, Roni, glad you could make it." He smiled back at me and stood up to be more formal.

With a toothpick in his mouth, he watched me for a moment, our hands continuing to shake.

"You girls eat yet? I am hungry. First, let's walk over and meet with my attorney and talk about your pending lawsuits and what ya'll need to do." He told us while moving from around his desk.

A real-life cowboy, from the hat down to the boots and belt buckle, with no problem corralling us like cattle out of his office to get his day of activities for us on the way. Staci and Laci started down the stairs.

"So how long have you been a bounty hunter?" Bernard asked while we walked down the stairs. He had had the whole day before to assess the girls, and it was now my turn, the Latin troublemaker of the group.

As we walked down the street to the attorney's office, I went through my employment history and explained to him why I was now in the bail business and my goals in the community.

"You see that building down the street," he pointed to a

building a few blocks down. "That is my law school, and if you move up here, I'll help you open your own bail bonds office and put you through law school. With ideas and dreams like yours, you need a degree," his offer sounded genuine.

Like my grandmother, his generation understood the value of education for Latins, and he held it in high regard as she did.

The offer was tempting, but there was no way I could relocate my life even if I wanted to.

He towered over me with his cool cowboy outlaw strut, like a country-pimp, walking down that street

We made it to his attorney's office and were welcomed by a sweet lady at the front desk who escorted us to an open-spaced office that looked like the office of a prestigious college dean in an eighties movie.

Jim, I believe it was, stood up and shook our hands with a smile ear to ear as if he had been waiting to meet us too.

"Jim, these are the ladies I told you about, they need some direction with their case, can you help them out?" Bernard said, now winded from the walkover.

Bernard, Staci, and Laci sat in the chairs facing the attorney, and I stood behind them to stretch my legs from the flight.

Too nervous and excited to sit comfortably anyway, I kept quiet and listened to every word Bernard, and Jim said.

Then Jim listened intently as Staci and Laci took turns explaining everything then handed him a copy of the lawsuit. He quickly skimmed through it.

"Well, you will have to respond, and even though most of

these are hard to prove, it may still cost you some money to get them all dismissed," his tone now serious.

He continued to explain each charge and how we could respond.

"We also sued him for slander and defamation," Laci said, pulling out the other stack of papers she brought to show him. He quickly went over those too.

"Some of yours will be hard to stick to him, he's an attorney, and trying to find someone to help go after him on your behalf won't be easy. Or cheap," he concluded.

Overwhelmed and hungry, I couldn't think straight anymore.

I tuned out the rest of the conversation and waited for my partner's cue for us to leave. Shortly after, we headed out the door, and Bernard's phone rang.

"I have to meet with someone after we visit the senator's office," he informed us while we headed to the next destination.

Senator's office? Am I meeting a senator?

I wasn't sure how Staci and Laci felt about it because we all had our game faces on, but I was elated.

As we walked, Bernard began to share some of his bounty hunter wisdom with me.

"In this business, you gotta know the right people, not necessarily a lot of people. A senator, an FBI agent, a U.S. Marshal, someone from immigration, and how to get in touch with a Federale (known as Police Officer or security) in Mexico because that is the closest international border to us. With these spades in your pocket and enough time, your chances of finding someone are a lot higher." Bernard and I walked in stride with one another now, and I listened intently to him. His knowledge could save my ass one day.

An opportunity to learn from someone like him comes around once in a lifetime if you're lucky.

POLITICAL POWER

We walked a few more blocks down the street to a deli restaurant. It was going to be a long day, and I was in desperate need of some greasy food. Bernard chivalrously pulled out the chair next to him for me to sit down.

"Coffee, please," all of us said at the same time to the sparkling older waitress who was extra friendly with Bernard.

"I will be back with a pitcher and give you a few minutes to order," she said politely, also with a country drawl.

"You already know what I want," Bernard said, showing off with a smile.

We all read over our menus.

"So Bernard, what do you think of the Watkins case?" I asked, still trying to chose which meal to order. He peered at me over his glasses that were now changing tint in the lighted room and smirked.

"I think you gals may have been set up," he said, trying not to chuckle.

"Fuck me too!" I said, with almost a gasp.

The waitress came back over to take our orders.

Bernard's phone rang, and while he took his call, Staci,

Laci, and I sat there in a daze while we drank our coffee, waiting for our food.

After we finished eating, Bernard and I discussed our search for Watkins at Davis house.

"I think I fucked up and missed Watkins in between the mattress, Bernard," I shamefully confessed.

"You're still new at this, and even if you did, there is nothing you can do about it now. What's his height and weight?" He asked, patting his pocket to look for the paper copy of the case on him.

"Five-six, maybe 140 pounds," I said.

"Oh shit yeah, he was in there!" he yelped.

Bernard chuckled, watching the wheels now turning in my head.

"I was so afraid to look under the bed and was emotional over the daughter being there." I started rambling.

He quickly put his hand up and stopped me in mid-sentence.

"Listen, that's not the time to get emotional because you can mess up," he lowered his voice and moved closer to me.

"You can get your head blown off or choked, or a bed dropped on you looking for someone under one." His tone turned serious, and not to scare me but to make clear the severity of the risk I took that night.

"I did look, but I moved too fast and didn't pay attention that the clothing and shit shoved in the corner was deliberately put there. I didn't realize it until after the fact." I continued confessing my guilt for not thinking like a huntress but like an irrational wife looking for her husband's mistress under the bed.

"Was she holding her little girl? Was the little girl crying?" Bernard asked curiously.

"Nooo," I said, unable to stutter out a better response and unsure where he was going with his questions.

"Then she told that little girl to sit there because that is where she was hiding him. Think about it. You have a little girl, right? A group of people is kicking in your door to get in your house to search it, would your daughter cry? Wouldn't she want you to hold her for comfort?" he said with confidence as he shifted his tooth pic to the other side of his mouth.

"You're right," was all I could say. Bernard solved the mystery in two seconds.

"See, had it been my case, I would have called CPS (Child Protective Services) to come to remove her daughter from the bed, move the bed, arrest both Davis and Watkins, and would have already been paid by now."

Putting a fresh toothpick in his mouth, he sat back in his chair like a badass cowboy who just dropped a microphone in my face.

As both a mother and rookie, I didn't think to call child protective services first. Not because I was weak but because it felt like a mom-code violation. You just don't do it unless the facts prove you must.

It wasn't just me who missed Watkins hiding in a bed, none of us thought it was possible. Hell, the police didn't look there either.

But combined, none of us had Bernard's experience with tracking and finding people.

I sat quietly for a minute and let the sting of my lesson wear off before I opened my mouth.

"I didn't even think of calling CPS because I didn't see she was in danger," I said softly, now replaying the scene over and over in my head again. Fast forward, then rewind and repeat.

"You don't think to let people kick in your door and assaulting them in front of your child while videotaping it all is grounds for a call to CPS? Didn't Watkins do something to a kid or have a charge that makes him dangerous? I don't know Roni, you sure CPS wouldn't have been appropriate in this case?" He said, looking at me like a prosecutor, trying to get me to see what he saw. And quickly, I did.

He was right. I allowed my personal feelings to interfere with the investigation and was way in over my head in my new-found profession.

We probably weren't going to avoid being named in a lawsuit at this point, but at least if we had arrested Watkin's, there would be less evidence to use against us.

Most importantly, we wouldn't have looked like we were harassing Davis, giving Greene more ammunition to win his lawsuit.

Bernard was a kind man to take the time for us, but he, too, had business concerns of his own. Our lawsuit could harm his bail business, many other bail companies, and the bail industry as a whole. If Greene won, it would breed more lawsuits and, eventually, bankrupt the industry.

"You girls ready for 'Inside Edition' tomorrow? They

should be calling you sometime this afternoon to go over your side of the story." He sounded excited. I could only cringe at the thought of going back on TV with Greene, now accusing me of racism.

Staci and Laci gave Bernard their game plan for the show.

Bernard would do all of the talking while Staci and I sat next to him. Bernard, known for making a bit of noise and challenging various groups, was more than up for the challenge.

"You have nothing to worry about because ya'll did nothing wrong," he assured us.

"Let's go to the Senate building for our meeting," he said, standing up to signal our lunch was over.

He paid the bill and opened the door for us to leave.

* * * *

The Senate building was one street over. We walked in, following Bernard's lead as he made his way through familiar faces and brief "good to see you" exchanges.

There was a team of young college interns moving around in the senator's office who, one by one, politely stopped to greet us. A couple of them recognized us from the news and eager to get some of the company chap-sticks Laci pulled out of her pocket. Bernard made his way towards the personal office of the senator, motioning for us to follow him.

Slowly, I moved towards the door, still in disbelief where I was and who I was about to meet. Bernard held the door open for me to join them. I felt starstruck all over again.

I had no idea who she was, nor had I ever heard her name

before, but she was a senator, and to me, that made her the biggest badass of us all.

These offices are where the real fight for justice takes place—wearing a skirt with fit calves and shoes that can conquer the world. Not in the streets or a courthouse wearing a badge.

She was a beautiful white blond woman, maybe mid-forties who reminded me of a Southern belle, accent and all. She smiled and kindly greeted us.

We sat, and Bernard got straight to the point. He began explaining the details of our lawsuit and how the penal code for private citizens to effect an arrest was deficient in the necessary language to protect bounty hunters and bail agents from being arrested or sued. I sat and listened while everyone took their turn, giving their input and experience, unsure whether adding my opinion would make much difference.

"If the police are with us and give the go-ahead, no one should be able to sue us." I heard the words fly out of my mouth, or something close to it.

The senator made eye contact with everyone to acknowledge all the opinions and suggestions given her, then nodded in agreement.

"The current penal codes clear us from criminal charges, but the gray areas in the language hurt us in the civil courts," Bernard added.

The senator assured Bernard that she would do all that she could to put together a draft proposal for review and get back to him. We talked a few minutes longer before her next appointment arrived.

Leaving her office, I'd made up my mind that the power position I needed to pursue was a political one.

The evening crept while we drove Bernard home. After grabbing food, we went back to the hotel room to rest for our interview first thing the next morning.

While driving back to the hotel, the journalist from "Inside Edition (Lachman, 1988-present)" called to go over the topics they would be discussing with us during their interview. I answered all the polite gentleman's questions, the same ones he asked my partners, except one.

"So in Greene's video it shows that you called the fugitive a racial slur, is that true?" he asked with a curious tone.

"No, that's not true, I referenced his behavior using a slang term that is used as a term of endearment, or to describe a motherfucker/bastard/asshole, etc.," I said fully prepared for a judgmental interrogation.

"My children are biracial and have fathers that are black, my husband is black, prior boyfriends have been black, and most people assume I'm also half-black. No, I was not using the term to be racist. I pointed out to Davis that her boyfriend put her and her baby in a shitty situation and was a motherfucker for doing so. I used 'nigga' instead of 'motherfucker'—period." I continued to sass at him.

If he was going to side with Greene, he was going to have hit me with something harder than a stupid video.

"That makes total sense, and I understand. I didn't see it as racial either, but we have to ask because that is the narrative Greene is pushing for us to air," he chuckled at how far my archenemy had gone to destroy me.

"We aren't going to bring it up on the show, but thanks for clarifying." We said our goodbyes, and I hung up the phone.

At that moment, I realized the same thing happened to Dog the Bounty Hunter. It was apparent Greene intended to discredit and disgrace me the same way Dog had been.

A clever move, indeed.

HOW UNFAIR IS A RACE

I didn't get much time to process the bigger picture of what was going on in the Blass case, and the role my race and ethnicity primarily played in fueling the flames of hatred targeted towards me.

Covered in a black and white myth, my race and it's *'ism* played a considerable role in my life. In each stage, there revealed more of sanctimonious shades of its gray. It's an antiquated strategy to control the masses that continues to curse our society because it works.

From birth, we are all placed in a race that keeps everyone ignorantly segregated.

One evening at the prison, I worked with a new white male guard who was very nervous to walk alone. It was difficult for those staff members without prior law enforcement or military training to adapt to prison life. I knew that guy wouldn't last very long, The prisoners were rotten to me, but the shit they used to say to the male guards made me more afraid for them.

When we came out of the last dorm, there was a group of black prisoners loudly playing dominoes a few feet from the door. The male guard left me and hurried, almost ran, to the Watch Office only twenty feet from where we were. I followed to be sure he was alright.

I assumed he got sick since it was over 100 degrees outside, but instead, he was talking to Sgt. Lowen, whom he didn't know, was married to a black man.

"We need more guards watching the blacks. There is a large group in front of dorm fifteen screaming verbal threats at one another. I think they are going to start a fight," he reported, trying to catch his breath.

This poor guy was scared shitless. I started to laugh.

"Dude, they are playing dominoes. You've never seen 'Boyz in the Hood (Singleton, 1991)?' That's how black men play dominoes. As long as they are talking shit to each other, they are cool, but what you didn't catch was the group of Chicanos standing quietly over by dorm eight. Them mofos are the ones you have to watch out for because they are too dam quiet." I couldn't help but mock him a little.

Lowen tried not to laugh at his ignorance as his supervisor. He stared at us, confused.

He was a square white boy in his late twenties who mistakenly thought it would be fun, and simple to wear a respectable pussy-attracting uniform while dispensing justice to the bad guys.

"Go with Faciane and follow her lead, if she says run—Run!" Lowen instructed him. He looked at me even more fearful.

Not only was his privilege more harmful than helpful to him, now he had to rely on someone like me, a non-white girl, to keep him safe.

He didn't last two months.

* * * *

Growing up in my house, the word nigger was the "mother" of all bad words. I could say fuck twenty times without much of a flinch from my parents, but that word was guaranteed either soap or a fat lip. No one ever used any racial slurs until I grew older, and we moved to an Army base at Fort Ord, California.

It was the early 1980s, I was about eight years old, and I remember my father using the word "gook" to describe an Asian woman driving who had cut him off. When I asked what it meant, all I got was the standard hypocritical parent answer, "Don't worry about it. It's a grown-up word, so don't ever say it."

It wasn't until I started the fourth grade that I learned what that word meant. It was the first time I had ever witnessed racism and prejudice. The Vietnam war was over for almost a decade, but its ghosts haunted our military base and its residents. Plaguing the country in general, but especially our armed forces and their families.

The most confusing part about being a military kid is the ironically diverse culture, the various "mixes" of interracial relationships, and the hypocrisy of its segregation.

All of us kids, no matter race, ethnicity, or culture, were subjected to the consequences of it in one way or another.

When I attended my first military elementary school in California, there were several Vietnamese kids in my class. Every lunch break, the black boys harassed the Vietnamese boys. Calling them gooks, chinks, and mocking their broken English. The harassment was relentless and widely accepted by the school and staff.

During middle school, after my parents divorced and my mother moved us to southern California, the Mexican girls gave me a crash course at being a Mexi-CANT.

A group of Mexican girls targeted me almost every day because a new and popular Mexican boy liked me. They soon nick-named me "guera" and used it to cat-call me like their pet whenever they passed me in the halls.

They didn't stop until they saw my mother drop me off at a school dance one night and saw her brown skin. They still didn't like me but left me alone.

During the same year, a boy told me I "had a butt like a black girl," and he didn't say it as a compliment.

A Korean boy shouted from a crowd of neighbor kids while we played soccer on our cul de sac, "she's cute, but she has a big butt."

In high school, I was surrounded by a group of black girls because one of the cute light-skinned black boys liked me. Thankfully I had a couple of Polynesian girls who had my back.

No one wanted to fight the Polynesian girls that went to my school.

The Latin girls treated me white, the white girls treated me ethnic, and the black girls were split somewhere in the middle of sisters of color and hating my good hair.

The only girls that didn't give me grief for my race were mostly of Asian and Middle Eastern descent or also bi-racial themselves.

Though the Latin women in my lineage made me strong, the black women, even the ones who hated me, taught me to be fearless. And white and Asian women demanded class and vocabulary.

It wasn't until I went to work for the prison that I learned what real racism looked like and the illusion of power it holds.

The first week was orientation and training. One of the days included a Q&A presentation from the Mac Reps. These were representatives of each racial group that mediated between the staff and the prisoners.

I was petrified.

There were four of them, one for the whites, one for the blacks, one for the "border brothers" (Latin Immigrants), and one for the Chicanos (Mexican Americans). The fifth for the others (usually Asians, Islanders, and other ethnicities who do not fit in the other groups) was not present.

While paying close attention to the Latin men, I watched and listened to them all give their do's and don'ts of prison life and personal stories.

It was interesting to watch these two men sit there like friends and almost proud of themselves to divide Latin culture behind whitey's wall.

Saucedo represented the Chicanos, an attractive well-preserved specimen of a man. He had salt-and-pepper gray hair and mustache, the build of a Sicario, and a Latin pride that could change the world.

They explained how we, as guards, would be "assigned" a race by the prisoners. Wait—what?

Yep, that's what he said, and that's what happened.

Up to this point, no one ever guessed my correct race and ethnicity. I reserve the right to be both. Italian, Puerto Rican, half black and white, and even Egyptian once, were always assumed.

"I'm half white and Mexican. What race does that classify me as?" I asked with inflated confidence so no one could see I wanted to shit my pants.

"Oh, we classified you as Chicana already," Saucedo immediately answered me, with a cocky machismo smile. It should've been a proud moment accepted as Latin without them having to see my mother, but it felt more like an invitation from the devil.

If we had been in any other room, I could've taken his dominance as a compliment, maybe even romantic, but not in this one. Instead, I paid close attention to him. There were too many stories and newspaper headlines of women getting caught up in sexual favors while working in prison, and this fucking guy wasn't going to use the "la Raza" card to get shit from me.

My mother, who also worked for a prison, had already schooled me on the basic rules of the prison. The first being there are only two races, green and blue. I wore green and Saucedo wore blue.

When the class was over, my training officer pulled me to the side to add, "In here, you'll be hated and set up by your race before any other, so watch your six Faciane," before moving towards his assigned post.

He was right. The *ism* gains more momentum in self-hate.

* * * *

From the first time I met eyes with Saucedo, I could see he was the smooth and manipulative player type. That's the game in prison, not just getting a guard to bring in drugs, cash, etc. but sex from the female cops for himself and sometimes, his ten best prison mates.

Saucedo had a suspicious rapport with the Captain, who worked the corporate side, and even as a rookie, I noticed it. Because of this, he carried an arrogant attitude towards the rest of the staff members.

Every time we spoke, Saucedo tried to "fish" or test me for weakness. He offered food, soda, and candy knowing damn well I couldn't take any of it just to see if I would. It wasn't personal

If he tricked me into breaking the rules, then he could blackmail me for personal use.

Soon my overzealous nature to earn stripes of respect pissed off the shot callers. Saucedo being first and foremost.

Weeks later, I tried to search a bathhouse with my training officer and gave Saucedo the perfect opportunity to make a warrior out of me.

She, I think her name was Fisher, despised doing bathroom checks and advised me against doing them. She was older than me and much weaker when it came to a confrontation. So far, I hadn't clashed with any of them, but not from lack of them trying.

They complained I invaded their privacy. I couldn't believe it bothered these hardcore men, who gave me hell all day, to take a shit in front of me. No other guard, female or male, received these complaints. Their shyness amused me.

Unfortunately for them, they showed me their weakness; lack of dignity in front of a pretty lady. I felt it only fair to use it against them as they were so eager to use mine against me.

When four-hundred and some odd people are watching, believe me when I say they know your weaknesses better than and even before you do.

My first training officer demanded that I inspect the bathroom stalls alongside every dorm room check, and I did as she instructed.

When I first started working there, the bathroom stall walls were full-length, giving them more privacy, but not long after someone had them cut in half.

For a bathhouse check to be thorough, I had to look in each stall and at every prisoner using it to be sure they weren't tattooing themselves or doing drugs. Most of the guards didn't like doing this part of the inspection, especially the female guards.

It was also my least favorite part of the job, but I did it anyway because I didn't want any of them, staff or prisoners, thinking I was intimidated by seeing their dicks or them taking a shit. I'd seen plenty of dick already.

When I entered bathhouse number three, without Fisher's assistance, Saucedo was coming out the same door.

"You can't come in here, Faciane," he scolded and blocked me from moving past the doorway.

His tone was usually flirtatious with me, but now it sounded threatening. Immediately it dawned on me why the prisoners didn't want me in the bathhouses.

"Move Saucedo!" I yelled at him. I was going inside that bathroom, and he was going to have to commit assault to stop me. Yes, there was a risk of getting my ass kicked, but he'd still have to be faster than me.

"You good, man?" Saucedo shouted to the backside of the bathroom while smiling and still refusing to budge. Within seconds, prisoner Johnson, a well-known gang member and low-key shot caller staggered towards us. Quickly, I moved away from the doorway in case he fell. He was a big boy, and I wasn't about to catch him.

"Yeah, man," Johnson responded, catching his balance with boxers hanging off his ass and one nut trying to escape.

He didn't acknowledge me and looked high on a narcotic. But even as a rookie, I knew Fisher couldn't back me up if I tried to detain either of them to prove it.

My best course of action was to let them be, document everything, and report it to my lieutenant.

"He did what!" Lt. Sadler screeched, almost gasping like he saw a spider crawling on my face. He wanted to protect me but knew the risk was mine to carry, and I had to learn to defend myself. Any other action on his part would've put me in more danger.

"I know there were drugs in the bathroom Lt. I could tell when Johnson came out that he was high and trying to avoid eye contact. He always makes time to speak with me," I reported confidently.

Johnson always spoke when he saw me. Usually, when I walked through the bathhouses, and he was taking a shit, he'd say something amusing like, "What's up, Faciane, it's a shitty day," and laugh.

He found it entertaining that an attractive woman could be so bold. But this particular night, he avoided me, and I was positive Saucedo supplied the high for him to do so.

The lieutenant had me write up a report to have Saucedo moved to another facility before any of the other prisoners could catch on. It's impossible to remove a shot-calling drug dealer unnoticed.

The next night when I came on shift and started an outer perimeter check, I noticed several prisoners grouped but quiet. It's never that quiet.

All the men stared and gave me the stank eye, not just the Latinos.

I strutted by them like it was a typical day with nothing to fear.

But just before I finished, my supervisors had me paged over the loudspeaker to the Watch Office like back in middle school.

"You OK, Faciane? We think for your safety, you need to work the control tower for a little while." Sgt. Lowen said, concerned. She was nothing like Sgt. Hanson.

Hanson wouldn't page me to the Watch Office. She'd radio me for my location, met me, and walk with me to be sure I was safe.

I think Lowen was afraid but not just for me, for what might happen with a prison full of pissed off detoxing prisoners. What I did was a big deal. I snitched. I snitched on a well-connected Latino drug dealing shot-caller in prison, a level 1 prison, but a prison nonetheless.

"You can't put me in control, Lowen. They'll think I'm afraid, and that will only put me in more danger. They can be pissed at me all they want, but if you send me to the box, it only proves Saucedo ran this yard and not us," I said, shaking with adrenaline.

Control, the box, was a guard post completely separated from the prison yard. Prisoners wouldn't have access to harm me working that post. Deep down, I wanted to go but knew what I said to her was true.

"She's right," Lt. Sadler mumbled.

We all waited for a moment in silence together, almost praying for my safety. "OK, Faciane, but I want you to check-in with Control every 30 minutes, so I know where you are at all times. Be safe!" She said like a worried mother.

My prayer was if the Chicanos chose to beat me up, rape and stash me in a corner somewhere, that it wouldn't take too long for someone on my team to find me.

With an absurd amount of bravery, I hurried back out the door.

SISTERS OF COLOR

I started with a dorm inspection and decided it was time to go balls to the wall.

Every group that I saw with more than three prisoners, I used the prison policy against 'grouping' to break them up, and I didn't care what race or ethnicity they were.

If they were going to hurt me, I was going to earn it.

"Hey, you want a write up for grouping to incite a riot? No? Then I suggest ya'll split up. Play with me if you want to, but I'm still going to do my job," I sternly shouted at the first group I saw. Pretty much daring them to make their move.

At five feet, two inches short I wasn't wasting time waiting for these fuckers to sneak up on me, I was going to instigate them in front of witnesses.

Fortunately, none of them ever flinched at me, but the

Chicanos stayed pissed at me for weeks. I was nervous every time I went to work that one of them was going to catch me off guard.

One evening a few days after, while assigned to stand post at the exit door of the chow hall, a couple of my Latino enemies passed me to leave talking shit in Spanish. I may not habla but could tell it wasn't flattering.

Coming up behind them was a black Muslim prisoner who was always polite and respectful, like most of the Muslims I met at this prison.

"How are you doing today, Faciane?" he asked.

I was stuck in a gaze plotting my vengeance of how I was going to get even with the douchebags that just passed me, and he caught me off guard. Not many prisoners had spoken to me voluntarily since I had Saucedo removed, so I wasn't sure if he was genuine or fucking with me.

"I'm good. How are you? You aren't trying to take anything out of here, right?" I asked defensively, and just in case this conversation was a setup.

"Not at all, Faciane," he chuckled, then said, "I just wanted to ask how your day was and to tell you to hold your head up my sista," He sounded genuine.

"Thank you, but I am not black, half Mexican, and white. Not that I wouldn't be proud to be black, but I'm not," I replied, trying to be culturally appropriate and respectful.

At this point, I was confused about where I fit in with my race. Both had made it clear I wasn't welcome. The Latins, as well as the whites, being two-thirds of the population, were now my potential enemies.

The 'brothers' and the 'others' were the only ones not giving me shit.

He smiled at me and continued his pep-talk with conviction.

"You're a sister of color, Faciane. Don't forget that," he whispered to me as he strutted down the steps to go towards the television room.

The Chicanos felt betrayed that I didn't back them as a Latin woman, but they couldn't change my race. Nothing ever felt like racism than this moment when my own sought to destroy me.

In prison, it's a strategic ploy not just to break you but to keep you that way.

Racism and ethnic exclusion are also profitable, and its agenda has little to do with skin color.

For almost two generations, people tiptoed around the word nigger, and somewhere it evolved to "nigga," leaving most people unsure where it could be used and by whom. Is it jive talk? Ebonics? Racism?

As a kid, I watched the movie "Airplane! (Zucker & Davison, 1980)" where the writers portray an older white woman as "bilingual" because she could speak "jive" to the black men on the plane.

In today's climate, that would be considered racist and culturally inappropriate, and perhaps that was its original intention, but I didn't see it that way.

My interpretation has always been that the black guys were way too cool to speak like white people, and the cool old white lady loved black people enough to learn their language. She was my hero.

'Nigga' isn't the same as 'nigger.' Even if you remove the history associated with the word nigger, it still sounds cruel and demeaning, but nigga sounds fucking cool. If it didn't, there wouldn't be so many fighting over who can and cannot say it.

As radical as it sounds, I have seen that term unify more groups of people than divide them.

I know Jewish jiggas, White wiggas, Machismo Migos, and Asian chiggas.

My mother and aunt were called niggers by white kids during their school years in Orange County, California, during the1960s. My grandmother went to a segregated school in the 1940s, also in Southern California.

It's a word, and like most words, it can serve for either good or evil.

"Bastard" was a term used to shame women who had children out of wedlock and has now evolved to a "despicable person" or something "no longer pure."

"Bitch" was used to define a female dog then evolved to a demeaning term towards women; now, it used to describe "a difficult situation" or to "express displeasure."

One author took it a step further to create an acronym of it, "Babe in Total Control of Herself (Sherry Argov, *Why Men Love Bitches*, 2000)," my favorite use of the term.

The meaning or expression of some words and terms evolve, perhaps we should too.

I remember hearing the word nigger as a kid from my dad.

Specifically, how mean and hateful he used it and how uncomfortable it would make me feel. When I asked mom what it meant, "it's a mean word and don't ever use it!" was the only answer my parents gave me. And I never used it, or its slang cousin, until my twenties.

While living in a small town in the late 1990s, I hung out and dated some gang-affiliated black men. Because I was new in town, and Latin, that pissed off a few black women. Ten-plus of them tried to jump me, but the guys stopped them. Still, I wound up in a fight with one of them—and won.

We all celebrated my victory with drinks and blunts.

Cain was like my big brother and was one of the men who protected me. He passed me the blunt, smiled, and said, "Roni, you's a nigga, and you'll always be my nigga." Him a few others were impressed with my scrapping skills and Latin pride. It felt like a right of passage because our generation wasn't bound to the same racial scripts as our parents before us.

* * * *

Various minorities have suffered from the curse of being treated like a nigger. In my opinion, any race or ethnicity that had a KKK chapter torment them has taken their turn at being a nigger in my country.

In 1848, a KKK chapter tormented Mexican people, with more than 600 men lynched. Mexicans were the hardest to classify as a specific race because they're were labeled "mixed"' stock. Leaving them also vulnerable to racial oppression. (Natalina Molina, *How Race is made in America*, 2014)

In Washington, during the 1920s, a well known KKK group targeted and tormented the Japanese farmers (https://depts.washington.edu/civilr/kkk_intro.htm).

Native Americans still face their genocide.

According to criminologists, Native American Indians are the most incarcerated per population and the most likely group to be victims of violent crimes. (Frank Hagan, *Introduction to Criminology: Theories, Methods, and Criminal Behavior-9th Edition*, 2017).

"Native Americans, unlike other racial/ethnic groups, are more likely to be victims of interracial violence (that is, between races). Sixty percent of those committing crimes against Native Americans were whites; most of these offenses were attributed to racism and alcohol. Native Americans, are, however, twice as likely as blacks and three times more likely than whites to be victims of rape or aggravated assault..."

"Native Americans are one of the smallest minority groups, yet they represent one of the largest percentages of prison inmates. There are 555 recognized Native American tribes in the United States, and, despite the well-publicized success of gambling facilities on some reservations, a third of the country's 2 million Native Americans live below the poverty line. This figure is higher than for all other minority groups (Blackman and Simmons, 1995)..."

"Native American youth are the largest category of youth incarcerated under federal jurisdiction..."

Author, Natalia Molina also references this Indigenous Racial Script:

"Manifest Destiny was used by politicians, officials, and journalists, beginning in the 1840s to justify westward expansion. As an ideology, it expressed a belief that those were taking over the land were spreading democratic institutions for those who were not capable of self-government. Jingoistic politicians, journalists, writers, and citizens alike singled out Native Americans especially, and those of non-European origin generally, as not fit for self-government. Furthermore, they argued that Native Americans would eventually disappear in the Southwest

after the U.S. takeover because they were not as biologically fit as white Americans."

Ain't that some shit?

We have to be classified, individually, fit (enough) for self-government. Probably why Blass believes we're all, still, niggers.

I'd bet my right ass cheek, had Beth Chapman been any other race than white no one would've cared about Duane "Dog" Chapman's private conversation.

HUNTING IN THE WRONG HOOD

We all got up early to be at the Inside Edition News station early for our interview, and Bernard was already there.

For whatever reason, the network didn't want Bernard included in our interview because of his reputation for being political and confrontational with the media. They knew pushing their narrative for Greene wouldn't be easy with him on our side.

So Laci got sick rather suddenly and stayed in the car while Bernard, Staci, and I did the interview. We didn't have to say much because Bernard said it all, and it was the shortest interview we had had yet.

I sat in my seat fearless and full of pride, listening as Bernard knocked down every bullshit question they threw at us with his knowledge and education. Making sure he adequately informed and educated the public, and our haters, that we didn't break the law with either the Blass or Watkins cases.

We left to eat and put together an itinerary for the rest of the trip. At some point, we still had to check out Oakland for Watkins and known contacts.

I called the Oakland Police Department to get their procedure for making a felony arrest in their city.

"Bounty Hunters, eh?" the on-duty Sergeant asked with almost a chuckle.

"We don't advise that anyone to serve a warrant to that area of Oakland without one of our units for backing, and I can't spare anyone until later in the week," he said concerned.

Why was I not surprised.

"Hey, the cops say they don't advise us to go into Oakland," I laughed. Staci had to hear it for herself.

I handed her the phone, and then Bernard added "this job is dangerous enough with a firearm, you girls are nuts for not carrying at least one" as he opened his office door.

"We' re going to drive through Oakland and just look, but we aren't going to knock on any doors or make contact," Staci said, hanging up her phone.

Regardless of the risk, we had to look for Watkins while in the area.

My partners tried not to show it, but it had become a little personal for all of us at this point. Finding Watkins was the key to shutting everyone up.

We packed up all our souvenirs, hugged our new legend friend, and left.

We were almost to the freeway when Laci reminded me it was Father's Day.

"I would give anything for my dad to be alive so I could call him, Roni. You might regret it," Laci said in her 'make you feel guilty" voice. She had skills for someone who didn't have children.

I was unmoved but eventually gave in.

"Hi, can I speak to my dad?" Mary answered the phone. I was polite but kept it short to avoid conversation.

"Hello?" my dad picked up the other line. We hadn't spoken for almost three years since I left his home. I called a couple of months after our fight to apologize for some of the things I said, but he refused to forgive me.

He always called for my birthday but purposely missed the last three.

"Happy Fathers Day!" I shouted, happy to hear his voice.

"Thanks," he said, annoyed at the sound of mine. His contempt for me was crystal fucking clear.

"How are you?" I asked to squeeze out as much conversation I could from him.

"Fine," he responded, annoyed.

The only commonality left to talk about was work. I was sure my current state of media attention would give us something to talk about.

"How are you?" he asked, to be polite.

"I'm good. I'm in Sacramento dealing with a case. I'm a bounty hunter. Did you see me on the news?" I asked, hopeful to rebuild anew.

"Yea, I saw you," he said in his disapproving tone.

It's possible that shooting a white supremacist with a paintball gun on national TV didn't make him so proud, after all. Or he just couldn't show it in front of Mary.

"Did you say hi to Mary when she answered?" he asked, irritated, and accusatory, now changing the subject.

"I asked if I could speak with you," I told him, now irritated myself.

"I have to go. Thanks for the call," Dad rushed off the phone, and I vowed never to make another call to him again. The next one was on him.

Laci meant well, but at that moment, I envied her and her sister. Their dad was gone and couldn't say cruel, life-altering statements that damage long after his death.

But we were on our way to Oakland with no time for mushy dad issues.

* * * *

When we drove by the address the bond agent gave us, there weren't visible cars or people associated with the case. Shortly after, we headed home more determined to find Watkins.

We looked for him almost every night. The night we searched for him at his parent's house, his stepmother was very chatty and compliant while answering our questions. The dad, however, was determined not to tell us a damn thing of any use. Not that I blame him, it's part of the game.

"You should go on down to neighborhood..." the stepmother named what sounded like specific gang-affiliated neighborhoods. I had no clue where these areas were, nor can I remember them by name for this story, but my partners knew them well.

"Oh wait, that is Blood gang territory, he's not associated with those gangs they're rivals," Staci said, showing off her former LAPD skills.

That woman had no idea Staci and Laci knew which territories each gang claimed, and they wouldn't be so easy to set up.

"They won't let us white girls in there," Laci said, chuckling.

"She can," the stepmother said, looking right at me. "They will let her there and talk to her," she smiled to acknowledge that my looks and ethnicity would guarantee our safety in these neighborhoods.

"Yea, maybe we will go by there," Staci played along to her. We quickly finished the search and left.

"She's trying to get us jumped," Staci told us when back in the car. "There is no way he is in those neighborhoods and associated with any Blood gang. And they know it," she continued while going through the paperwork to confirm his background and known gang affiliations.

Watkins had many connections in this community. He had people watching out for him every dam where we went in a five-mile radius, and the residents knew which cars belonged there and which ones didn't. If we had used a rental car or any other unmarked vehicle, it would have stood out more. Making contacts was useless because no one would speak to us about Watkins either. Even with a five-thousand-dollar reward, no one talked.

One night we had perfect timing, and his known vehicle

was parked in front of his grandmother's house. Less than ten minutes later, the car pulled away from the street. It was too dark out to see whether Watkins was driving, but Laci followed the car anyways.

I'll be damned if three more cars appeared out of nowhere to cut us off and divert our direction.

While we played chase with the cars, we passed a local bar too many times, and one of its patrons, an older black man, walked out to the middle of the street like he was about to draw a gun on us.

He screamed at us like an O.G. out of a John Singleton movie. "WHO THE FUCK ARE YOU, AND WHAT ARE YOU DOING IN THIS NEIGHBORHOOD!"

Laci made a quick left to avoid him, rolled down the window and shouted back to him, "WE'RE LOOKING FOR HER HUSBAND!" then pointed to me.

He still looked pissed but didn't say anything else. Laci hit the gas and got us down the street safely.

I tried to get pissed at her for being so fucking insane but laughed instead. I had to give it to her because that was some quick award-winning thinking on her part. She may have kept us from being killed.

We didn't dare drive back down that street again, but it caused us to lose all the cars in the process. I can't deny it was a thrilling chase, but the extent this man had gone to avoid jail disturbed me. Not to mention how many people supported him in doing so.

In the last days of the case, we played more shadow games

but never located and arrested Watkins and the bond company had to pay the court.

Greene continued to threaten us with a lawsuit for this case but didn't officially file one.

He continued to hire people to harass my mom's house to treat my family and me like fugitives to avenge Blass.

BRIDGING THE BIG ASS GAP

Even with Greene doing what he could to slander all of us, customers still wanted to work with Staci and Laci. They received numerous requests to help with missing persons and process serving. One requested they help enforce a civil court monetary judgment. But after we pissed off some Russian mob types because of said monetary judgment, the stress became more than I could handle.

After a few weeks, a bail agent and bounty hunter, we all knew, tried to arrest one of his clients and was detained by the local police. He asked Staci and Laci if they would join him for a meeting with the Riverside County Sheriff to discuss how to better "bridge the gap" between the local law enforcement and bounty hunters.

They declined but sent me instead. I wasn't sure how to feel about the idea, both excited and frightened. It was another rare opportunity to network in a room full of political power.

This bounty hunter, Sam, physically saw his fugitive inside the residence, but because his bail application didn't list that particular address, they arrested him.

"I don't know what the hell to say them," I said nervously before agreeing to attend on their behalf.

Of course, I was lying to myself because I knew what to say, exactly, but grew tired of repeating it to those who could care less.

They all needed to quit their pissing contests, implement black-and-white procedures, and add clear language to the penal codes for bounty hunters. When I took the required laws and arrests class with the Sheriff's department, there was no mention, or any curriculum, regarding bail, bounty hunting, or fugitive recovery, etc.

Bounty hunting was a "custody" job and not just a "snatch and grab" so there should have been more "custody training" required, in my opinion.

In 2013, California law allowed bounty hunters to legally detain a fugitive for up to 48 hours after the arrest, before turning them over to the custody of the sheriff.

If that isn't some outlaw shit, I don't know what is. However, since it was legal, how people were cared for and treated while in the custody of a civilian was pretty dam important in my book.

I sat in the lobby of the sheriff's office, watching all his staff in suits and uniforms shuffle around. Thankful, I no longer had to wear pantyhose and heels to work.

A double door opened to my right, and inside was a group of older official-looking men gathered around a table. Sam, the Latino gentleman I recognized from the company's social media contacts, came out to greet me.

"Hi Roni, I'm Sam. Nice to formally meet you. I see Staci and Laci didn't come after all?" he nervously shook my hand and looked behind me in hopes of seeing them.

I understood his nervousness, being that I was the rookie with none of the experience and knowledge that Staci and Laci had may make him look even more incompetent in his plea.

Not to mention we were both Latin and, recently in the news for "questionable" acts during the scope of our duties. Might defeat the purpose.

Sam didn't give me a chance to respond before he pulled me into the conference room and introduced me to everyone. We all sat down, and the men began their meeting.

Everyone took their turn to speak, and I listened intently to all they had to say.

Sam explained the awkward position his arrest put him as a licensed bondsman and certified bounty hunter. He emphasized the difficulties of having "tied hands" as a bondsman in a county that does not educate their police force in bail law. His request of the lawmen was that they add bail laws and guidelines for bounty hunting to the curriculum at the Police Academy.

The men all agreed it made sense.

"I attended the State required classes and noticed a couple of problematic issues," I blurted out before it was my turn to speak.

"I'm not sure why it's required to attend training with the Sheriff's Department if none of the curricula includes who we are or what we do. We arrest people and should be required to have extensive custody training like peace officers do." I added to assure them the inconsistency was noticeable even to me.

None of the men mentioned it, but Greene exposed a weakness that went all the way up their chain of command.

After they all agreed I had valid points, the gentleman who worked with the Corrections Academy mentioned they'd also consider adding bail law to their curriculum.

For the sake of the bail industry and its clients, I hoped they'd follow through.

DIVERSION 101

Investigators meticulously train to see what's hidden in plain sight, and most of the time, people think you are deranged if you can see what they cannot.

The first time I saw a prison fight and tried to break it up, the state supervisor, Sgt. Macke stopped me.

"Hold on, Faciane, don't be so quick to jump. The fight may be a diversion," he instructed.

I hadn't heard any of my training officers use the term before and anticipated his next move.

"Prisoners know that fighting will only get them in trouble, normally they prefer to handle their physical business when the guards aren't watching them. I'm positive that fight is to draw all the cops to one place so another group can do something somewhere else. You need to be looking somewhere else right now." He schooled me then shifted his toothpick to the other side of his mouth with a confident grin. Toothpicks must be a badass guy thing.

The smooth sergeant looked around and moved away from the dorm areas. "Come on, let's go check some fences."

We checked the outer perimeter fence, and I saw nothing suspicious right away.

“You see that?” Macke asked before he stopped dead in his tracks.

“See what?” I asked irritated because it was hot, and I couldn’t see shit.

“The straw that’s sticking out of the ground,” he whispered as he moved towards the gate to get back inside the dorm area.

I still saw nothing, and my eyes were younger than his. Once back inside the gate, we moved towards the target area, and Macke called the lieutenant on duty to meet him at the closest dorm.

As we approached, I saw it.

These fucking guys buried their pruno stash (prison-made alcohol) and put a straw in it for ventilation so it wouldn’t blow up. They created a diversion to hide it. It made total sense when I remembered the two squares who fought.

Because of this lesson, I learned to read between the lies.

When the dust of the Blass’ case settled, I realized we were just the tip of a bigger fight.

* * * *

In 2012, the city attorney in San Bernardino, California, the largest county in the state, fell under scrutiny when he told residents to “lock their doors and load their guns” during a council meeting. Officials forced to cut its police force, created longer response times, and an influx in crime. (https://losangeles.cbslocal.com/2012/11/30/city-attorney-tells-san-bernardino-residents-to-lock-their-doors-load-their-guns-because-of-police-downsizing/)

That same year, at least three major cities faced bankruptcy. (https://finance.yahoo.com/blogs/daily-ticker/three-california-cities-bankrupt-tip-iceberg-says-fmr-155121281.html)

The U.S. Senate introduced the Assault Weapons Ban of 2013 for stricter gun control. (https://www.congress.gov/bill/113th-congress/senate-bill/150)

The AB109 Prison Reform, in its second year, statistics showed only a shift, not a reduction, of offenders from prison to county jails. (http://www.pasadenastarnews.com/general-news/20130203/socal-police-chiefs-on-ab-109-this-is-dangerous)

Governor Jerry Brown pushed, for a second time, to revamp the cash bail system in California. (https://www.scpr.org/news/2018/08/28/85760/california-becomes-first-state-to-end-cash-bail-af/)

Our story wasn't just sexy; it was the perfect weapon to fit their narrative and swing votes.

I can't deny that three bitches shooting rubber bullets and a taser at a dangerous felon in a public restaurant was kind of irresponsible, though legal.

But posting it on Youtube made it easier to prove their point and use us as their diversion.

Anyone who didn't agree with stricter policies and saw our 'one-sided' story might be inclined to change their vote.

Blass was out of jail on four separate bonds, that's four different pending criminal cases. He also had prior cases for violent crimes. A fact none of his supporters ever mentioned.

He shouldn't have been out on parole from prison in the first place, but no one seemed to care about that. AB109 may have changed how the state assessed their risk, but still, they managed to release high-risk offenders.

It made no sense to go through all the risk to arrest someone only for them to be released a few days later on their own recognizance.

Of course, to the public, we looked more like domestic terrorists than professionals.

5.

Bullet 5

BULLET 5 -FEAR

SEARCHING FOR KIANNA

There is always that one cop, usually a guy, in that one movie that had that one case that fucks them up for life, rendering them obsessive, and almost delusional of what's real and what's not.

They appear almost heroic in their failures to get justice for a stranger, but in real life, it's not that noble. Or is that kind of trauma reserved for just the guys.

One night reviewing cases while eating dinner, Staci noticed one was a solicitation case and mocked the bondsman's negligence.

"This bondsman knows better, bailing out prostitutes and escorts is a high risk," she chuckled.

"Because their pimps might bail them out?" I ignorantly asked.

I couldn't think of any reason that would make them a higher risk than the other cases.

"No, because they move around in the state, and state to state, practically live in motels/hotels. If they miss court, you usually never find them." Laci said while reading the file.

Assessing the risk is a vital skill to being a bail agent, and Staci and Laci's assessment of solicitation cases was an experienced one, not a prejudicial one. They both worked VICE, the police unit for moral crimes, i.e., solicitation, while with the LAPD. They experienced both sides of this coin.

Staci read off the client's name then began to read the notes in the file when Laci interrupted her, "Kianna? Kianna Jackson?" Staci nodded while staring back at her sister.

"She is one of the four girls missing. The story has been all over the news. You guys haven't seen it?" Laci asked, then grabbed the iPad from Staci's side to show us the news article.

There it was, the same booking photo of Kianna that the bondsman sent them with the file.

Kianna and three others had just made national headlines as missing persons and possibly linked to human trafficking.

You gotta be shittin' me?!

When I was in my twenties, I didn't hear about human trafficking, only "white slavery" and mostly white girls (blond hair and blue eyes) in Las Vegas were rumored to be the victims of it.

I didn't fit the description, but it frightened me and kept me from partying like a rockstar in Las Vegas for many years.

Kianna was twenty-years-old, almost the same age as my son, biracial, and looked as if she could be related to my daughter.

I was speechless, and we all sat quietly for a few minutes to eat our food.

"You know, it's a good thing that she's also a fugitive now. We can do what the cops can't do to find her. We can legally kick in the doors," Laci and I nodded in agreement listening to Staci put together a tentative strategy.

With all the media attention we already had, getting involved in this case may do it some good. We weren't hunting a fugitive now but searching for a missing young woman who may be a victim of human trafficking.

For the first time in months, I felt rejuvenated and my passion for this gig redefined. If we could bring Blass's ass to jail, we could find Kianna and bring her home.

I was ignorantly optimistic.

We ran through all the possible scenarios we could use that would help us find her.

It would take a lot of time and research, but we were determined to find her. I was petrified and had no clue of the rabbit hole I agreed to throw myself down, taking all those that I love with me.

* * * *

We started our search for Kianna and used all the usual tactics, posted fliers, and made phone calls, but we didn't have much to go on.

One night about two a.m. and a few days after getting the case, Staci and Laci drove us through the area in Santa Ana, California, known for its solicitation. Kianna and the other missing girls might have worked the same location before they disappeared.

We hoped to find someone willing to talk to us as investigators searching for a missing person, not as bounty hunters or police.

Two people were walking towards us from across the street. “Excuse me,” Staci asked in a normal tone not to attract the wrong attention to us.

We were near a motel, and it was very dark out. So dark, I can’t tell you where the hell we were to this day.

“Hi, we’re investigators looking for a missing girl,” she lowered her voice in case someone in the motel heard her.

The gal stopped walking and turned towards us. The gentleman with her stepped in front of her to protect her. We moved closer, and I saw he was a black man, early fifties, and her a white woman in her mid to late forties.

She told us she was pregnant, and the gentleman with her was the father and not her pimp.

They both made that clear upfront.

Staci pulled out one of the fliers with Kianna’s information and handed it to the woman while her man watched us closely, still untrusting of our intentions.

“I haven’t seen her before,” the gal said, staring at the photo while Staci held her flashlight over Kianna’s face.

“Many people come and go around here,” she hinted to the challenge finding anyone in this area.

The couple let their guard down when they saw our flier, proving we weren't there to bust them.

The woman explained that she was a working girl, and the gentleman was her boyfriend, who walked with her at night to protect her.

A cool breeze filled my jacket as I listened to my partner's exchange questions back and forth. I tried to put myself in Kianna's shoes to feel how frightened a young girl would be out in this area, desperate to find her next meal and a warm bed.

The woman explained there was a rumor amongst the local working girls in the neighborhood that a black man who drove a black car had grabbed a couple of women, in broad daylight, off the street and put them in his car the drove off. No one had seen them since. Then she added;

"And that hotel right there? If she's in there, you won't find her. We all know not to end up in there, or there's no coming back out." The woman pointed to the tall, sparkling building a few blocks over from us.

I stood there frightened as every imaginable and horrific threat to a vulnerable young woman ran through my mind and tortured me. They flashed between her face and my daughter's.

The woman was right. If Kianna were in there, it would be damn near impossible to find her. To gain access to a motel or hotel for an arrest isn't easy, and if someone took her for trafficking, we were already at least two weeks behind them.

Staci and Laci talked to the couple a little longer then gave them some t-shirts and snacks for their help.

"Time to go," Laci said as she and Staci walked back to the SUV. My almost frozen, numb body lagged behind them.

Once we were in the SUV, I asked how we could access the motel.

"It's very hard with motels without any hard evidence," Staci answered, frustrated. "Especially since we got our intel from a source considered questionable. I'll call and let Kianna's mother know what we found out tonight so she can pass it on to the investigator for the case." She said and then answered her phone for a bail call.

I put my hands over the heater to try and thaw out then began to panic. How the hell were we going to find her? We had nothing.

But if it were my daughter, I'd want someone to be just as obsessed with finding her as I had become.

****

Unfortunately, a couple of weeks later, a woman who'd been reported missing at the same time as Kianna was found and confessed she wasn't missing but hiding to avoid a warrant.

After this, the air time for Kianna's story became almost non-existent. It isn't illegal to go missing, but it is illegal to hide from the legal ramifications of one's actions.

The public loses interest and empathy, especially for sex workers, and the media soon moves on to the next headline. Our case turned colder and colder.

After developing a strong rapport with Kianna's mother, I learned that Kianna had big dreams to move to the city and build a life. At twenty, she met a man who became her boyfriend and then seduced her to be an escort for him.

Pimps come in all races, genders, and backgrounds, their

lifestyles are glamorized by mainstream society. Both pimp and rape cultures have paved the way for human trafficking to become a lucrative business by desensitizing the public to the massacre of hundreds of sex workers.

In the 2016 docu-series "The Killing Season (Zeman & Gibney, 2016)," journalists, authors, and law enforcement officials investigate the deaths of several girls that are suspected to be victims of L.I.S.K., the Long Island Serial Killer. To date, the only evidence is the suspicion of an uncaught serial killer believed to have killed over fifty young girls.

According to Mark Safarik, a former FBI profiler, the FBI unit that helps solve these crimes now consists of no more than ten overwhelmed profilers for the entire country and the world.

Since the attack on the twin towers in 2011, all government agencies became focused on terrorism. Which forced the FBI to focus more on intelligence than investigations.

Over the years, several citizens savvy with the Internet created an online criminal profiler group that combed through countless online records and helped police and families identify two hundred-eighty nameless victims.

Some believe that because there's a large number of victims, there may be more than one killer competing for hunting grounds and media coverage.

Serial killer Joel Rifkin murdered his victims, known prostitutes, at the same time and in the same location as Robert Shulman, a postal worker, and also convicted of killing five young girls, known prostitutes.

During his interview for the series, Thomas Hargrave, an investigative journalist, tells the interviewer;

"Its a documented fact there are more than 200 killers in the FBI's highway serial killer initiative, and this number accounts for only 1 type of serial killer."

Experts are confident there are far more active serial killers than we, the public, can imagine.

Merna Quinn, the author of 'The Missing, Missing," adds during her interview that her efforts to get more attention on killers who prey on prostitutes has been ongoing since the 1990s.

Her research shows that in the 1970s, only sixteen-percent of female victims of serial killers were prostitutes, and now between 2000-2009, thirty years later, seventy-percent of female victims of serial killers are prostitutes.

We've created the ideal underworld for serial killers whose prey are sex workers.

PIMPS AND PREY

Prisoner Lewis was the first pimp I'd ever met. I found pictures of him dressed up for what looked like a "Pimp of the Year" contest when I searched his locker one night.

I tried not to burst out in laughter when it reminded me of the scene in the movie "I'm Gonna Git You Sucka (Wayans & Craig et al, 1988)". The pimp just released from jail in a loud-yellow outfit with goldfish swimming in his platform shoes.

Lewis was a good-looking, dark-skinned black man and maybe a couple of years older than me but no more than twenty-six years old.

He never gave me the impression that he was the thug type. He wore big ass curls in his hair for gosh sakes, and until then, I didn't know any black male gangster that did that.

Not sure how our debate started, but Lewis and I went back and forth over the level of romance roses ranked one night. He argued that roses made every woman melt no matter how angry or hateful she felt towards a man. I debated he was full of shit, and that not all of us women forgave so easily.

"Roses die in days, betrayal can last a lifetime," I sassed at him.

I'd forgotten all about it, but a few nights, he strategically proved his point.

As I unlocked the gate to enter the pod to get to the dorm, I noticed a group of Latin prisoners standing against the bathhouse wall watch me but didn't see Lewis come to the gate.

When I went through the gate and turned to lock it, I looked up, and Lewis stood about five feet in front of me with a dozen roses, hand made out of tissue paper in his hands.

Latinos are romance artists and made these beautiful pieces of art to sell and mail to their loved ones. The group who stood by the bathhouse must have made them for Lewis and wanted to see my reaction.

He stood there, smiling and waiting for me to react as he predicted.

What a fucker! I felt my face get hot, and blush to remind me a mushy woman hid under my uniform, but I didn't dare flinch.

"Oh, fuck you, Lewis!" I chuckled and hurried past him.

"Aw come on, Faciane, aren't they beautiful?" He giggled and followed behind me, now headed towards the Latin group. I had to get rid of the witnesses.

"You'd better get to your dorms, its count time. Don't make me write ya'll up for snot rag roses!" I shouted, to assure them I wasn't impressed.

All of them looked genuinely disappointed. They may have had intentions to mess with me as a guard, but I'm positive they also wanted me to appreciate the beauty of their art as a woman.

Regardless, I couldn't show them that side of me.

Lewis got the hint and went to his dorm. I didn't talk to him until the next day and made it clear that his actions were unacceptable. Not just because he was a prisoner but because he was a pimp.

Blushing uncontrollably at his gesture, scared the shit out of me.

Months passed, and I'd forgotten all about the tissue roses until a co-worker told me that a transgender prisoner who worked for me, Tambouché, a 6'4" tall, attractive, young and black, was gang-raped. He named only one of his attackers, prisoner Lewis. They grew up together, and his violent betrayal would stain Tambouché's life forever.

"This isn't something I'm allowed to share with anyone because it's private, but I know you have a good rapport with him, and he works for you. If you see him experiencing any emotional distress, please encourage him to go to medical. He won't press charges because he doesn't want anyone to know." Miller whispered, looking over her shoulder to be sure we were alone.

She was a petite white woman in her forties, and I watched the sadness settle in her tiny face when she finished. Just to know his story traumatized her, and it circled in her eyes as she stared at the wall behind me.

I stood there and tried not to imagine what this man had endured. He wasn't a small man or easily bullied, and it would take a group of men to hurt him.

Even in prison, a gay man is still a man and will beat the shit out of someone if deemed necessary. Tambouché had ass and hips that could make a black woman jealous, and I knew they didn't take him down without a fight.

It dawned on me right then his rape was around the same time I found a pair of ripped jean shorts on the cement block of a dorm not far from the TV room.

They looked like they had been ripped off someone's body, from the zipper down to the leg. When I asked my training officer what to do with them, he instructed me to take them to the laundry room to have them thrown away.

I never followed up and didn't hear that anyone reported a rape. It bothered me not to know what happened to the person wearing them that night.

Miller couldn't confirm if the ripped jeans were Tambouché's, but my experience as a victim didn't need her too.

We hugged, something we usually didn't do but did so that day to share our emotion for Tambouché.

Even with our alleged "power to protect" as women, we were both powerless to help a man and rape victim.

It isn't enough to put a man in a cage and call it just. Our society also condones prison rape as a special bonus for their punishment. A twisted "boys will be boys" club that breeds violent predators and then unleashes them into our communities. When we ignore the crime of rape in prison because its victims are men, it doesn't make it less of a crime, just a double standard by hypocrites.

I've never looked at roses the same.

* * * *

Not long ago, at an adult birthday party with children, I overheard a little boy arguing with another little boy. Neither were older than ten yrs old, and one of them yelled that "he" was going to make the other "suck his dick."

When I told the child's closest relative, they asked me to keep quiet, and they would speak to his mother.

For me, it wasn't a coincidence, that he used this form of communication to establish dominance because his dad went in and out of jail since before he was born.

A pattern destined to repeat.

VIRGINITY: THE UNEQUAL VIRTUE

The closest to church I got growing up was an anonymous "beverage" recovery program where its members shared their spirit, strength, and hope. And a shit-ton of politically incorrect personal life stories that inspire greatness.

My grandmother and mom befriended many prostitutes in the program and created a shame-free perception of sex work for me as a young girl.

I was always fascinated with the ladies of the night walking in their leopard print skin-tight outfits when we drove down their tarty street.

Mom didn't gasp in disgust or judge them. Instead, she'd

shout, "Look at the hookers Roni!" excited like she, herself, was starstruck.

The women of her generation still faced shame for their sexuality, and to my mom, prostitutes were almost like superheroes.

But when dad returned from Korea, and my parents divorced, the inequality of my feminine virtue soon defined me.

Dad came back with an eclectic porn collection, most recorded on the same VHS tapes labeled "for kids." He also stashed dirty magazines, noticeably, under the bathroom sink. I'm still unsure whether he'd forgotten he no longer lived with a group of men or intended to piss mom off.

He regularly made sexist and sexual remarks about women he saw either on television or walking on the street.

His chauvinism had no regard for the impression it left on me, nor did my watching and listening gave him pause. At fifteen, he called me a prude when I refused to wear a skirt.

Unfortunately, it didn't matter that mom came from the generation that led the sexual revolution, sex for pleasure was still taboo and so was talking about it.

When I asked where babies came from as a young girl, she used her Persian cats as examples instead of the birds and bees. Later as a curious teen, even more confused, I got up the courage to ask how humans have sex, and she freaked out.

"Why do you want to know?" she answered irritated.

"Nevermind," I whispered and went back to read my book. Eventually, I did the worst thing a kid could do and asked my peers, who were already having sex, for advice.

Dad's sex talk sounded more like advice better fit for one of his military troops.

"Roni, sex is good between people who love each other. Well, sex is good with people you don't love too, so make sure you use a condom," he said, matter-of-fact then changed the subject.

At fourteen, I had my first mother-approved boyfriend, Victor, a Mexican boy, one school grade behind me, and like all the after school specials of the 1990s, it started innocently. After a couple of months of hovering over the third base, the pressure for us to have sex began.

We were both virgins, at least I was, and he said it would make it more special and memorable. Blah blah blah.

When I chickened out, he gave me the horny teenage boy ultimatum, "if you don't, I'll find someone who will," and I gave in.

It was disastrous. I bled through both my mattress and box spring. The stains left behind only confirmed mom's suspicions of my deflowering later.

After she found out I had had sex, she hadn't a clue what to say to me, and when she finally spoke, her words were in shame and disappointment.

"What are you going to give your husband now?" she screeched at me.

Give my husband? Was I supposed to give something to a husband? No one ever told me I had to save my virginity for a husband.

Mom had missed something between her applause for the

ladies of the night and the award-winning sex talk of how to breed Persian cats.

She then used some choice words to imply I was no different than my "slut" cousin on dad's side of the family. She had lost her virginity too just before I did.

My grandmother was pissed. I took a big shit on her plans for me to attend Pepperdine University, become a lawyer, and marry a wealthy white farmer.

But neither one of them was going to let me ruin their plans, not without a fight.

My grandmother decided that mom's demeaning insults weren't cruel enough to stop me from having sex again until my honeymoon.

She demanded that mom take me to the home of the heathen who deflowered me and make me tell his mother that I had sex with her son.

Mom agreed.

Victor and I both had abusive parents, and I was worried us showing up at his house would get him in more trouble. Even though he met my mother, I had never met his mother before.

* * * *

Victor's mother opened the door with a look of surprise. She was a petite Mexican woman, and behind her was a taller Mexican man who must have been his stepfather.

"Hello?" she said and looked annoyed.

"Ahh-hi Mrs. Lopez, I'm Roni—Victor's girlfriend."

I couldn't help but stutter at her; she was already irritated we were at her door.

"Yes, what can I do for you?" she asked, bracing herself for whatever shitty news we came to deliver.

"Hi, I'm Roni's mother, and I wanted to come by and let you know that your son Victor has been at my house without my permission, and I need him to stop. They both ditched school together," mom interrupted me to snarl at her first.

"Yes, I know," his mother replied angrily. "I received a call from the school today, and you won't have to worry about him over at your house again because he is going to live with his father tonight."

Tonight? My heart raced, and I began to panic that I'd never see Victor again.

Mom nudged me to confess my dirty secret. I opened my mouth and started to talk, but nothing came out. After several seconds I heard my own words betray me.

"We had sex the day we ditched. We didn't plan it; it just happened." I mumbled then put my head down in shame.

Disgusted, she replied, "As I said, Victor will no longer be a problem for you and your family. Thank you and goodbye."

She shut the door on us.

Mom walked away, satisfied with me sulking behind her back to the car to go home. I wanted to crawl in a hole and die.

I gave up my innocence, and an unequal virtue for a future husband, to a boy I'd never see again. At fourteen-years-old, I felt like the words 'damaged goods' were branded into my flesh.

My grandmother and 1980s feminism encouraged mom to believe that the only other cure to my promiscuity was to send me to live with my father.

The resentment I grew for her would also change the course of my life. I needed her those years, like all teenage girls need their mothers, for guidance and protection through my development as a young woman.

Dad hadn't a clue how to raise a teenage girl, and I ended up in more shit living with him.

STALKED LIKE PREY

In the early 1990s, the term 'stalking' wasn't associated with a crime or much of a mainstream topic yet. At sixteen years old, I met Giovanni, a nineteen-year-old, six-foot three-inch, almost three hundred pounds big ass, Samoa guy from the neighborhood. We crossed paths in my apartment complex one afternoon, coming home from school and exchanged phone numbers.

I had no intention of anything more than friendship with him. One night he showed up to my house while dad was at work and kissed me, and I, regretfully, kissed him back.

Within days it began.

He started to show up at my house unannounced, and I caught him a couple of times hiding outside my window, watching and listening.

Dad caught him one night too, but Giovanni knew to immediately apologize then gave a believable excuse for why he was out so late.

I don't remember ever agreeing to a relationship, but after I introduced him to dad, he presumed I belonged to him.

One evening after dad went to work, he came over and asked if we could talk in my room, which I found to be an odd request, but I complied nonetheless.

He started to claw at my clothes, and when I tried to push his hands off of me, he pushed me so hard that I flew back onto the bed. His strength still frightens me.

There was no way I could stop him at five-foot-one inch short and one-hundred and eight pounds soaking wet. Without flinching, he closed and locked the door.

He grabbed my legs and held them there until he was on top of me. I tried to fight him while he pulled my pants down, but he just squeezed me harder.

"You're mine, don't fight me. Let me show you I love you," he whispered to taunt me. I tried to bite him when he pulled my leg out of my pants but failed. He pushed his weight onto me, and when I realized he was inside of me, I began to cry.

He pounded my tiny body under him until he was satisfied, got dressed, kissed my forehead, and left. My defiled body lay there stained by the stench of his sweat.

From that day forward, Giovanni forced himself on me every time he came over, and my dad wasn't home.

Eventually, I learned it was much easier, and faster, just to allow him sex and not waste my time or energy fighting. But my permission only made things worse.

He'd show up at my job, walk around and stare at everyone. My story looked nothing like a Lifetime movie. Giovanni wasn't a crazed-looking white guy, but a crazed-looking muscle-bound Samoan guy.

When I started my junior year of high school, he showed up during lunch one afternoon with a pair of handcuffs in his back pocket. No one dared tell on him.

"What are those for?" I asked, pointing to his pocket.

"Those are for you," he smirked.

"Me? What do I need handcuffs for?" I asked, confused at his humor.

Quickly, he pulled them from his pocket, slapped one on his wrist, and then grabbed my hand to apply the other. I tried to resist, but that only made him bend my wrist the other way to gain control over my arm.

"I'm going to show everyone who you belong to," he whispered in my ear as the handcuff tightened on my wrist.

Once both our cuffs were secure, he paraded me around my school.

My schoolmates stared when we walked by them, some laughed, some looked confused, but most were startled.

I laughed to pretend to enjoy his twisted romantic gesture and hid my humiliation. It didn't take long to learn how to hide my feelings and pretend what was happening to me was normal.

Even after he took the handcuff off of me, I felt like his prisoner.

One girl watched him handcuff me and said, "he must love you, girl." Sadly, I wasn't the only young girl who hadn't a clue this was abuse.

"Yes, he must," I shrugged.

My only out was to keep quiet until dad, and I moved eight hours away, but Giovanni followed me there too. We moved to Riverside, California, and he had family less than fifty miles away in Westminster, California.

I feared that if I told dad what happened, he'd try to kill him, and because of his size versus Giovanni's, I wasn't sure he'd succeed. Giovanni had already threatened to hurt my family and me if I left him.

I kept quiet to protect both of us.

It wasn't until Giovanni made the mistake of taking a credit card my grandmother had given for emergencies, that I was able to get rid of him.

My grandmother made me file fraud charges on him, and he disappeared.

My saving grace was either he had a criminal record already or didn't want one, but the effects of what he did to me were everlasting.

* * * *

By the time I was twenty-one, and a mother to a child of my own, I could give two shits what my parental units had to say about how I lived my life.

My rebellion towards them for unintentionally setting me up to fail was at an all-time high.

Anything they had planned for me, I sabotaged it in every way that I could. My vision board for the future consisted of all things— "fuck that and fuck you!"

When I couldn't find a job that made enough money to support my son, I decided to move to Las Vegas to become a stripper. My cousin worked as a stripper at the time and made more money than anyone I knew.

My priority was to make my own money, and if it pissed off my parents in the process, it was even more appealing.

I was disappointed when I told mom, and her reaction was so calm and calculated.

"Mija, how are you going to take off your clothes and dance naked in front of a bunch of old men jacking off?" she gently mocked me.

With only one hit, mom penetrated my wall of rebellion, and immediately I grew disgusted at the thought

I hadn't been honest with myself whether I could dance nude in front of strangers to earn money. At the time, I couldn't reveal more than my belly button in public.

It was hard for me to believe that my mom knew me better than I knew myself at that moment. This time, and without shame, she crushed my dream to be a sex worker to spite her—the wrong reason to become anything.

She didn't want that life for me and not because she was against sex work but because she didn't raise me to be good at that kind of hustle. It's almost impossible for a parent to prepare their child for a life they haven't experienced themselves.

The irony was, I still ended up with a job where a bunch of creepy men could jack off to my body, but I was fully clothed and wore a badge.

As much as I'd like to credit her psychology, it didn't save my life. I'm not that special.

At twenty-one, I didn't make better decisions or take fewer risks than Kianna.

I was lucky not to be killed by a prisoner, a lover, a one night stand, or a stalker myself.

WHEN PREDATORS ARE SET FREE

On April 14, 2014, it was all over the local news that police arrested two men for the deaths of Kianna and four other young women. The men were friends in prison, then released to the streets as homeless registered sex offenders who wore ankle monitors.

Frank Cano, a Mexican man, twenty-seven years old, and Steven Gordon, a white man and forty-five years old.

Dumbfounded that not one, but two men killed these young women. Not to mention it eerie that they were the primary colors of my mixed race. It was beyond my comprehension how a killing spree of prostitutes, while the assailants wore tracking devices, went unnoticed.

I sat on my bed in utter shock with my phone in hand, scrolling through the article. The police had found one of the girl's bodies, but it wasn't Kianna. That detail alone made it impossible for me to believe she was dead.

In my inexperienced and ignorant Hollywood entertained mind, the rarity of two killers with five victims and only one body recovered (not Kianna's), equaled a police department that had to have made a desperate mistake.

Staci and Laci worked with bail agents that used the same type of software to monitor clients, and the odds that two people, not just one, could murder five other people while monitored was inconceivable.

I was sure, Kianna was out there somewhere.

With countless hours spent sat in courtrooms over the years, I'd witnessed plenty of judges get it wrong and allow predators back on the streets.

One predator, in the early stages of his craft, in particular.

* * * *

I had to be in Compton Court by 8 a.m. and ready to present a bail motion for a request to extend the due date on a bond. Since I hadn't been to this court yet, parking delayed me by thirty minutes.

Once inside the courtroom, I heard the judge read instructions to each defendant already in custody waiting to be released, then dismissed them.

After the court took a mid-morning break, then resumed, the first case called was for a young Latin male defendant in his late teens, early twenties. His attorney was an older white man, mid to late sixties.

The judge begins the hearing, and the defendant's attorney requested a continuance then gave a brief explanation of why.

The attorney was undergoing surgery and concerned his recovery time would interfere with his client's right to a speedy trial. He asked the court to either grant the continuance so that he may defend his client himself or allow the defendant to appoint himself another attorney.

The judge asked the defendant whether he wanted to continue with his current attorney or to hire another.

The young pony-tailed man nodded his head while standing nervously with his hands crossed in front of his waist.

"Alright, I will grant a continuance for the date and time as per the request of the defendant. Does opposing counsel have any objections?" the judge asked

"No, your honor," one of the attorneys on the prosecution side mumbled, looking up from her paperwork.

"OK, Mr. Martinez," the judge said, focused back on the defendant. "You need to stay away from Jessica Hernandez, and you're not to be alone with anyone under the age of sixteen. Bail now set for two-hundred thousand dollars!" He ordered before dismissing the case.

His last words rang in my ear like a bell, and I have no idea what anyone said after that.

The judge lost me when he added an age restriction, a girl's name, and a large bail amount. There had to be sex abuse charges against this defendant, and still, they allowed him to walk out that courtroom.

I had to see this young man's face. With this kind of leniency, if he were guilty, I would see it.

True to form, he had a shit-eaten-ass grin on his face, and strutted off passed me and out the courtroom doors confident he got away with his crime.

He was a predator, free from consequence, and I was powerless to stop it.

They didn't even slap his hand and released him on an O.R., his own recognizance. Nothing more than a legal pinky swear.

Mr. Martinez's wicked smile and proud strut proved he knew he was free to abuse again.

Mortified that the defendants before his case had mere warrants for traffic violations and minor misdemeanors. Nickels and dimes compared to this kid's bail amount, and he was free to walk out of the courthouse before any of them.

It was a tragic reminder of how the system allows predators to continue devouring their prey.

Cano and Gordon were both sex offenders on parole, and Gordon was also on federal parole. They each had prior convictions for lewd, lascivious acts on a child under fourteen.

Neither of these men should have been allowed to roam the streets homeless. It only made it easier for them to act like animals looking to devour anything and anyone for survival.

It would take a couple of years before either of their trials began, and I stayed in touch with Kianna's mother with the hope she was found alive.

THE PERFECT PATSY

Late 2013 I attended a bail agent conference, and one of the speakers was a local investigator for the sheriff's department. Not far into his speech, it was clear that he had a major hard-on for bounty hunters. He was a white male, possibly mid-thirties and stood no more than five feet six inches tall. He was cocky and immediately reminded me of Sgt. Beecher.

As he spoke, I could see he was asserting great effort to appear charismatic and informative to warm his audience. The bail agents watched and listened but paid no attention to his subliminal warnings. He playfully listed the consequences he'd inflict on those who hired bounty hunters to revoke bonds based on reasons he felt weren't defined in the bail laws

What I heard him say, in cop-speak, was bounty hunters

wasted and abused the systems time and, more importantly, his time. He had made it his mission to dispense the proper justice to such faulty businesses in his jurisdiction.

I'm unsure if it was the energy of the people in the room or that we were on a known haunted ship (the Queen Mary in Long Beach, California), but I urgently had to pee in the middle of his speech.

While washing my hands, a Latin woman, I assumed another bail agent, came in the door.

"Hey, you know he just showed your video," she told me while she washed her own hands.

"What? I was just in there," I gasped with hands still pressed together under the running water.

"I know it was rude of him. He showed it as an example of how "not" to bounty hunt, referring to you and your team being on the news and facing a lawsuit." She explained while adjusting her shirt in the mirror.

My rage grew. I turned off the water, straightened myself up, then stared at the mirror to decide my next move.

It was a coward move for him to wait until I left the room before talking shit about me to a room full of my business associates.

The whole situation became a conflict of my moral interest. I understood the bail agents and their financial risks and also agreed with some of the investigator's points.

I agree, bail companies shouldn't treat bond revocation like buyer's remorse, but its almost impossible to affirm a person's credibility with a state ID, a short application, and ten percent in collateral or cash.

Nonetheless, whether the little guy had good intentions or not, he didn't know shit about the facts of the Blass case.

Strutting back to the conference room, I decided to be a professional and politely confront him at the end of his speech during the Q&A. I was curious how he, himself, would've handled the arrest.

But, by the time I made it back to my chair, the tv monitors were off, and he was discussing a whole other topic. Quite the sissy move for someone so confident in their agenda.

Standing directly in his view, I watched him like a prisoner.

Ready to confront him, I raised my hand, and he ignored me with a smirk to call on someone else.

When he finally called on me to speak, an uncontrollable grin exploded all over his face, like a mischievous child. Either he was immature or starstruck.

"Yes," he said, pointing at me to give me the floor.

"I understand you showed a video example of misconduct by bounty hunters? It was unfair for you to do that not having all the facts of the case, and me not being in the room to defend myself." I tried not to yell at him. My body shook to control my anger and finish the sentence without cussing.

The entire conference room of agents reacted with either a gasp, mumbled smart-ass comments amongst one another, or just their dirty looks. I was stunned at their ignorance, and blatant despise for me.

For all, I knew these bastards were the trolls making death threats at my children and me on YouTube.

I pushed my ass out like the black girls taught me, squared my shoulders back to face the aggressive crowd, and waited for the investigator to find the courage to berate his villain to her face.

"Well, you have to admit—that looks bad," he chuckled like a schoolboy looking at his first booby magazine while pointing up towards the blank screen where he'd aired the Blass video.

Staci and Laci were with these same people the night before and claimed to have had a "blast." The hate in this crowd had brewed for me and me alone.

All I could do was stand there and make them tolerate me until I finished what I had to say or until they kicked me out. Whichever came first. The disgust in the faces of the women and the judgment in the eyes of the men was undeniable.

Perusing the crowd one more time, I chose my words carefully to keep from a mutiny.

"Do any of you know what's going on with our civil case?" I screeched back at them.

It was all I could muster out of my mouth without stuttering, but none of them cared.

So I waited to speak with the investigator, one on one after his speech was over.

When he walked away from the podium and noticed me, he saw it in my face that I wasn't done with him yet. We locked eyes, and I moved steadily towards him like stalking my prey. He watched me nervously.

Not because he feared humiliation but because he knew

his dick would get hard as soon as I got close enough for him to smell my shampoo.

Perhaps my wardrobe was his problem. I didn't have on my usual tactical uniform and gear that we, as a team, always wore. My tight jeans and flowered tank top hugged my assets perfectly.

His weakness glared at me, and it was only fair that I exploit it.

I moved every inch of my body with intention and demanded the investigators respect with every step. My strut would make even Kevin Bacon proud. With the sway of my hips and the bounce of my breasts, I had his complete attention.

It was all fun in games watching me on video and insulting me behind my back, but now I was in his face wearing my woman suit. He reminded me of my dad, attracted to strong women, but also felt emasculated by them.

Almost inches from him, the conference host stepped in front of me to shield him.

"I'm sorry, but the investigator isn't taking questions now," she smugly snapped at me.

The investigator smiled and flirtatiously sassed the words, "Give my office a call later in the week," at me over her shoulder.

Bastard. And typical of his type.

In public, I wasn't worthy of his respect or time, but in private, he probably wanted me to disrespect him and spank his ass like a bad boy. He wouldn't be the first.

I quickly made my way back to the table to get my things and leave. Even more determined to make every one of them eat their word and especially the little guy with the badge.

Then it happened two years later and almost to the date.

* * * *

"Man who sued Lipstick for $52 million is arrested for murder." (The subject line of the email starred at me like a shotgun.

What the fuck? I assumed my former partners were pranking me but still clicked on the link. It was now 2015, and we hadn't worked together in over a year.

Immediately after I clicked it, Blass's face flashed over my computer screen. It included the story of a family birthday party that turned deadly.

Blass and his uncle got into a verbal altercation over his mentally ill cousin, and the uncle retreated to his car out of self-defense. When he caught up to his uncle, he pulled out a handgun, a tactic he was known for, then fatally shot him in the back. Blass returned to the party, didn't call for help, and left his uncle to bleed to death in his car.

All three of us knew it was only a matter of time before he caught another case. Still, I didn't imagine it would be for murder and not his blood relative. At the worst, maybe, a battery or aggravated assault on a minority or an immigrant.

My emotions were conflicted with joy and sadness.

Had everyone listened to us, Blass's uncle would be alive and had Greene not promised him millions, maybe Blass wouldn't have felt so above the law.

In my opinion, Greene cost two people their lives in his shenanigans to take down the bail industry; his client Blass's life and Blass's uncle's life.

Most of the public hasn't heard this story, but what would be their point? I made the perfect patsy.

If the industry believed I tarnished its good name and contributed to its demise, no one would ever have to discuss the real issues plaguing it.

Blass was a high-risk offender who shouldn't have been out of prison on four separate bail bonds, legally, just because he found a way to pay for them. The bondsman shouldn't have made the desperate decision to bail him out, and Assembly Bill 109 shouldn't have co-signed it.

From my understanding, before implementing AB109 (California Prison Alignment), Blass wouldn't have been out of prison with several pending cases. With his prior convictions and the weapons charge from the first bond, the judge should have kept him in jail until sentencing.

On August 4, 2017, the judge sentenced Blass to eighty years in prison for first-degree murder. But even as a convicted murderer, the local judicial system showed just how far his supreme white privilege ran. After he murdered a family member in cold blood, the judge agreed to postpone his official sentencing to be sure Blass saw his ill father before going back to prison. Guess I found their stash of pruno after all.

My dream to be a hero, now turned to a nightmare, and the pressure of it all left me no choice but to quit.

GOODBYES AND AFTERSHOCKS

I woke up the morning after the last case I'd ever work, and my body felt like a mack truck had run over me. My daughter sat on the floor with her cereal and cartoons while I watched her. A colossal wave of remorse came over me, and I uncontrollably began to cry.

I'd thrown away a real estate career, one I had worked hard to be successful at, for a business of my own that now made me feel like a disgruntled employee. And I couldn't afford to fire myself.

My intentions to help people and give my daughter a hero may have been noble, but mostly I risked my life for some bullshit.

I had lost all perspective of what had mattered the most to me. All of these insane sacrifices and risks were supposed to be mine to carry and not my child's.

When the women reporters would look at me in judgment for leaving my child to risk my life, I'd become sarcastically defensive towards them. My defense, like many others, was always "do you ask the men these questions?" and they would pivot me to another question. But at that moment, I finally got it.

Having other career options and professional skills meant I didn't have to risk my life to provide for my family. This career path was supposed to make me a better person, mother-woman, etc., not worse.

We were packing our things to move to Seal Beach, California. I'd also taken the week off to get settled in our new place and spend quality time with her.

A few days in, and still knee-deep in boxes, Staci sent me a new video from our last arrest to review and give my feedback, but I had no desire to watch it.

I was sick of seeing my face and disgusted with what I had come to represent.

Unfortunately, there's no graceful way to bow out of any relationship, especially one in which your financial livelihood depends.

It became harder and harder to suit up and work without a disgruntled attitude, and it didn't take long for my partners to notice.

Like that traumatized cop in the movies, I was too distracted and could no longer focus. Every time I entered someone's home, all I could think of was Kianna and possible trafficking scenarios.

Was she in this house?

Does this child belong to this family?

Are they hiding traffic victims here?

It was maddening and made me a danger to myself and my team. Staci and Laci agreed it was time for me to step away. It was their stage, and I couldn't pick the parts I wanted to play. The bail business belonged to professional men and women who could set their emotions aside and do the job, which I no longer could.

Barging into homes to arrest people who weren't real threats, just debts, no longer made sense for the risk. The thought of ending my life to a laughable tragedy was more than my ego could bare.

No matter how much I tried, handing out toys to traumatized children, could never clear my conscience. I was dangerously close to another life-long regret where there'd be no coming back and chose not to lose myself in that kind of self-destruction. Within a few days, we, the team, parted ways with a minimal amount of drama necessary.

I'm grateful for Staci and Laci's training, life lessons, and unforgettable humor.

Them blasting the "Jeffersons" theme song while driving

through Crenshaw, California, and its residents laughing their asses off at us is a memory I will keep forever.

* * * *

It wasn't such a smooth transition from superhero back to civilian life, though.

I'd given up my privacy, faced shame and humiliation, and forgotten all about the priorities of being a mother. Like all great disasters, my road also paved with the best and most unrealistic intentions. It was time to get back to the fundamentals of my life.

After I dropped her off at school a few days later, I also had to drop my truck off at the mechanic for an oil change.

I walked to the Denny's a couple of blocks down the street, ordered breakfast, and waited for the mechanic to call.

Skimming through the news updates on my phone, I saw an article with an update to Kianna's case. I read as many pieces to the story as I could find until my breakfast was gone, and it was time to retrieve my truck.

My senses were on high alert, with a paranoid state of mind, walking back to the mechanic's service station on the north side of Long Beach.

Many months prior, while looking for Watkins, I drove through this section of town numerous times but never walked through it. For at least four blocks, on both sides of the street, were commercial businesses and one run-down motel.

It wasn't a safe place for any woman of any age to walk alone. I walked faster.

At my height, five-foot and one and a half inches short, wearing a baggy T-shirt, jeans, tennis shoes, no makeup, and my hair tied in a ponytail, I could have easily passed for sixteen or seventeen years old.

Luckily, Staci and Laci bought me a JPiexon pepper gun months before we parted ways, and I always kept it in my purse. From a distance, it passed for a firearm and held two pepper balls with a laser attached. It was just as effective in deterring an attacker.

After two blocks, I noticed a Latin man walking behind me, about twenty feet back. Half a block in front of me was a black man standing against a street sign waiting for the bus. Quickly I slowed my stroll to be sure the man behind me wasn't following me.

The oncoming traffic was on the opposite side of the street, and I noticed a black sedan quickly make a u-turn to get on the same side as me.

The driver pulled onto the same street where the black man waited at the bus stop and parked. I could only see the trunk of the car.

My mind raced to remember what the woman told me months prior, looking for Kianna about a man taking women off the street in broad daylight and forcing them into his car.

Was the Latin guy coming up behind me in on it?

What about the black guy at the bus station? He was now looking down at his phone, possibly texting.

Damn! Is he talking to the guy behind me? Or the guy in the car that made the u-turn?

The footsteps of the Latin guy grew louder, quickly I turned, and he stepped around me.

"Excuse me," he said as he continued to walk down the street.

I was now ten feet from the guy standing at the bus stop and saw that he was no longer on the phone.

The black car that had made the u-turn and parked was still there, but I couldn't see the driver through its dark tinted windows. The vehicle matched the description of the car the woman described.

Sliding my hand in my purse, I gripped the handle of my pepper gun. Resting my finger on its trigger.

I soon passed the guy at the bus stop, and he moved to unblock my way but didn't say a word.

Phew! The Latin guy and the black guy weren't threats after all. But what about this prick in the car?

Once upon a time, I was that young girl that walked around the neighborhood, and there were always guys, older guys, who pulled their cars over to talk to me.

The ones that did still showed their faces before giving me some crafty, or cheesy, pick-up line.

But not this person, now parked at least two minutes without making their identity known.

I crossed the street and could feel the driver watch me.

An alarm sounded in my lizard brain that I was in danger.

No one took the time to pull their car over for me, was this mysterious and silent afterward.

I stopped walking a few feet from the curb and stood next to the closest building to block their view of me.

The car engine started, and I saw the car pull away and flip around, possibly to start following me. Or as my mind played it, move to a better position on the street to get me in the car.

Whoever they were, they were about to get a real-life lesson in stranger danger.

I turned to look at the car, and the window of the passenger side was down, exposing that the driver was a black man. I pulled out my pepper gun and held it down by my side.

Moving steadily towards him, I shouted, "Are you fucking following me?"

I didn't give him enough time to determine whether my weapon was a real firearm or not. He looked at me surprised and tried not to laugh, but then quickly realized I was a woman and not a young girl.

"Oh, shit!" he screeched and slammed on the gas, then darted through the intersection to get away from me.

I stopped and watched him drive off, relieved.

OK, I felt a little badass to scare some of the piss out of him. At the same time, empowered to walk safely down any street without a badge to do so.

I'll never know whether I was right or wrong in my instincts, but I know there's at least one guy out there who now thinks twice before pulling his car over for a stranger.

Driving home, I had to face I wasn't just a loca Latina but that I might have a post-traumatic disorder

CAN'T ALL BE QUEENS

Being a single parent is a lifestyle that requires a special kind of sacrifice. It's not easy, it's undervalued and not perceived as heroic, but it still makes one a badass.

It took some time to find steady work again after being labeled an Internet villain, but eventually, I found a gig doing what I loved in real estate with the option to work from home.

It was a perfect opportunity that allowed me to be present and supportive throughout all the phases of my daughter's development.

Let me insert here that going back to middle and high school emotionally with your child makes you a ginormous badass.

Mean kids you can't beat up, or their parents, are the worst.

I decided to do something with my trauma and became a certified life coach to educate parents and their children about human trafficking. It was frightening how many were oblivious to the possibility and disinterested in learning more. Their ignorance and resistance to the facts made me more paranoid.

A terrifying fact permanently branded on my psyche as a woman is Ted Bundy claimed to know his prey by their walk. It was vital to me that my children were well informed and protected by any means necessary, even if that meant tainting their innocence to do so.

For the record, there's no fun or graceful way to do this.

Whether she chooses to be a scientist, an engineer, a cop,

an attorney, or a sex worker, she'll be more successful in defending herself. Yeah, I said sex work.

Kianna taught me that I am powerless to protect her any other way.

She'll be kind but never nice to please anyone.

I'm pretty sure discussing rape was the hardest, but as a victim myself, I knew it was vital to lay a foundation of insurmountable support and raw data to build her assertiveness. The horrific reality a rape victim faces in a courtroom, is having to defend themselves for "implied consent."

I added a scoop of consistent safety habits, a table-spoon of situational awareness, and a dash of self-defense training. Not just to stop an attack but to prevent one. Girlfriend got a mean left punch.

I'm confident my knowledge of the law, safety habits, and some krav maga, have cut the odds of an attack as an adult woman in half.

It also never hurt that I wore tight ass jeans out on the town and probably stopped a few bad intentions, along with some of my bad choices.

Like it or not, the law is only as good as the time and money you spend for a chance to fight in court. It's much easier and less expensive to avoid situations and people.

I can't express enough how important it is to teach our children state and federal laws. Then have them learn how to make changes when their adults.

* * * *

But, in my ignorance and Christian self-righteousness, I still failed to protect her from the evil we both already knew.

It had been two years, seven-thousand-dollars, and once again, my daughter became a victim inside Tyrone and Toni's tormented home.

I listened as my daughter described the secrets, once again, forced to hide from me, and felt my guilt consume my soul. She sobbed while pleading never to revisit them.

Toni micromanaged every moment Tyrone spent with my daughter and disallowed them any alone time together.

Tyrone drank regularly and was only home for a couple of her waking hours during her weekend visits.

She witnessed several fights between them all hours of the night. But when she described how Toni made her watch her brother get beat for putting on her bathing suit.

I was over Christianity and co-parenting.

Toni didn't dare touch my daughter again but abusing her little brother while she watched recycled the fear once more.

As my daughter saw it, Toni abused her brother to keep him from becoming gay and shame them in their church. He was five, and she was eight.

I decided then to pluck that seed of hate before it had a chance to grow. Neither society or Toni would brainwash her sexuality and whom she chose to share it.

Toni's threshold for the perfect blended family had reached its boiling point. She needed to be queen, and in doing so, she had to treat my daughter like a peasant girl.

I never felt qualified to wear a crown myself, mostly because the only queens I knew fit dress drag.

Her need to control the king blinded her madness and blurred the pecking order of our children. My daughter was the firstborn, and that would always anger her just as the doctor assessed years prior.

As much as I want to blame Tyrone once more for not standing up for our daughter, I couldn't, because he made no promises to do so.

My ludicrous obedience to religion caused me to ignore the real-life consequences forgiving deviant and abusive behavior breeds. Jesus wasn't going to save me from the judge's decision if anything happened to my daughter for a second time. They'd take no time to classify me as an unfit mother.

Both left me no choice but to suspend all visitation indefinitely, better known as, never fucking again.

A few days later, I noticed how upset unable to see her father and brother made her, and felt it time she know the whole story. I sat her down with the court folder, two-inches thick, with every court document filed for her case and told her the ugly truth of how her life began.

Tyrone and I met at a club about a month after I became a Christian and a bad break up. After a week of phone-play, we went on a date, and I'm pretty sure her conception was the next morning.

Three weeks separated Tyrone and an ex-boyfriend, and I wasn't exactly sure which would be her dad.

I was about to turn thirty-years-old, had my life together,

and was ready for a baby, but I didn't want a husband or to co-parent.

It was the cheapest artificial insemination I could ever get.

"I wanted to have you and didn't care whether he was around because I never wanted to share you with him anyway. We tried to make things work for you, and they didn't. What's important is that you who he is, what he's capable of, and how unfit as a parent he is for you. You get to choose not to feel abandoned and unwanted by him. He does love you, but he can't protect you, and because of that, he's no longer welcome to be part of your life."

I held her and gently rubbed her head to comfort her while we both quietly sobbed. My hope in sharing the truth was she'd avoid developing daddy issues altogether, and choose to focus on her life without any abandonment issues.

Those die with me.

It wasn't easy for her to unlearn their hate, but I made sure she had access to the positive sides of her black culture. I filled her library with books written by great black authors, Malcolm X and Maya Angelou, to grow her confidence as a young afro-Latina. She needed to understand that Toni's abuse wasn't about her, but Toni herself.

Neither was going to break her or make her feel unlovable for being only half black. Because she's not a half.

LOSING MY CHRISTIAN-INSANITY

In my daughter's own words, this is her story:

There was a lot of tension between my father and I, as a little girl, because I was very overprotective of my mom. Every time he took me from her, I would scream bloody murder, and probably

why he let me get hit.
It's not like he dropped me on my head or hurt me physically, but maybe I knew what was going to happen.
I don't remember much between the ages of ages two and four, but it was during my summer vacation visit at my dad's where Toni would hit me a lot when he went to work.
She hit me until my skin was purple. Every time she came around me, I would sit or stand in a stance to be prepared to get hit or pushed.
My dad and Toni told me to lie to everyone and say I fell off the couch, and that's why I had bruises on my arms and legs.
I remember the court case had finished, and I only saw my father under supervised visitation with a therapist.
The judge then decided to give custody to my mom.
At five, I would cry without reason. Now I know it was my way of coping with what happened with my dad, like an aftershock. Every time I would cry, I 'd say that I missed my dad because I didn't know why I cried.
When I was six, I remember Toni calling my mom and asking for me. I talked to her for a minute or two and felt that she changed. I went to one of my dad's union events for his job after a long time, not seeing her and my dad.
She was kind to me, let me play on her phone, and had a real conversation with me, which was more then she used to do.
When I was with them, Toni said mean things to me and made me keep secrets from my mom.
She even told me once that she'd never hit me and that the court case was all a lie. But when I told my mom, who called and told her off, my dad yelled at me later for no reason.
The first couple of times, I started to go to my dad's house again, I would still cry, and it would upset them both.
Toni would make comments when I would leave my mom and even counted how many hugs I gave her.

"You shouldn't hug your mom that much." She told me that once

when I got in her car. As usual, my dad defended her no matter what.

I use to pretend that I was asleep so they would leave me alone, and I didn't have to talk to her. When I was there, I wanted to go into a coma and never wake up.

Toni would spy on me like I was going to hurt my brother, her son. She would stand in the hallway and listen to our conversations.

They always accused me of having an attitude towards them, giving them a reason to be upset with me.

Like I was Cinderella. They were "royals," and I was a peasant.

While she washed my hair one visit, she asked that I call her Mrs. Wilson instead of Toni. I felt that she was trying to make me feel inferior to her and her family.

They treated me separate, I was my mother's kid, and their kids were their kids.

Many times, my dad pressured me to move in with him and leave my mother, Toni would encourage him. Just talking to either of them felt like psychological warfare.

I felt set up to fail with Toni no matter what I did, and couldn't trust my father to protect me.

In the second grade, a boy bullied me at school, physically hitting me, and my mother told my dad. He sadistically chose to scold his six-year-old crying and looking for comfort. When I say crying, I mean weeping.

I remember it like it was yesterday. Dad looked me in the face and said, "You need to understand that not everybody is going to like you," with Toni nodding her head behind him.

They dismissed my abuse as me being dramatic. At this point, I no longer cared if I got in trouble or not. I just took the abuse.

Most of the time, I day-dreamed about running away to go back home to my mom's house. My dad was either drunk or at work. So, most of the time, I didn't talk to him.

Looking back at these moments, I can see that I was the child my dad never wanted and also, not black enough to be accepted as his kid or Toni's stepdaughter.

To be sure I didn't get too close, she got pregnant again.

The day I found out I was so angry. Toni had the sonogram picture of the baby, about four weeks old, and I asked, "Who's baby is this?"

She said, "It's mine."

I said, "No, it isn't."

She said, smirking, "Yes, it is."

I just sat in the passenger seat of her car and put my head down sad.

I can remember him telling my mom, and could see her smiling in the corner of my eye. She was pleased that I felt replaced by another baby.

As she got further along in her pregnancy, both she and my father would tell me I'd be responsible for their new baby. No way I'd carry the pressure of their replacement of me on my shoulders.

I had been afraid to tell my mother and them all start to fight again, but I couldn't take it anymore.

My mom gave me her cell phone to take with me to call her whenever I wanted while visiting with my dad.

I put it in my bag and did not tell either of them. I had it. They found the phone during a visit and accused me of hiding it from them.

Toni called me "sneaky" to my dad. They were both always worried about what I told my mother about them.

When I told her I wasn't sneaking around with the phone, she told my father that I wasn't going to see "them" anymore. My dad didn't say anything.

They dropped me off with my mom, and that was the last time I saw them. Not because of Toni's threat but because mom promised to protect me.

My dad called when my new brother was born to tell me he was going to mail me my toys and things since I wasn't going back to his house, but he never did. He was just cruel.

My last words I yelled to my dad were, "You ruined my childhood."

He denied and probably still denies the abuse to this day. As I got older, I learned that blood might make someone related to you, but loyalty makes you family, and unfortunately, dad still hasn't shown me any loyalty.

My advice for other children who are victims of child abuse, especially by a step-monster, please tell someone. No matter how they make, you feel it's not your fault. Because, on some levels, I do regret not telling my mom about the abuse sooner. She would've stopped them, and I knew but allowed them to abuse me anyway to have my dad in my life.

Do your best to keep your spirits up because a positive mindset is important to have, and don't be afraid to tell somebody what you're going through.

* * * *

I shouldn't have handed my forgiveness out so freely to Toni and Tyrone. Or anyone for that matter. An apology can't cover the severest of indiscretions, nor should it.

Before I decided to get "saved," I'd never forgiven or stopped inflicting my vengeance on either of them. The ignorant belief that somehow I could turn back time with my good acts and forgiving heart made me delusional.

My all-powerful deity gave me a false sense of security to forgive the evils of others.

"Forgive them for they know not what they do!" Luke 23:34

"Forgive them 77 times 7..." Matthew 8:21-22

"These trials will show your faith is genuine" 1 Peter 1:7

For years I desperately clung to these words, and because I never questioned any of them, my dumb-ass handed my baby back to her abusers. That kind of stupidity could have gotten her killed this time.

I failed because I believed Toni wouldn't hurt my daughter again. I failed because I forgave based on my beliefs and belief, isn't knowledge.

The danger in that kind of child-like trust as an adult is it requires no logic or rationality to give it. Then the traumatic, even criminal, indiscretions are ignored and often go unpunished.

It didn't matter what I believed because I knew Toni and Tyrone were abusers, and no amount of prayer or forgiveness was going to change that.

Forgiving them, or anyone, seventy-seven times seven expecting different results is the very definition of insanity.

I wanted religion to fix our lives, make it easy on me, but instead, I opened the door and unintentionally invited evil back in our lives.

From that moment forward, as a mother and a human being, I made sure to base my core principles on facts and not the inspiration of an imaginary entity.

6.

Bullet 6

BULLET 6: ANGER

LOVE AND WAR

I stood in my newly rented hallway, and watched the last decade of my life flash through my mind.

"You're so stupid, and will always need a man to take care of you," dad's words bubbled over my head.

My husband packed his things in the other room while shouting his cruelty at me. We married only two years prior.

William Macke was a black man in his fifties and who I'd loved for more than fifteen years. He was eighteen years my senior and the perfect storm for my daddy issues.

The only black man I ever knew to attend the Million Man March, and immediately he earned my respect.

A dashing older man who handled his badge like a weapon, to watch him as a young woman in training felt like a privilege.

For almost two decades of my life, I relentlessly pursued him to win his ring, but less than two years after our wedding, we found ourselves in a "War of the Roses (DeVito & Brooks, 1989)" showdown of our own.

"I know you were out having lunch with someone!" Macke shouted at me.

"You know I wasn't," I yelled back.

It was just days after I quit working with Staci and Laci and had no idea how I was going to pay my bills.

I turned in my badge to preserve my sanity, devote more time as a mother and wife, and it was about to make me homeless. The distress of it all spun me out of control.

He slammed the dresser drawers to make his exit dramatic. I couldn't help but be suspicious that he'd made plans to be with someone else.

We spent years mind-fucking each other and denied marriage could repair the damage we'd already done to one another. Many nights I longed to be older, wiser, and more mature in hopes that he would see me as his equal.

Fear and betrayal boiled in me to the point of the unthinkable, and I couldn't stop myself. War was about to break out in our new, sacred, and now married space.

We were both professional abusers but had never raised our hands to one another before.

But this day, the very thought of taking his shit so he could leave for a play date, guilt-free, made me snap.

* * * *

Before I could even calculate my next move, I was in his face yelling and pushing him. Unimpressed, he stepped back without dropping the shirt he was folding to dodge my tantrum.

Pushing him again and again, and still no reaction. It's difficult to admit, but I understood people who satisfied their rage by killing their spouse at that moment. Until death-do-us-fucking-part takes on a whole new meaning.

I pounded at his chest with my fists until satisfied, and then he pushed me away from him towards the bed. He allowed me to be violent to avoid any guilt later.

I felt deranged, leaving our room, adjusting my clothes and hair. There was no more denying our apathy for one another.

The ugliest part of this relationship had finally come to a head, and it didn't matter that the wife in me felt just or not. I had assaulted my husband, a retired peace officer.

The fact that no one escorted me from home in handcuffs made me a hypocrite. Had I been a man, I wouldn't have been so lucky.

Waiting to hear him leave, I sat on the couch, pulling my emotions together before picking up my daughter from school.

No way was I going to let her see me so frazzled. She'd been through enough.

"In a way, what goes wrong with someone who becomes infatuated – and thinks it's love – is that they are operating with an insufficient range of emotional categories. Perhaps when we are so eagerly searching for the profundity and security of reciprocal love, we can hardly stop ourselves from promoting each attachment to the higher grade...The better option – but it is one which requires a degree of maturity – is to

align infatuation with friendship, not with romantic love."— John Armstrong, *Conditions of Love*, 2002.

THE THRILL OF A SCANDAL

A month after I started working at the prison, I met Sgt. Macke. There was no romantic interest at first because I had never dated a cop before or saw the appeal. At twenty-three, I preferred bad boys and hustlers because the un-square parts of me enjoyed the rush.

Remember prisoner Saucedo? Macke watched him, too, and also noticed the favoritism displayed.

Because he also had intentions to get Saucedo transferred to another facility, I couldn't help but brag that I got the job done before he did.

That's how our love story began.

He took pride in his job and our safety. And it didn't matter whether it was a prisoner or another cop, he dispensed the right amount of justice when deemed necessary. Growing up on the south side of Chicago in the 1960s, he didn't fear retaliation. Not to mention he was a sexy specimen of a man.

Macke could command respect from anyone in a room using a minimal amount of words necessary, and I wanted that kind of power. There weren't real advantages to being feminine and attractive in that environment.

The one consistent with the men in this prison, the male staff, included, they lacked self-respect and respect for others. Their parents must have lost control of them the minute they could walk and talk.

As guards, we spent most of the day de-escalating egotistical pissing contests and immature tantrums. No matter their age, they acted like kids. I learned to be fair, firm, and consistent at the job and home.

Soon, Macke and I became quite the team at work. He felt like a spunky young cop again, and I felt like a grown, invincible woman in her super suit.

And man did he wear the hell out of his uniform. Walking with him felt like walking with the head of the pride.

Very rarely did I walk with co-workers because I didn't feel safe with most of them. Some guards have enemies by proxy of their partners, but with him, I was safe, and the prisoners showed me respect.

After a couple of months, we decided to have dinner with no expectations. Because I was nervous never having a real date before, I did what any other twenty-something year old would do. I got stoned about thirty minutes before he showed up.

Technically, I was a corporate corrections officer and didn't have to adhere to all the off-duty rules a real peace officer did. At least that's my story, and I'm sticking to it.

Nonetheless, in 1998 getting stoned was illegal. Which only made me more paranoid when he arrived to pick me up. Fortunately, he didn't notice.

"Come on, let's go eat. I want to show you off," he kissed me then whisked me out the door, almost skipping.

The debonair man led me out of my front door like the lady I never knew I wanted to be.

He drove us two hours out of the way to San Diego, California, to dine by the ocean. It was the most romantic time I'd ever had.

* * * *

We didn't see each other again for a couple of weeks, and our first shift together we spent on different sides of the yard.

My post for the day was in the administration building outside the prison yard, having to answer phones and keep track of the prison activity log.

I was busy multitasking and twisted up in the phone cord with one leg on a stool bent over when I noticed a reflection in the window in front of me. Startled that someone was watching me, I turned around and saw it was Macke leaned up against the doorway of the entrance of the building.

The director's office he worked in was just next door.

He was smoking a cigarette, grinning, and thoroughly entertained watching me juggle my tasks.

"How long have you been standing there?" I asked, now blushing and unraveling myself from the phone chord.

"Long enough to know how good you are at your job," he winked and walked out the door, teasing me.

Later that night, he called and asked me to visit him and to wear very little clothing.

I should have said no, but the thrill to be deviant wouldn't let me. I did just as he asked, and pulled up to my place of employment, wearing nothing but a hoodie.

We crept in the director's office like teenagers breaking

into the principal's office. The lights were off, but the crack through the window blinds left our silhouettes free to play.

Macke's hand slid through my jacket onto my waist and pulled me close to him. I felt his warm lips touch my neck. Before I could kiss him, he pushed me onto the desk, ran his warm hand up my cold thigh, and gently pulled my legs apart.

He kissed, nibbled my ear, and whispered, "I've wanted you like this."

The other handheld me up while he devoured my breast in his mouth, and then moved his other hand in between my legs.

I felt trapped in a state of euphoria as he unleashed the freak in me, and all I could do was moan, one I had never heard before. He gently rubbed my clitoris while opening my legs wider and pulling me further off the desk, now exposing both my breasts.

He slid his finger inside me as he pulled me towards him, then ravished my lady parts.

When he stood and kissed me again, I heard him unbuckle his uniform pants.

I wrapped my legs around his waist and felt his hard shaft waiting for my permission.

Pulling his waist closer to mine, I opened my legs wider to let him inside me. He was a perfect fit.

His breath moved fast, but his body was gentle. Deep and complete.

Within minutes he stood me up, turned me around, and bent me over the office desk. He moved my jacket up over my backside then used his knee to spread my legs like he was about to pat me down.

In a complete state of ecstasy, I leaned over and let him have his way.

When he climaxed, he grabbed me and pulled me towards him, and held me tight a few seconds before letting me go. I felt the coldness of his badge pressed against the back of my shoulder.

We quickly hurried to straighten ourselves up, and the desk, then I got the hell out of there before someone walked in on us doing a late-night building safety check.

That's all I needed was to get caught naked with the state sergeant by one of my co-workers.

Later we agreed it better to keep our relations private to avoid drama.

For months we balanced our professional and personal lives pretty well.

Then, I was pregnant.

* * * *

Unwanted babies make for toxic and abusive parents, and I refused to birth a child I wouldn't love. Plus, to add another child to my life would've been financial suicide. My son deserved better than that.

Macke didn't pressure me either way, but, in the end, I made the decision that was best for my son and me.

After working all day in a cage with many who were once unwanted children, I didn't risk cursing the seeds of my womb with the same fate.

Prison is more cruel and inhumane than abortion.

CODED FOR HONOR

A couple of weeks after I terminated the pregnancy, I learned my supervisors were gossiping amongst one another about it.

Men gossip just as much as women. Don't lie. I've heard it for myself.

Macke's militant support for the black prisoners pissed off a lot of the white corporate staff, mainly my supervisors, putting me between them.

Men have to pee on every damn thing.

"What did you say?" I gasped in shock at my drunken lieutenant, Bradley, trying not to drop the phone.

"Bradley, did you just tell me that the captain accused Macke of forcing me to have an abortion?" Bradley said nothing. I waited anxiously

Seconds later, I heard him sigh, and the words slowly slurred out of his mouth "Yes, that's what they're saying."

I felt anger, then shame, as I tried to recount my steps of who betrayed my trust to start such a rumor. Unsure whether Bradley intended to be my friend or foe, I hung up the phone abruptly.

Bradley had always been cool with me, but he, too, was known to be a good ole boy that wore corrupted stripes.

"Macke, they are trying to set you up. Lt. Bradley just called me and said my captain, along with someone in your department, has concocted a rumor that you forced me to have the abortion," my words shot out at him like bullets.

"WHAT!?!?" He shouted back in the phone.

"I'm not going to let them win," I assured him. They had no idea of the battle they just begun..

Fortunately, he scheduled vacation time with his kids and would be gone for a week—enough time for me to raise hell.

The only person capable of such defamation was my supervisor on the graveyard shift, Sgt. Hale. I only disclosed to him that I was pregnant because he threatened to write me up for calling off sick too many days in a row. He had to be the source.

The next day I went to work ready to confront this man like a prisoner, and his rank over me didn't deter the ass chewing he was about to get.

I don't recall my exact words, but I remember the look on his face when he heard them. Regret filled his eyes that he betrayed my trust.

I was disgusted by these cowards and their need to make me a victim to sabotage Macke's career. Punks.

No way I'd let them take him down by using me. I'd sabotage my career first.

My vengeance was to file a harassment complaint and humiliate the gossiping penis clan in front of their superiors. I then sent a memo to every State and corporate supervisor to request a meeting. Including el jefe who had to make a special trip from Sacramento, California.

Little more than a week later, and after Macke returned

from his vacation, they called me to the Captain's office to attend the meeting.

They kept silent when I walked in the office. There were six men and one woman who was my HR representative.

I sat down, and el jefe began the meeting. It pissed me off when I heard myself explain why I chose to have an abortion. Quickly, I changed course and accused them all of using me to destroy the career of another employee, Macke. Who was also in attendance, listening, and watching.

I continued to snarl at them for playing with our lives for their amusement and racial agendas. The Captain was the only one who defended his actions.

"I thought you were being harmed and was only trying to help" he tried to sound empathetic.

"If you were so concerned about my well-being, Captain, then why didn't you offer me time off? Or if you truly thought Macke forced me, then why not come talk to me about it first?" My interrogating tone made him shrink in his seat, and his eyes filled with shame. All the men in the room turned to look at him to wait for his response.

My human resources rep was the same woman who told me about Tambouché's rape, and she started to sob on my behalf.

"I wasn't forced to have an abortion. I did so for personal reasons that I don't have to share with any of you. What I will share with you is that Macke and I love each other as friends, lovers, and co-workers. None of you had the right to accuse him of such a monstrosity and threaten his job. I request that those involved reprimanded." I demanded without allowing him to respond.

When I stood up to leave, I glanced around the room and looked them all in the face before turning to Macke. I had avoided eye-contact with him the entire meeting to stay in control of emotions. Those men wouldn't get the pleasure of seeing me vulnerable. I moved closer to him and touched his leg while they all watched us. We smiled at one another, and then I turned to leave back, dismissing them. I could hear a pin drop when the door closed behind me.

If only that had been the end of it.

Just months before this incident, there was a raid at a meth lab in a local town not far from two other State prisons, less than an hour away.

During this raid, they discovered that a few local police and correctional officers from one of those state prisons were involved.

Days later, they raided the prison and found large quantities of drugs, cell phones, and other contraband. Only the guards, with an extensive operation, could be their source.

It was a disgusting display of corruption that shamed the system.

* * * *

Many assumed when I left the prison, they fired me for fraternizing with a prisoner, but I resigned. See, what had happened was...

Ricky, was his name, wasn't just a prisoner but a friend whom I knew long before working at the prison.

He was a former boyfriend who had a drug addiction. And

because I still cared for him, I wasn't going to let my shitty job stop me from staying in touch with him when he went to jail.

I decided to visit him at the city jail, where someone recognized me or my name on the sign-in log and informed them at the prison.

We lived in a small region, and anyone who wore a badge within a fifty-mile radius was subject to know one another.

Because I filed an additional request for monetary compensation with the HR department after the meeting, my jailhouse visit allowed them to simultaneously get rid of my complaint and defame my character by branding me "fraternizing with the enemy."

They gave me the option of being terminated or resigning.

My forced resignation was a crafty move by the same group of men who were out to get Macke.

They weren't giving up to get rid of him, and I naively put a target on my back by not knowing how to play this game of man-chess. All of them were determined to keep me quiet.

Their treachery confirmed by another director of which department I can't remember, and who called me as soon as I got home from signing my resignation.

"I'm going to talk to them, Faciane. You just made a mistake. This is nonsense. You're good at your job." He sounded confident and optimistic he could save my job.

But within a couple of hours, he called back to let me know they wouldn't budge no matter how hard he tried.

Their next step, on that same day, was to open an investigation on Macke to tie him to the state officers caught in the meth lab raid.

And I quickly foiled that shit too after a brash phone call to his supervisor to set things straight.

"How dare you allow this? What I do on my off time is none of your damn business! Or corporate, or sergeant Macke's. He had no clue I went to visit someone at the jail. All your investigation is going to do is waste time and money. It may even get you investigated for trying set Macke up; again! And I'll help kick your ass all the way there." I yelled. Or something close to it before slamming the phone down to hang-up on him. It was the 1990's, and we could still do that.

Macke called less than an hour later to tell me they dropped the investigation, and his supervisor personally apologized.

I was humiliated that no one knew the truth about what happened but had to face that I overplayed my hand. Instead of quitting on my terms and with dignity, I let them take it from me.

Still, it was better than them finding out I played butt-naked leapfrog all over someone's desk.

BATTLE SCARS

As the years past, I evolved out of law enforcement to a real estate career, while Macke continued his in a cesspool of corruption.

They may not have liked Macke, but they couldn't keep the prisoners calm as he could. He managed to keep many riots from breaking out on his own.

Except for one.

This particular riot ended with the deaths of two black men, and shortly after they closed the prison. In my opinion, to cover the shady details of it up.

It was all over the news, and I immediately called Macke to be sure he was safe. The reports hadn't mentioned if any staff members were injured.

We hadn't spoken for months.

"Are you OK?" I asked.

"NO!" he shouted back at me in distress.

"Call me later if you want to talk," I offered.

"K," he said and hung up. It would be another week before I saw him.

After a few drinks, Macke told me what happened.

Something had shattered in him, and watching him cry, I felt powerless to comfort him.

A young black prisoner, no more than twenty-five years old, informed Macke that he needed to be transferred to another prison because his life was in danger. He asked a day before the riot.

Macke was on his way to visit another facility for a meeting and then would be off work for the weekend. He assured the prisoner when he returned in a couple of days that he'd have him transferred to another facility.

The negligent prison misclassified their violent felons and hired inexperienced guards, causing the tension to brew for months.

He warned the bigger brassed supervisors that a riot was inevitable if changes not made immediately. They ignored him.

* * * *

On October 25, 2003, more than one-hundred and fifty inmates rioted on that unarmed and ill-equipped "Camp Snoopy" yard. Because of the inexperienced guards, the prisoners gained access to any and every weapon they could find. Knives, meat cleavers, broom handles, etc.

What you won't read are the details that would forever traumatize him.

The prisoners involved made sure to riot when they knew Macke would be too far from the facility to stop them. This prison didn't have a gun tower, and the only guns available were locked up in the director's office, the building across from where the prisoners lived.

The other problem was only a state officer could access them, and the only state officer badass enough to stop anyone was Macke.

When he got back to the facility a few hours after the riot, he had to assist in processing the victims' bodies. There were two men total killed.

One was the prisoner who came to him for help and young enough to be his son.

A group of El Salvadoran immigrants (unsure if they were illegal or not) brutally killed the two black men. Why they selected these two men for death was unclear, but I believe it was both racial and cultural.

Immigration is and has always been a complicated subject,

but the one place it's most dangerous, and deadly, is in prison. Male prisons, to be exact.

Our judicial system is merciful compared to other countries. It attracts violent immigrants looking to avoid punishment, who then end up in our prison system.

It's impossible to lock up savage killers with petty thieves, and no suffer fatal consequences. I don't care who you hire to supervise them.

They chased one of the victims up a vendor gate, his last desperate attempt to escape death was to run up a fucking fenced gate, and the group, as Macke described it from having to watch the gruesome video footage, "hacked at him until they could pull him off the fence." They used a large knife from the kitchen to hack at him.

It was his job to analyze, document, and report the incident for the state. Listening to him describe it all terrorized me for life too.

He's still haunted even two decades later.

Many nights I tried to comfort him while he whimpered in his sleep at the ghosts that chased after him.

No one is immune to pain or emotion, including law enforcement. Those who've never had the courage or stupidity to put on a badge and put their life on the line for pain in the ass strangers, I challenge to be more open-minded.

The Stanford Prison Experiment in 1971 proved how dangerous the social structure of prison is, and almost thirty years later, nothing has changed.

People, even good people, will do vile things to one another when put in a position of authority to do so.

During my psychology course, I read this excerpt from their findings (Laura King, *The Science of Psychology: An Appreciative View*, 2016):

'The experiment continues to inform our understanding of human behavior in prison contexts and to inspire controversy.'

The experiment was initially scheduled for two weeks but lasted only six days before they had to stop it over safety concerns.

The people assigned to be "guards" were attacking and dehumanizing the people assigned to be "prisoners" when the research staff wasn't watching them. The researchers themselves became corrupt by power while role-playing.

All of the participants were mere students and faculty from the college.

If I had my way, I'd classify the experiment a success at proving the delusion humans are fit to police one another without corruption.

Within weeks the prison prepared to close, and Macke informed me he was moving up north, eight hours away to another facility.

I had just begun my real estate career and couldn't follow him.

UNEQUAL PARTNERS

A few years later, he transferred back to San Diego, and in 2012 we married. Our wedding was a romantic ceremony where we rode in a gondola through the Venetian hotel in Las Vegas, Nevada.

It was perfect, and I felt like one of the lucky ones. But before we could get out of the honeymoon phase, my bounty hunting career took off, and he seemed emasculated by it all.

Plenty of men warned me how it would bother them their wives out late at night, chasing and arresting criminals while they were home asleep.

He only expressed his concern for my safety because he wouldn't be around to watch and keep me safe this time.

My running into strange houses in dangerous neighborhoods wasn't the same as walking around in a controlled prison environment.

When my short-lived career was finally over, I hoped he and I would open up our own investigations business, but he planned to retire and live a chaos-free life.

I couldn't help but feel like we'd made a mistake settling down with each other. Settling down always felt like, well, settling.

Neither one of us knew how to be married or how to walk away from one another.

Marriage felt like a burden that eventually tightens around one's neck like a noose. Having to define our roles to feel equal constantly was maddening.

The obligations, the obedience, the humility, the obsession, and all that friggin jealousy turned me into a mutated version of myself. One I couldn't stand being trapped in the same skin with—a trap doomed for failure.

I eventually had to accept that real love is allowing a person the freedom to make choices, at any given moment, about their happiness that won't include me. And vice versa.

No matter how much I wanted to honor my own written promises, I couldn't be the wife he needed. Nor did I want to be.

The truth was, I had expected Macke to make unrealistic sacrifices, and when he wouldn't comply, my resentment brewed towards him.

When I got back home after assaulting him, both he and most of his things were gone. He didn't come home for more than a week. When he finally did, I saw a faded bruise on his chest from my fist.

My visible abuse reminded me of what I'd become and that we both needed to abandon our sinking marriage-ship before it crippled us.

We hung in there another year before we finally divorced.

* * * *

As a teenager, my favorite Hollywood love story was "Streets of Fire (Hill & Gordon-Silver, 1984)." The sexy singer gets kidnapped, her handsome old boyfriend comes back to rescue her, and their love rekindled.

But in the end, no matter how much she loved and needed him, he left her ass and rode off with the chic who was handy with the pistol.

The woman who wore combat boots, no make up and well trained to cover his ass. The one he needed by his side, and not who fed his needy superego. Not to be mistaken for a "needy, super big-ass ego," but Freud's psychoanalytic theory (Laura King, *The Science of Psychology: An Appreciative View*, 2016).

The superego is the moral and ethical component of our personality. In development, it absorbs family and society traditions and serves as a moral compass of what's acceptable and unacceptable behavior.

Just because a woman chooses to rescue herself, and a few men, doesn't make her unlovable or deserving to be stamped crazy.

"In a way, what goes wrong with someone who becomes infatuated – and thinks it is love – is that they are operating with an insufficient range of emotional categories. Perhaps when we are so eagerly searching for the profundity and security of reciprocal love, we can hardly stop ourselves promoting each attachment to the highest grade...The better option – but it is one which requires a degree of maturity – is to align infatuation with friendship, not with romantic love"-Conditions of Love, pg. 82.

GIRLS WILL BE GIRLS

There were no specifics on gender when the topic of getting married came up because it was just understood.

I was a tomboy up until high school. My hair was short with a tail, and I dressed like the boys. In sixth grade, a classmate, who thought I was a boy, slipped a note in my locker to confess her schoolgirl crush for me. When all the kids shamed me for it, I felt forced to act attracted to boys before I was ready.

The assumptions of my sexuality didn't come up again until I entered law enforcement. Someone with my looks in a masculine field had to be lesbian or at least bisexual.

Years later, a lesbian friend of mine told me, "Roni, you should be gay. We need more strong and independent women in the gay community."

Her words only further confused my 1990s feminist brainwashing. Even women equate being strong and independent with being lesbian? WTF!

Being a single mother, I had to hustle like a man, and somehow that classified me not feminine enough to be heterosexual.

Not long after my split with Macke, my daughter chose to write about Frida Kahlo for a project at school. I had never studied this woman's life myself nor heard much of its details, and decided to watch Salma Hayek's performance of this honored artist, Frida (Taymor & Hayek-et al, 2002) to learn more.

I couldn't relate to the physical tragedies she suffered, but the heartache she endured for the man she loved was a perfect reflection.

I was surprised how empowered I felt watching Salma's confidence as she pursued both men and women playing this character.

Frida didn't have to make a "switch" from masculine to feminine; it was who she was. I watched in awe as she sparked a memory of myself as a little girl.

When I was seven or eight years old, my friend, a neighbor girl, stayed the night at my house for a mini slumber party.

Unsure who started what, but I remember our hands in each other's underwear while hiding under the covers. Within minutes the lights were on, and my mom had pulled the covers from over us, revealing our sin.

She said nothing about what we were doing but told my friend to gather her things and come out of the room. My father said nothing.

The little girl's parents came to get her, and I don't recall playing with her again. My parents never spoke of it, but their silence was understood.

It was inappropriate to put my hands in another girl's panties or allow any other girls' hands in mine.

* * * *

It was just weeks after my divorce was final that I started to question everything I thought I knew about myself. I hadn't planned or prepared for life after marriage and assumed Macke, and I'd be together until one of us died, or we killed each other. After at least twenty-five years worth of boy-crazed sex all of a sudden, I was unsure if only the boys tickled my fancy.

Maybe I didn't have to pick a gendered-team after all.

I was still attracted to men, but my homophobia towards women had dwindled and found myself sexually aroused, not jealous, watching them.

Perhaps, now that I was out of my territorial baby-making years, I didn't have to avoid my urges and could abandon all those archaic principles that limited my sexuality.

Lying in bed tossing and turning, unpaid bills, and the mess of my life danced in my head, a strange text rung my phone at about two a.m.

"Hi, its Brookie, how are you?" I quickly sat up to read it. Immediately paranoid that I was unable to recognize the caller. After all the media attention, I changed my phone number.

"Who is this?" I wrote back, annoyed.

"We met a few months back, you helped me," the next text read.

I was in no mood for a booty call, and before I got the next text, it dawned on me who it was.

Brookie was a young woman that my former partners and I arrested for solicitation a year prior. She had scammed the bail agent to bail her out of jail with no money.

The arrest was very emotional for me because she was so young and far from her loved ones who lived in North Carolina.

It was a cold night, and she had on only a short one-piece shirt-skirt that barely covered anything. I covered her with one of the marketing T-shirts then tried to sit closer to keep her warm.

She was a stunningly, beautiful, petite young white woman, twenty-three years old, who reminded me of a young Liv Tyler. She looked like she hadn't slept or eaten in a couple of days, and the mention of her mother only made her more apathetic.

Staci called her grandmother, the cosigner, who brought tears to Brookie's eyes while she spoke to her.

When Staci and I walked her to the county jail reception center, I felt like a piece of me was going inside with her. It was the first arrest where I wanted to bail out a fugitive myself. She needed help, not shame and blame.

We sat and waited for the deputy to come out and take her inside while I filled out her booking information. I was scared for her and put twenty dollars on her books for food and a phone call.

When I asked if she had anyone locally to call to bail her out, she told me no, and why she skipped out on the bail agent in the first place.

She had a friend in Los Angeles from high school who

told her about all the money they could make together performing porn if she moved to California.

Being from a small southern town, she was desperate for any way out. By the age of fourteen, she was a full-blown heroin addict and by fifteen, put on methadone.

She hoped the fast cash in a big city would offer her a better life, but it didn't happen that way. The friend hadn't contacted her in months.

I wanted to hug her but wrote my phone number on her arm instead.

"If you need help getting into rehab or finding a job, place to live, whatever. You call me, and I'll do what I can to help you," I assured her.

She smiled, and tears filled her eyes. "My father raped me when I was eighteen. He got me drunk and had sex with me. I was never the same."

Her confession hit me like a ton of bricks, and I had no idea how to react. I desperately tried not to show any emotion on my face to avoid her feeling judged.

"You're a strong young woman, and you get to live any life you want. That doesn't have to be your only story. Please call me if you need me and be safe." I told her, standing up to greet the deputy approaching her from behind.

She stood up slow with a frightened look. The female deputy also noticed how frail Brookie was and made sure to pat her down gently before switching out my cuffs for her own. I stood by the exit door and watched them walk back inside the jail.

An unforgettable image to remind it could have easily been me.

By the time I got back to the SUV, I was emotionally exhausted and in no shape to continue to work. After we went by the bondsman's office to turn in the paperwork, I asked to go home for the night.

Driving back to the office to wrap up the evening, I kept thinking about Brookies confession about her father and how it reminded me of my incident with my dad. He, too, may have been waiting for the right moment but never had the chance to act on it.

At thirteen, I had just begun to menstruate, and my parents had already divorced. Dad and I were lying on his bed together watching TV when his hand rubbed my hip, then slid to my waist. Immediately, it felt creepy and wrong.

I was still very ticklish, and when I squirmed to move from him, he asked me, "What are you going to do when you get a boyfriend, and he wants to rub on you? Are you going to squirm and giggle too?"

Being too young and trusting to question him, I just laid there a little longer, then made an excuse to get up and go to another room.

As I got older and developed, he continued with little subtle inappropriate acts. Like rubbing on my butt when I stood next to him or sticking his tongue in my ear when I'd hug him. All of these incidents, I passed off as him just being playful.

The last time he tried to pin me down and tickle me, now sixteen-years-old, I kneed him so hard in the ribs (by accident) he didn't touch me again.

Now, having listened to Brookie's story, I was left to wonder.

LOVE BROOKIE

A couple of months after her arrest, Brookie contacted me and asked if I'd help her find an outpatient rehabilitation facility. Once I gave her the information to a few I called for her, we spoke a couple more times briefly and then nothing. My assumption had been she was on her way to a better life. I'd forgotten all about her.

"Brookie? Did I arrest you months back for a bail bond?" I asked in my text back to her.

"Yes! That's me! I had lost your number. I have so much to tell you," the text read.

I text back, "So good to hear from you, let's chat in the morning, and we'll meet for lunch, yeah?"

"Yes, I'll text tomorrow. Good nite." Her text agreed.

Knowing that I helped save at least one soul made the chaos of the last two years of my life slightly subside. I fell back to sleep.

I was excited to see her and hear all about her new life. We met for lunch the following day, and she was now a glowing pregnant woman who looked healthy and happy.

Though I still felt bitter about my divorce and layoff, spending time with this vibrant young woman gave me hope that I, too, could start over and be happy again.

She proudly boasted about her "Pretty Woman (Marshall & Goldsten-et al, 1990)" movie fairytale ending with a man much older than her, a former client who had offered a new life and now carried his child.

I smiled and gulped my bitterness down with half my soda then cheered her brave decision. After lunch, I took her back to her apartment, and we recorded a vlog for my website to show off her new life.

We'd been recording for about two minutes when she stopped in mid-sentence and stared at the man behind me watching us.

After a quick introduction, she told him she'd return to their apartment once we finished with the vlog. I stood up to shake his hand and saw he was a white man in his early fifties. He was polite, but his presence made her uncomfortable. After he made a sarcastic remark to her that I don't recall, he disappeared behind the pool.

"I love him, but I don't trust him," she whispered, still watching to be sure he stayed gone. Sadly her situation wasn't so ideal after all, but I had to applaud her efforts.

I didn't have the heart to discourage her by adding my relationship resentments. It didn't matter to her that she didn't trust him, and I wasn't going to tell her it should.

We wrapped up our video, and I packed up my things to leave.

"I'm here for you if you ever need me. Both you and the baby," I assured her with a hug.

Though she'd made progress, I saw the cracks above the surface. No matter how much I wanted to reclaim my youth and save her from the obvious, I decided it best just to be supportive and listen.

It didn't take long for her to become a woman I trusted more than those I'd known for years. She reminded me so much of myself at that age and continuously having to prove worthy of a place in the world.

We didn't speak for another six months. She called from a sober living house, and her baby girl was only weeks.

"She's beautiful, Brookie!" What did you name her?" Before she could say the name, I already knew.

"Graylyn, after my grandmother," she answered proudly. She shared a special bond with her grandmother, who died before her daughter was born.

Then I asked how the hell she ended up in sober living after giving birth.

"Yeah, they told me I had to be at court, and I showed up late. They told me I had to come here or they'd take the baby from me after I gave birth to her. So I came here." She rambled off, embarrassed.

Her explanation didn't sound like the whole story, but I didn't want to scare her away with the impression I judged her by asking questions she was too ashamed to answer honestly. It wasn't any of my business anyway, and I was more proud that she swallowed her pride to ask for my help.

"I have to take the baby to the doctor's and don't have a ride. Do you mind taking us?" she said with a hint of humiliation in her soft voice.

"Of course, doll, text me the address and time, and I'll be there," I assured her. She sighed with relief.

I picked up her and her precious bundle of joy and drove them to their appointment, and then spent a couple of hours with them. We shared secrets about motherhood and men. She, too, was raised to marry a man and have children but grew more attracted to women with age.

"Most women who are in the sex industry prefer women, that's how we can turn the emotions off," she added while I listened to her intently.

She paused, then turned the topic to her man and the baby's father.

"I think he sees an escort," she told me then dropped her head. She sounded heartbroken that after changing her life and birthing his child, she still wasn't worthy of him.

"How do you know?" I asked, genuinely concerned. In her fragile postpartum state, it would be easy to go back to using drugs.

"Well, if they carry a bag with an extra set of clothes in their car, that's an obvious sign," she chuckled with sarcasm.

Obvious? Shit. A couple of men I dated did this very thing, and I had assumed it was a gym bag used to carry gym clothes.

"Couldn't they be gym clothes?" I asked before the light turned on over my head. How did I miss the bag wasn't for the gym but the John? I tried to stay positive to avoid adding my well-seasoned baggage and arouse more of her suspicions but also didn't want to help her dismiss her instincts either.

All I could tell her was, "You know the telltale signs of men who see escorts, and you know your man. Trust your gut, even if it hurts."

She reached towards the backseat to give the baby her

pacifier and said, “Most guys wear their gym clothes to the gym and go home to change after,” matter-of-fact.

Damn, checkmate! I had no comeback. We both sat in silence driving back to her temporary home now exhausted from over-analyzing John bags

“When can you get out again so I can take you to lunch?” I asked her to change the subject before leaving them.

She immediately perked up and said, “We have another doctor’s appointment next week if you don’t mind taking us.”

“Of course, I’ll be here.” I parked my truck and helped her get the baby out. We hugged, and I left home.

A month later, Brookie left the rehab facility to start a new life with her new baby and the father. Our communication was sporadic, but we kept in touch as time went by.

Unsure what exactly it was that inspired me, Frida, or too many bad online dates, but during a conversation, I asked her if she would go to a gay bar with me.

“For real? Finally, decided to cross over the penis line, eh?” She giggled at me.

I explained how unsure what, or who, it is I wanted, but I had become open to the idea of dating women.

“Do you have a preference for age or type of woman you want to date?” she asked and caught me off guard.

I hadn’t gotten that far yet. Did I have a type?

“Someone attractive, around my age or a little younger and my size. I’m not sure I can handle a woman bigger than me with my short woman’s complex!” We laughed like school girls.

It felt like back in high school and exploring my virginity all over again with my BFF.

"Well, if you're comfortable with it, I'd like to volunteer to be the one for you..." her words came towards me softly and bold.

I heard her smile through the phone, and it turned me on. Immediately I became lost for words. I'd had many women come on to me before, but none appealing enough to turn me on.

Brookie wasn't like any other woman I'd met before, and even though her young age intimidated my moral fiber, I knew she wouldn't judge my sex-ploring

Still, I felt torn between my home training and quest for a different kind of intimacy. And orgasm.

I worried about crossing a line, but after running many scenarios through my head, I heard the words of my porn crush, Nina Hartley, echo in my head.

"They want to have sex with me? Why not?!" The sexy adult film star exclaimed when asked about doing porn with people half her age.

"Are you serious? Do you think it would ruin our friendship?" I asked her nervously. Friends like her were hard to find, and I didn't want to lose her to my possibly fleeting curiosity.

"Hell, no, it'll be fun," she giggled confidently to put me at ease.

We made plans to meet for lunch later in the week before hanging up, and later that evening, she sent me a pic of her partially nude, with the words "can't wait to see you." I was mesmerized by this beautiful woman and her fearless sexuality that shined even brighter than mine. I felt the rush of my blush.

I accepted her invitation to play and sent out my first partially nude selfie text. The excitement alone, one that had been taboo for so many years, was orgasmic.

She was more experienced than me, and I was in total awe of her.

* * * *

When we met for lunch, she confided that her life had become complicated since she left the rehab facility. Not long after she moved in with her man, she learned he'd become financially unstable and that he wasn't as dedicated to fatherhood as she'd hoped.

They moved from the prestigious townhouse in Irvine to a run-down apartment complex in Anaheim. To provide for her daughter, she had to go back out and escort.

And unless she paid him, he wouldn't watch their daughter. She tried to find a legit gig that covered the bills, but with her record, it was dam near impossible.

My heart broke for her, and my anger brewed. I wanted to find him and kick his old ass. Brookie and I both wanted to believe she'd be free from her past, but a criminal record with solicitation and drugs made her life difficult, no matter how white she was.

"I'm seeing a new guy now. He's a little older than me. And married," she mumbled, taking a bite of her sandwich.

Her new mystery man was also a client and another she'd become too personal with and invested her emotions. Even professionals still pursue the idea of a happily ever after. I wanted to warn her but didn't' want to spoil our time together with my paranoia.

"Please be careful. If his wife finds out, she may not handle his infidelity with such grace. I don't want you to get hurt," I pleaded with her.

She smiled at me and leaned over her plate to be sure only I could hear her.

"I knew when we met that I was going to have you. It was just a matter of time," she winked at me, sitting back in her seat.

I almost inhaled my food through my nose, trying not to burst out laughing and blush at the same time. Brookie's approach was admirable, seductive, and thoroughly turned me on.

She gave me lady-wood, and I wanted to kiss her right then and there. We finished eating shortly after, and I had to cut our conversation short so that I could beat the lunch traffic back home for work.

When I took her back home and slid towards her seat to hug her goodbye, I had to kiss her.

Her lips were soft, and the more she teased me with her tongue, the deeper I wanted to kiss her. My breath panted nervously. She placed my hand on her breast, and I felt feel my entire body get hot as I followed her lead. Like an inexperienced teenager, I caressed her nipple, hoping I was doing it right.

When I started to kiss her neck, she turned her lips from mine to let out a sigh of pleasure. I wanted to bite her as my hunger to explore more grew. Without realizing my hand was in her lap, I felt her legs open up, inviting me to touch more of her.

I didn't want to stop, but the cop in me remembered where we were, and quickly pulled her skirt back down before sitting back in my seat.

"We could so go to jail for this," I sighed, then we both giggled like teenagers.

"We need a bed," she added, with a matter-of-fact snicker.

She gave me one more sensual kiss and hopped out of my car. "I'll text later and let you know what day I can get free," she said, shutting the door.

"I can't wait, be safe," I said, smiling back at her pulling.

Driving home like a teenager with a crush, I replayed our kiss and smiled at her scent still on me.

HEARTBROKEN

A few days later, Brookie sent me a text to tell me she was going out of state to visit family, postponing our next rendezvous. Weeks past and her text responses became shorter and shorter, then eventually not at all.

Six months passed, and still nothing. All I cared about at this point was her safety. Since I knew she started escorting again, I became obsessed with hearing back from her.

I remembered that when Staci and Laci found her, she had a website, so I Googled her. The one guarantee I had was Brookie wasn't a good criminal and got caught almost every time she broke the law.

Sure enough, the first thing that popped up was a mugshot of her arrest in another state about a month prior. The airport police busted her for possession and transporting narcotics.

I waited a month to text her again, and it took her a whole other month to respond. I concluded that she turned back to drugs and started the cycle of addiction all over again.

By October of 2017, I was desperate and sent her one more message "Girl, where the heck are you? I miss your face! Let's have lunch ASAP. I have so much to tell you! Call me!"

Finally, after a few days, she wrote back, "Hey, yes, let's have lunch, where and when?"

Relieved that she responded, I didn't bother to ask any questions. I just wanted to see her face.

"Let's meet this week, your choice of anywhere you want. My treat," I quickly typed back.

I wanted to pour out my heart and tell her how much I missed her but feared she'd been too embarrassed to say to me my girl kissing skills sucked.

"I hope I didn't cross a line in our friendship because if so, I truly apologize. Only care about your friendship and safety at this point." That's when the shame and guilt I had no idea was there came flooding over me. I never wanted to make her feel like I was manipulating her time or her body like others had.

"Oh no, lovely, you didn't push me away. Been busy out of town. I enjoyed our time together and have been wanting more time with you. You could never lose my friendship. Let's meet at Coco's down the street from my house next Tuesday." she replied within minutes.

It felt like a huge weight lifted off of me to know she was safe and still wanted my friendship. My heart was full as I typed back, "Can't wait" with a heart emoji.

"Hey girl, do you need me to pick you up, or are you meeting me there?" I emailed her about nine o'clock Tuesday morning. Unsure what time she wanted to meet, but we usually met before one o'clock in the afternoon.

No response.

I emailed her again at half-past eleven o'clock. "Yo, we still doing lunch, doll? I'm starving, LOL!"

No response. I began to worry.

Two hours later, I sent another email that sounded like a mother desperate for a response, "OK, now you know how I have PTSD with girls disappearing! Don't make me hunt you down again, girl! Seriously, let me know you're OK. Please."

Nothing.

Fuck.

I watched the clock for the next twenty-four hours like my kid didn't come home.

Unsure if she was in trouble, busy or out of town, I couldn't help but think of the worst. We had no mutual friends or contacts, leaving me no other choice but to wait to hear from her.

Another six months passed, and I had a bad feeling she wasn't out living a happy life. This time I sent a message through social media, but still, nothing from her.

My last resort was to Google her once more. This time I feared she caught a case with real prison time, and why she was a no show to our lunch, but that's not what I found.

There it was, her obituary.

Jacqueline Brooke Jernigan, age 26 of Newport Beach, CA, and formerly of Whiteville passed on Thursday, November 16,2017.

What?! No, no, no, this isn't happening.

I scrambled back to her social media account to see her last post.

How did I miss the banner over her name that read, "celebrate her life" and "in loving memory of"?

My chest tightened, and my heart raced, all I could get out was a long agonizing scream. I felt tears run down my cheeks while I rocked myself back and forth and sobbed on my couch.

I wanted to throw my computer and pretend I didn't read the words. What the hell happened to her? Did one of her clients kill her? Did she also die at the hands of a serial killer? Did she have a drug overdose? Car crash? Every horrible scenario ran through my head.

Final rites will be held at 11:00 a.m. Saturday at Worthington Funeral Home with Reverend Ricky Donaldson officiating. Interment will follow in Pleasant Hill Baptist Church Cemetery. The family will receive friends from 6-8:00 p.m. on Friday, December 1, 2017, at Worthington Funeral Home.

The date of her death was a month after she missed out lunch, and probably why I never heard from her again.

I skimmed through her media page to find anything that could tell me what happened, but nothing stood out.

Devastated, I'd never see her smiling face again, hear her laugh, or watch her eyes light up looking at her daughter.

Searching through the Google feed looking for more articles and any clue to what happened to my friend, I found two more booking photos from the year before, where she looked heroin sick again when they arrested her.

I started to sob. Her eyes were empty and lifeless like she'd given up, but her most recent social media picture post showed a healthier her.

Was she hiding her misery? Did she flirt with death for one last high, and it cost her her life?

It's impossible to believe she intended to leave her baby no matter how undeserving she felt. My heart broke for her.

And it still does from time to time when the waves of grief wash over me. Being a hero is overrated and a delusion, no one can rescue anyone from themselves.

I didn't save Brookie, but in many ways, she did me. She made me a better woman and mother by allowing me the freedom to explore all aspects of my womanhood.

A courageous soul who guided me through to a place of shameless self-acceptance that I'd never arrived at on my own. The small-time I had in her presence changed me forever.

She turned me on, and then she was gone.

7.

Bullet 7

BULLET 7-SADNESS

KILLER JUSTICE

"Hi Roni, we'll be in Santa Ana next week for Gordon's trial, if you're still interested in going with us. Our hotel isn't far from the courthouse, and you can meet us there," Kianna's mother text me one afternoon in December 2017.

I looked forward to meeting her for almost four years now, but right before the trial of one of the men charged with killing her daughter, Kianna, wasn't how I planned it.

Unsure whether I could handle any more trauma, I agreed to go anyways.

For so long, I believed Kianna was still alive and out there somewhere. This trial would be my only opportunity to find out what happened to her.

I met her and her husband at her hotel for a quick breakfast before driving to the courthouse. I hugged her tight like we'd known each other for years.

She wasn't much older than me, a white woman in her forties, and astonishingly calm for a mother who had lost her daughter to such tragedy. We started some casual chit-chat, nibbled on a small continental breakfast, then I followed them to the courthouse. I'd only have time to stay for the morning part of the hearing.

I sat in several courtrooms, in different courts, listened to many hearings, but never for a murder trial before. When we made our way through the court halls to stand with clusters of people and wait for the elevators, I felt an urge to cry.

Once we were in the elevator, Kianna's mother pushed the top floor button, one I'd never been on before. The old dank odor greeted us walking in, and we all sat down on the uncomfortably designed chair like benches. Looking around, I couldn't believe how plain it looked for a place that decided the fate of one's life or, in this case, death.

I expected more ambiance of drama. Seriously, I watch too much dam TV.

It felt cold and, the energy, restless. I sat in the circle of the victims' mothers, who each exuded their rage and despair. It was day two of the trial.

"There he is. See him sitting at the table?" Kianna's mother whispered and nudged me to look at the defense table.

Steven Gordon, one of the accused, sat at the table alone, staring down at some paperwork.

I sat there and stared at him in disbelief to be that close to a serial killer.

There was nothing about that fit the description of a cold-blooded murderer. He wore glasses, had a clean shave, combed back hair, and no visible reflection of creepy I'd expected.

"He's representing himself, did I tell you that?" she whispered.

Wait—what? I couldn't believe what I was about to witness. Ted Bundy was the only serial killer that I'd heard of that represented himself in his capital murder serial killer case. I wondered if Gordon was about to put on a show for the history books too.

I watched him, both disgusted and intrigued while thinking, "Where the hell are all the TV cameras?"

The court came to order, and Gordon started to call witnesses to the stand. Kianna's mother was calm and absorbed every word while she watched Gordon ask his witness questions. His current witness barely spoke English, a Mexican woman also in her late forties, who appeared frightened to be in the courtroom.

He asked her a couple of questions regarding his friendship with her son, and co-defendant Frank Cano. If I listened correctly, he wanted the jury to account for a history of friendship, to prove them two didn't merge into a killing a machine overnight.

The woman answered his questions, and then he excused her from the stand. The state's attorneys sat at their table, flipping through papers and whispering back and forth with one another and the lead detective to the case.

They didn't appear to an interest in the witness, and I don't recall them having cross-examined her, perhaps to save their loaded questions for Cano's trial.

Gordon called a black woman, early thirties, and one of his former parole agents, to the stand. I recall most of his questions to her pertained to how the Board of Parole and their agents monitored transient sex offenders.

She explained that were specific locations, under freeways, alleys, and industrial areas, where transient sex offenders were allowed to "live" legally as a registered resident.

So instead of keeping sex offenders in prison, paroles make them register to live under a fucking freeway? Who the hell authorized this monstrosity? I grew more frustrated, listening to her answer his questions.

Gordon asked about the rules sex offenders must abide by while living in these open spaces. I remember her mentioning they weren't allowed to share any space, not sleep in the same car, cardboard box, etc. Friendships were also forbidden.

He then asked her to confirm when parole agents loosened those restrictions, even encouraged transient offenders to stay in proximity to one another for protection.

She confirmed that it was an actual, emergency, procedure implemented in 2011 because a serial killer preyed on transient people in that same area. All transient parolees/sex offenders were told by their parole agents to "group up" for protection. After a couple of more questions, he dismissed her from the stand. I don't recall the state's attorneys ask her anything either.

Gordon called the last agent assigned to him before their arrest for the killings, a white man in his late thirties. His superiority complex was undeniable.

As soon as his ass hit the seat, he defensively crossed his hands then leaned over the modesty panel in front of him, to establish control.

It angered him that the same felon, tuned serial killer, he

was employed by the state to monitor was grilling him about his job performance.

POVERTY IS A RACE

Gordon took full advantage of the moment and used his self-representation to settle a score with the people who were once an authority over him.

Many saw this as an intention to place blame elsewhere for his crimes, but not me. What I saw was a person who felt those responsible for watching him helped provoke his evil, and he wanted them held publicly accountable for it too.

It's no secret that Gordon choosing to represent himself in his capital murder trial was a guaranteed death sentenced.

He wanted to prove this agent negligent, and to do so, Gordon had to get the agent to admit that he was aware Gordon and Cano hung out regularly and ignored their GPS monitored activities.

The agent answered Gordon's questions cocksure, then shrugged his shoulders to show his disgust for Gordon and his implications that he too, as a state parole agent, played a role in his victims' deaths. Even if only by extension.

The tension between these two became almost combative, and I lost focus of their words to assess their body language. Gordon, fighting for the little honor he had left before they locked him in a dungeon for life, and the agent fighting for his judicial pride disallowed to admit that even the best of us make mistakes. Watching them, I grew respect for Gordon's efforts to put the system on trial and ride out in a blaze of glory.

I didn't hear his last question but, the last words out of the agent's mouth were, "I don't know," and Gordon yelled back at him an unforgettable and heart-wrenching response "Yeah and if you had five girls would still be alive wouldn't they?" His voice was loud and dramatic.

I watched the agent and waited for him to throw up from taking that kind of a blow in public. Even I felt sick, and it wasn't me on the stand. Had it been me with the responsibility to monitor these two men and my negligence, or lack of training and knowledge, created a monster, or contributed to a monster terrorizing other human beings, I'd be haunted by it forever.

Then I remembered I had. Had I been honest with myself about the risks instead of filling voids for personal reasons, maybe Blass's uncle would still be alive.

I sat there perplexed with who the real devil in the room was.

Before I knew it, it was lunchtime, and the court staff dismissed us to resume after one o'clock p.m. There was no way I could sit and listen to more now.

Driving home mentally exhausted by my logic and irrational emotion, I felt betrayed. Betrayed that I ignorantly and sometimes, arrogantly, believed and enforced, a system that lacked accountability. A soldier's kid taught to follow orders without question.

****

The Milgram experiments started in 1961 at Yale by Stanley Milgram. (Frank Hagan, *Introduction to Criminology: Theories, Methods, and Criminal Behavior-9th Edition*, 2017.)

After the trial for Nazi crimes began, Milgram wanted to study those who obey authority figures even when instructed to perform acts that conflict with their morality, values, and conscience.

They instructed the subjects to give electric shocks ranging from light to intense and weren't allowed to watch the person they were shocking, but could hear screams, requests to stop, or sometimes, nothing at all.

They concluded all the subjects administered at least three hundred volts as instructed, even if they were uncomfortable, hesitant, and remorseful.

Without question, each person followed the instructions because they were told to by someone of authority.

Proof that even to be "good" is a delusion.

The majority of these careers are glorified and sought out by those from lower socio-economic backgrounds. Wealthy people don't breed civil servants.

Turning poor people against one another by dividing them into teams is just as genius as racism.

* * * *

It was the fourth day of trial, and the last I'd attend. Gordon scheduled with the court to play his confession tape continued from the day before. I had no idea what to expect but very curious about his strategy in playing it for the jury.

It was almost eerie that I'd already missed one full day of Gordon playing this same video for the jury, and it began that morning with his actual confession to the murders.

Finally, I'd find out what happened to these girls after three years of obsessions and assumptions. But, instead of feeling relief, my anxiety consumed me sitting in between their grief-stricken mothers. Like a child, I wanted to scream and run out of the courtroom with my hands over my ears.

Instead, I forced myself to sit there, push my fears aside, and listen intently for what Gordon wanted everyone to hear. Like most people who've been imprisoned or are mentally ill, they speak in code.

The video interview showed both the lead detective in the case and Gordon in what looked like the interrogation room of the police department. She asked him questions, and he answered in detail. He appeared anxious, frightened, and stuttered some of his words. Every other sentence, he repeated that he "wanted to die right now" and how he "deserved the death penalty."

For those few seconds, he reminded me of that scene in the movie "Seven (Fincher, Kopelson-Carlyle, 1995)." The man forced to put on the leather strap suit, with a knife in place of a penis, to have sex with the prostitute.

The hysterical man wanted not only out of the suit but out of his skin. Not just for what he'd done, but the images that now wickedly danced in his head destined to drive him insane.

That's the reaction Gordon had when he answered the detectives' questions. Like he wanted to jump out of his skin for what he'd done to his victims.

As the tape played, I couldn't help but have a smidgen of empathy for this man. Not pity, but mercy for his self inflicted terror. He'd spend the rest of his life cursed with a living spirit, surrounded by walking dead.

Gordon then started to describe what happened with his first victim, Kianna.

NOOO! I wanted to scream out when he said her name but instead grabbed her mother's hand.

Gordon explained how he and Cano picked her up, and that she'd agreed to have sex with them, but it angered them when she tried to take their money and run without following through on the sex.

He explained that they took her back to the alley behind his place of employment to have sex with her.

My mind raced with questions. Is it because Kianna tried to get out of the deal that they killed her? She must have been terrified.

The detective interceded gently with more questions to keep him talking.

Gordon confessed to strangling Kianna and then began to describe the details. I squeezed her mother's hand, moving closer to her for comfort. She clenched her husband's arm with her other hand and buried her head in his chest to brace herself.

The detective asked how they disposed of her body, and I felt her mother's hand go limp. She leaned closer to her husband, and I leaned on her. It was the moment this mother, and all the other mothers waited three years to have.

As I listened to Gordon, describe how and why he strangled Kianna, my body filled with adrenaline and fear.

The memory of being choked, to the extent that I feared death, ran through my mind.

THE RAGE TO KILL

When dad retired from the military, it was hard to find a decent paying job. He felt the burden and stress of single parenthood to provide and survive in a civilian world that had no use for his military skills.

He'd spent almost two decades training for war, and it infuriated him when treated like an ill-equipped relic.

We'd just moved down-state away from all of my friends, and because I hated my new segregated school and ditched a couple of classes, then forged his name on the note to excuse my absence.

An act I can't deny as a parent myself was worthy of some discipline. It was the wrong time to add a "rebellious teen" to my daughter's profile.

He started his lecture, and I tried to explain my side of the story. I knew I was wrong but didn't care because I was miserable and wanted him to care more about that.

I never saw his hands come towards me. Dad grabbed me by my neck, with precision, and proceeded to choke me as though I was his enemy. His hands tightly squeezed around my neck, and me in place for what seemed like forever.

Then he let me go.

The bloodthirsty look on his face stared back at me like dissatisfied I'd suffered enough. Within seconds, and no time to catch my breath, he grabbed me again and choked me harder and for even longer.

It took my aunt, who'd watched us the whole time, to intervene and shout out his name before he'd stop. He showed no remorse, and sat down, to dismiss me to the other room. I'm still baffled about how my actions warranted a death sentence to this day.

The next day driving home from the grocery store, he apologized but wouldn't look me in the face. Only a small tear fell from his eye when he said the words. He'd never physically abuse me again.

It left me always to wonder if he'd chocked other women like that before. Well, not my mom. I watched her knock his ass to the floor the one time I saw them get physical.

Dad never went to combat, and yet he choked me with a murderous experience. His sadistic act to threaten my life as my parent, not once but twice, proved him capable of snuffing me out whenever he deemed it necessary.

* * * *

Gordon described how 'they' (Cano and himself) stripped her body and belongings, cut her nails, wrapped her in plastic, and dumped her in a garbage bin. He insisted that "no one" would find the bodies.

Gordon continued to explain what made him snap to kill her.

When the detective asked what made him "snap" and choke Kianna, Gordon said it was because she had lied about her name and that the name she picked was his daughter's name. The same daughter was taken from him by her mother, also the victims in his prior kidnapping case.

His words finally broke me, and I began to sob. I believed that Kianna was out there somewhere and to hear her death described in detail, how a stage name to protect her identity may have led to her demise, was mortifying.

I could hear the other mothers weep and sniffle behind me. Looking over at Gordon, who had his head down, I saw him sad too. To listen to the painful groans of these mothers was difficult for everyone in the room.

After he explained, I realized that Gordon and my dad weren't so different from one another. Dad harbored some of his same resentments and possibly a sociopath cloaked in a cape of military honor.

Gordon was right—Kianna's body, and the others, hasn't been recovered.

The tape played and continued with the details of other girls' deaths. The scenarios were similar in that the girls were working and mostly young.

The last girl, however, Jarrae Estepp, somehow snapped him back to the reality that he'd been role-playing this evil killer after all. He wanted her to stay with him and not kill her, but Cano told him they had to. Gordon made sure that Jarrae's body, and her body alone, was found. I believe his intent, conscious or not, was for the authorities to stop them.

The tape played and would continue to play with more details of the murders and the girls' identities. The identity of one victim wasn't known when the trial began because they killed her in one county, but she lived in another. It wouldn't be until after Gordon was convicted, the detectives were finally able to confirm the young woman's identity. She was a beautiful, nineteen years young, woman named Sable.

I couldn't listen to it anymore or attend another day of the trial. The final verdict wasn't going to bring any of them back.

When they dismissed us for lunch, I hugged Kianna's mother, said goodbye to the other mothers, and made my way to my car. I felt like someone kicked me in my soul. Everything I'd believed now turned upside down. The evil, in this case, was no longer black and white. What happened to make Gordon seek justice for his victims?

He made sure to fast-track his trial to death row, when he could have pled not guilty and drawn the case out for years, like his co-defendant, but he didn't. I saw the reflection of his remorse most while describing Kianna and Jodi, the first and last victims. The pinned-up rage he felt towards the women that betrayed him, enabled him to act out deviant fantasies concocted while incarcerated. And having Cano along for the ride made it easier to add more victims to the list.

For days I couldn't shake that Kianna's white lie had pushed someone to kill her. Just a small white lie. But that's what lies do, and even small ones can push a situation too far.

After I moved with my dad, I told my friends that I'd lost my virginity by rape. I feared that the truth would cause them to think of me as slutty and unworthy of respect. Being humiliated for having sex so young, I learned it was better to be a victim than to be a slut. Months later, Giovanni came into my life.

For years I blamed myself and felt deserving of his rapes because I told that one lie. I'd forgotten all about that lie and the impact it could have made on that young man's life until I that day in court. A lie like that destroys lives and infects them with hatred.

Gordon was found guilty of all four murders and received the death penalty. He accepted his fate, and while he spoke his last words to the jury, Gordon, a serial killer, wept. He demanded the death penalty, made sure to get it, and still, he wept.

Watching the news clip, I remembered how sad all the victim's mothers were, and an overwhelming sadness came over me again.

Though I was grateful not to be one of them and mourning the loss of my daughter, I couldn't shake the question of how I'd feel if it were my son sentenced to death?

What if it were my seed to sit in that courtroom and explain why he chose to murder five women? Would I feel it just to serve him death?

The thought of losing my daughter to a killer was just as horrific as losing my son to the antiquated system of cruel inhumanity for the rest of his life

My daughter isn't worth more to me than my son.

MAMAS BOY

As a young girl, I never wanted children, but on my eighteenth birthday and a month before graduating high school, I found myself pregnant.

Staring at the woman sitting in the chair across from me at the women's clinic as she explained my options, I tried to calculate when it happened.

It didn't take long to remember the motel room on prom night.

Everyone had my life planned for me already, and all I had to do was submit and follow it. Looking back it is quite possible I fucked it up on teenager purpose and cost myself a law degree from Pepperdine University

MJ, my first ex-husband, and I were horny teenagers who didn't use birth control on that romantic and infamous night. He'll tell you it was my fault, and it was.

He was a cute and sweet Creole boy that I met my junior year of high school, and weeks after Giovanni disappeared. Damaged and traumatized, he was the gentle landing I could never appreciate.

An artist break-dancer who enjoyed spray-painting buildings illegally and who could've cared less about grades and SAT scores. I also worked part-time at a pizza restaurant to help out at home and attend social events and envied his irresponsibility.

Both high schools I attended had daycare facilities, for its students, that created a shame-free environment to birth babies before accomplishing anything else in life.

We were a new breed of feminists.

Quite a few of my classmates were already parents or about to be parents, so my predicament wasn't unique.

* * * *

When I got home from the clinic, I called MJ to tell him I was pregnant and wasn't ready to have a baby. He didn't agree but respected that it was my decision.

One of the pamphlets the nurse put in my stack of paperwork had the words "qualify for alternate abortion services" written on it, and I assumed they meant financial help with abortions.

Now already at six weeks, I called and made an immediate appointment. They only had one opening during the morning a few days out, and I'd have to ditch my morning classes to make it.

When I walked in the office, an attractive white woman in her mid-twenties, who looked fresh out of college, greeted me at the door.

"Hi Roni, I'm Amanda. Please come in," she opened another door to an office and motioned for me to enter and have a seat. I sat down as she closed the door behind me.

There were several affirmations posted on the walls along with pictures of a family; a mother, father, and little boy. When Amanda sat down near one of the pictures, I realized it was her family in the colorful frames.She began with what sounded like scripted questions, much like the questions asked at the clinic. After I answered what I could, she asked what supplies I already had for the baby.

Wait—what? Supplies?

"I was under the impression you offered financial help with abortions. I can't afford one right now, and can't ask my parents for money," I mumbled at her.

"I'm sorry for the confusion, sweetheart," she said, then gently put her pen down to make contact with me.

"We don't provide any abortion services here. We assist women with their medical needs and baby supplies for people who can't afford them to help abortions." Her smile was nonjudgmental.

Seriously? No way I was fit, or intelligent enough, to be a mother after trying to get financial help for an abortion at a clinic that doesn't support abortions!?

She pointed to the pictures of her son and shared a couple of stories as a young mother. At eighteen, she too became a mom, and still found success.

Listening to her, I felt guilty for not embracing teen motherhood with the same bravery as my classmates. When I left her office, I was on the wait-list for a car seat and crib fully prepared to sabotage the plan already in place for my future.

I was petrified to make the mistakes my parents did, but

chose to try anyway. I could hear MJ smiling through the phone after telling him he was going to be a dad.

"On one condition," I added.

"Anything," he shouted.

"No matter what happens between us, we always do what is best for the baby," I demanded. He quickly agreed.

It wasn't unit after I graduated and moved out of my dad's house, then into MJ and his parent's house, that I told my family I was pregnant. Five months later. Mom was devastated and heartbroken. Dad was disappointed and disgusted, and my grandmother was fucking pissed.

"You're so stupid," my grandmother yelled at me.

"You'll always have to sacrifice and worry about someone else. It will never end. You didn't even give yourself or this baby a fair chance in this cruel world," she scolded. She was right. I had no idea the disservice I was about to do to my unborn child and myself.

Positive we were having a girl, I had a name and colors already picked out, but MJ was sure a son was in our midst. So over-confident in my want for a girl that I'd never considered how I would react to birthing a baby boy.

When the woman who performed our ultrasound announced our bundle of joy was a boy, I felt immediately disappointed. MJ was ecstatic.

To celebrate, we grabbed lunch and a cheap movie. "The Good Son (Page & Ruben, 1993)" had just been released to theaters, and I picked that movie to accept the news of having a son because McCauley Culkin was the cute little boy in my favorite movie, "Home Alone Columbus & Hughes, 1990),"

What a big fucking mistake that was! Leaving the theater, I was scared shitless to have a son.

Ironically, since I ate nothing but a poor junk food diet my entire pregnancy, his birth almost killed both of us. Who knew Chips Ahoy cookies and Snickers bars caused toxemia. Well, mom, the nurse, warned me, but what did she know?

After thirty-six hours of labor, I had barely dilated to three centimeters, and the doctor decided to take my baby by emergency C-section.

Never will I forget the excruciating horrific pain I felt when they made me walk afterward. It was the best cure for not wanting any more children.

The pain was so great that my hands shook, and I couldn't hold my son for the first twenty-four hours of his life. The next morning I waddled to the nursery to hold him and rock him in my arms. For nine months, I imagined that moment would make me feel so attached to MJ, but it didn't. I wanted our baby to myself.

By the third day, they found blood in my son's stool and moved him to the baby NICU at another hospital. My young blossoming mothering spirit was devastated, and I still don't eat Chips Ahoy cookies to this day.

When we finally brought him home, a week later, I did whatever it took to keep him safe and healthy.

My mom and grandmother decided we needed to make things right and get married. I had birthed a prince, and they were going to see to it I honored him as such. It was the 1990s, but a shotgun wedding, as my grandmother put it, was just punishment and "what you get" for having sex then getting pregnant.

She, too, married my grandfather because of her pregnancy with my mother.

Neither MJ or I wanted to get married but did so to be obedient and do what we could to give our son a fair chance. Even with the gut instinct that a civil union between us would fail, I proceeded anyway.

But gaining eighty fucking pounds during the pregnancy was the cruelest part of the journey. I went from my one-hundred and five-pound athletic teen figure with abs to a one-hundred and eight-five pound, rolling thunder-thighed young mom with an ugly Cesarean scar. Surprisingly I held no post-partum resentment towards my son but only for MJ.

SINGLE MOM SACRIFICE

Being a young mother was hard, but I found the little rewards that made it worthwhile. Being a wife, on the other hand, sucked, and I grew to despise it.

A few years prior, my grandmother tried to teach me essential duties fit for a husband and family, and I remember being disinterested watching her show off her skills as a domestic goddess.

We were from different generations, and her old-fashioned approach to marriage would eventually leave me joyless in mine. Like it had with my parents.

I resented that MJ's sole responsibility was to provide. Not to cook or clean, or even assure our baby was clean, clothed, or nourished, just go to work. It felt unfair that he didn't have to work hard in high school and now, in marriage and fatherhood, either. Not to mention that now I was fat, and by default, he became the pretty one getting all the attention.

It brought out the worst in me when he was around, and when he wasn't, I was happy alone with my son. This tiny baby had zapped all of the selfless young love right out of me, and I had none left to give his dad, now my husband.

After seeing myself on video celebrating my son's first birthday, I became determined to lose weight and focus on myself and my son.

It wasn't long after I got my sexy back, that I completely lost the enthusiasm to perform my wifely duties and soon threw in the towel. Just before our son turned two years old, we decided to separate.

MJ moved almost an hour away, and I stayed to make myself a full-time single mother. For the next two years, I did the job irresponsibly. Threw late-night parties, hung out with drug dealers and gangsters, and allowed strangers to come in and out of my home. How the millennial generation survived us dumb ass 1990's moms, I'll never know.

Fortunately, my mom and grandmother made sure I never needed daycare or anything else for my son.

They even encouraged some of my shenanigans because they knew I was young and needed to "punch myself out," so to speak.

Though my grandmother and I were close growing up, when my son was born, it brought out her aggression towards me.

* * * *

After my son turned 4, I received a promotion to a manager's position at the restaurant I worked for and felt accomplished. My mom came to pick my son and me up to take me to work and then my son to my grandmother's house for the night.

She watched a couple of male friends of mine leave my house was angry with me when I got to her car.

"You shouldn't have those men in your house," she snapped at me while I buckled my son in his car seat.

"That was my friend Tasha's boyfriend and her brother dropping off some mail from her mom," I responded, annoyed.

"I don't care who they are. You shouldn't have gang members coming in and out of your house," she continued, determined to pick a fight.

It was possible my bad decisions and questionable associates could harm my son, but I was too rebellious and careless to see it that way.

I ignored her and tried to keep quiet until she dropped me off at work.

We pulled up to my grandmother's house, and mom went inside. My grandmother came running out, screaming and yelling at me with that old-school-ass-whooping voice that smacks you when you hear it.

I was sure she'd stop to grab a switch off one of her trees before getting to me.

Now, before I describe the next course of events, keep in mind that my grandmother was not and is still not the calm, mild-mannered Mexican grandmother, you see in movies making homemade tortillas.

My grandmother is Yaqui Indian and an old school

Pachuca with no problem fighting and hitting anyone no matter her age or theirs.

Even now, in her eighties, she still knows exactly where her gun is.

She made her way to my wide-open car door, and I braced myself for her verbal assault. But she leaned into the car and slapped my face, grabbed me by the hair, and began to shake my head like a rag doll in the mouth of a pit bull.

Somehow and from some unknown place, I got enough strength to stand up and get out of from between the car door she had me pinned in.

"Let go of my hair, grandma," I screamed at her, feeling her squeeze me harder.

Before I could accept that I was in a physical fight with my grandmother, of all people, both my hands were full of her hair. I tried to shove her body against the car door in hopes she'd let go of her grip, but she didn't.

Mexican grandmas will throw chingasos until they can't lift their arms. Even when I tried to get away from her, she continued towards me to fight.

Frightened, I may have to punch her in the face out of self-defense, my grandfather thankfully appeared out of nowhere to break us up.

Unsure at what point mom pulled my son out of the car to keep him from witnessing the monstrous Jerry Springer-like showdown starring the loca women in charge of his life, but they both now stood on the porch of my grandmother's house.

I took my son from her hands then demanded that she drive us back home.

"We want what's best for the baby. You can't see the danger you have him in?" mom said under her breath, driving me back home.

We were all fighting for what was best for him, and she couldn't choose between her loca mother and pendeja daughter over her precious mijo.

She dropped me off, and I ditched work. No one wants a crybaby waitress.

I cried and vowed to move as far away from them both as soon as I could.

AN UGLY TRUTH

A couple of weeks later, I was out at a local bar, with Tasha and her boyfriend having drinks and dancing.

We lived in a small town where everyone knows everyone, including the gangs.

I knew the black gang members of both gangs, Crips, and Bloods because most of them lived near my apartment building. The Latin gang members were on the other side of town.

Tasha and I, and a small group we invited for the after-party, began to walk towards the alley to take our shortcut back to my house. We just walked outside of the bar and passed through the parking lot when a Latin woman came storming out of the exit door. To this day, I don't know who she was or what she looked like or her age. She started to scream at a group of guys standing against the wall, talking, and smoking cigarettes.

I knew all the young men in this group, and the person

she was yelling at. The guy next to him, Cain, was a neighbor and close friend who hung out at my house with my son and me almost every day. His mother and he, along with most of his relatives, were like family to us. It was no secret that Cain had a hell of a temper, but I had no idea to what extent.

Cain walked away from the woman, and the group then headed towards us. I noticed there was a forty-ounce bottle of beer half full about fifteen feet between the both of us. For a moment, I assumed he had put it down and forgotten about it, even though that didn't make any sense. He never left his beer.

The look on his face made me nervous because I'd never seen him so upset. Even now, I'm unsure why, but without thinking, I ran towards the bottle, and met him almost second for second.

"Cain, you don't need to drink that, I'll buy you another one," I said playfully to distract him.

His eyes were bloodshot, already intoxicated, and it took him a few seconds to realize it was me standing in front of him.

"Don't worry dog, I'm not going to do anything" he smiled back at me as he picked the bottle up.

"Have a good night dog," he slurred then turned to walk back to the group. I stood and watched him walk away.

"Come on, girl, it's freezing out here," Tasha shouted now yards ahead of me. Trying to ignore the bad feeling I had, I started to walk back towards my friends and turned back to watch Cain every other step.

The woman still yelling, but now at someone else, when he approached. He moved the bottle behind him to conceal it from everyone, and when he got close enough to the screaming woman, hit her in the face as hard as he could with it. Hard enough that not only did it echo, but when she fell, and her body slid backward, and her face scraped along the gravel.

I stopped dead in my tracks petrified of what I'd just witnessed and, for a moment, couldn't catch my breath. Then I heard Tasha yell, "Come on, Roni!" and snapped me out of my trance. Running as fast as I could to catch up, we all then ran to my house to avoid the police. They, too, saw what Cain had done, and none of us wanted to be witnesses against him.

A few nights later, I was at a different friend's house, a Mexican girl, drinking and smoking weed with a couple of other friends and her brother.

All of us girls hung out with Cain and his friends, but her brother was a member of the Latin gang and kept his distance.

"Did you guys hear about one of the home-girls getting clocked in the face by some black guys at the bar last night?" her brother asked.

Completely unaware of the consequences, or their extent, to the conversation I was about to get sucked in.

"Yea, I saw a chick get in someone's face before I left," I answered as his sister passed the joint to me.

Both friends were stunned by the way their eyes widened in surprise, then slowly shook their heads to warn me to shut the fuck up.

"You see him punch her or hit her with something?" he asked, trying to keep his cool.

At that moment, it was clear why my friends cautioned me and that I was about to have my first real moral conflict. If I told him that Cain hit her, the Latins would retaliate, creating unnecessary and, maybe even, fatal violence. If I didn't, the victim would never get justice for her assault. Cain was my friend, and I didn't dare betray him, but he deserved some form of restitution

"No, I didn't. We were already down the street before we heard yelling. It was too cold to walk back and see what was going on ." I answered to sound casual.

Disgusted to hear my own words betray me, I took another hit off the joint, passed it to his sister, and changed the subject.

* * * *

A couple of weeks later, a woman I knew, who worked for a private prison forty-five minutes away, gave me an application to apply as a corrections officer. She knew I took a couple of criminal justice classes at the college the year before.

Sitting on my couch going over the application, job description, and benefits, I saw that it was the most perfect, and only, opportunity to escape most of my bad decisions. And my loca family.

They offered free housing within driving distance of the facility, medical benefits, and there was a local school.

As much as I wanted to hate my mom and grandmother for their obsessive, controlling behavior, I had to accept that they were right about the environment I had ignorantly submerged my son and me in.

While Cain and his crew were cool friends, but the ugly truth was they weren't role models, and I put my son and myself in danger every time we were around them.

But could I go back to being square after having tasted the

life of a bad girl rebelling her sheltered roots? I'd have to give up my careless freedom to be held accountable for my actions, and it felt like choosing between good and bad witch.

The only silver lining was when I turned badge Cain, and all my other friends respected me for it. It wasn't a spoken rule, but an understood boundary had formed between us.

I stayed away from their trouble, and no one invited me to any.

SHE-WOLF AND HER CUB

It didn't take long for me to understand why my grandmother reacted the way she did. She was willing to do whatever it took to keep my son, her great-grandson, from becoming a resident in state prison.

When I started work on day shift, they assigned me to supervise one of the cleaning crews, and not long after taking the position, a very young Latin kid, barely nineteen years old, applied.

Because I saw the resemblance of my son in his young face, I hired him to be sure he gained work experience before being released.

He followed me everywhere, trying to make himself my assistant, and the other prisoners would tease that he had a crush on me. I admit, at first, I suspected the same until one afternoon while putting supplies away, he started to talk about his mom and how he missed helping her around the house. He may have found me attractive, but more than that, it was a familiarity in the routine for him. It wasn't often he showed a softer side around me, mostly he was vatos-locos all the way, but when he did, it appeared to be genuine.

The thought of my son locked up in prison frightened me, obliterating my original perception of what kind of woman I needed to become to raise a man.

When I signed my rental agreement, somehow I missed that the maintenance crew, who would attend to our housing needs, would be a crew of low-risk prisoners and not a professional maintenance company. It was a self-defining moment coming out of my home in tight jeans with my adorable four-year-old son in hand and a group of prisoners less than twenty feet from our house. I'd never feel safe to walk out my front door or any other door, ever again.

They ogled at not only me but my son, and the fear of it all pulled a she-wolf out of me. I was still very naive about predators and the dangers for little boys, but at that moment, it was all crystal fucking clear.

What flowed throw my veins was nothing I'd ever experienced as a mother up to that point. Like a wild animal with no remorse, I could've torn the flesh off those men in that state of terror. I moved slowly not to show fear, then quickly put my son in the car and drove away.

The next day, the administration department confirmed that they carefully screen the outside prison work crews to be sure they weren't high risk and were legally allowed to work outside of our homes. And sometimes inside. I'm pretty sure I missed this detail in between my hostage training and checking fences. But working at the prison made me feel like a real provider for the first time, mostly because of these crazy-ass sacrifices I had to make.

When I resigned and had no job to turn to, I understood the pressure men felt. I had four options; find a job, and commute forty-five minutes one-way, move to my mom's house, turn tricks, or commit a federal felony transporting a few pounds of methamphetamine with friends. Finding a job would take time, not having suffered enough yet, I wasn't ready to move us back to my mom's house. I still couldn't turn tricks, but in a moment of desperation, I agreed to transport the drugs.

Fortunately, I had enough sense to chicken out at the last minute. No matter how much I tried to be that gangster about my situation and pretend I didn't care, I knew the law, and that a federal indictment wasn't worth a drug dealer's wage.

I got lucky and found a job working as a security guard for a casino in Palm Springs, California, less than a month later. Soon, our lives were as stable as they could be, considering I was still learning the ropes of adult-single-parenting.

* * * *

At the age of eight, my son was accused of "inappropriate behavior" because another child at his daycare saw him helping another younger child, a girl, pull her pants up in the bathroom.

Once all of us parents spoke and cleared up the misunderstanding all was right in our little daycare world. Though I was impressed by how well the child's parents educated him, I realized I needed to do the same for mine to be sure he fully understood why his behavior caused such a harsh accusation. Without any criticism towards him or his actions, I sat him down and explained rape, molestation, std's, sex, and then prison.

My only intentions were to educate him and keep him safe and free as an adult man. I'd have to live with sacrificing a portion of his innocence to do it. For the next twenty years, and by the seat of my mom-pants, I did all I could to be sure he avoided predators and prison.

BOYS GROWS UP TO BE SOLDIERS

Unsure which time it was, somewhere around preteen age, that my son threatened to go live with his dad, and for the first time, I considered the idea.

MJ was now married to Terri, a wonderful black woman my age who believed in a secure family unit, even a blended one. She'd shown her love and loyalty for my son and me over the years.

It was because of his marriage to her that I couldn't deny MJ the parental role of full-time dad. The only reason I hadn't already sent our son to live with him was because of my fear of the unknown.

Who would I be if not a stressed-out single mother? My biggest accomplishment thus far was having a kid too young and keeping him alive. A most selfish reason to keep a child from living with their dad.

The day had come, and I finally understood how Riva from "Boyz In The Hood (Singleton & Nicolaides, 1991)" felt. I wasn't willing to bet my son on my pride and accepted that my baby grew to need his dad more than me. Granted, MJ was no Lucious by any means, but he grew up in Los Angeles, California, and knew how to keep our son safe.

I was a proud mother when he graduated from high school and not a father-to-be. Although he was a borderline genius, he never wanted college. Unsure what he wanted to do after high school, he picked up a couple of part-time jobs that seemed to contribute more to the lack of his motivation.

When he turned nineteen, he came to visit for a few weeks and announced that he was going to join the Army.

My first thought was, "Whose fucking fault is this?" to

blame someone, but my second thought was, "Bitch, yours!" And shut my self up.

I kept silent for the first few seconds after his announcement, and it made him visibly uncomfortable. He could never shut me up.

"Not active duty mom, only the reserves for now," he added.

"Doesn't make me feel better, but thanks," was all I could say. I'd be a hypocrite to say much else since I chose to risk my life to wear a badge too. A couple of them.

It'd been six months since I began to work with Staci and Laci, and needed to choose my words very carefully. All his years growing up, I had nailed every speech a young boy needed. From shaving to fighting, masturbation, and porn, even what happens to a man's scrotum when cold, but this one I never expected. I assumed that by watching me live a paranoid, paycheck to paycheck, traumatized life in a uniform, he would want better and chose a better career and life.

During his rebellious teenage years, I feared that he'd veer off course to a prison career and advised him to join the military to find something positive to do with his life. It was old school advice I once heard my dad give to one of my cousins. Without even thinking, I blurted out the words in complete desperation.

My son's face anxiously waited for me to impart some wisdom upon him, and I scrambled my mental Rolodex of what to say next. All I could think to say to him was something I once heard Macke tell his son when he too joined the military. The most honest words someone can offer another when choosing to become a soldier, no matter their gender.

It was the hardest conversation I never thought we would

have. I sighed and took a deep breath to control my emotions, looked him in the face, then spoke to him like any other man and not my son.

"You do understand that the military trains killers? They will expect you to engage in violence, and kill when instructed to do so. That includes women and children. Are you prepared for that? Do you think you're capable of that?" Fighting the mom in me, I paused.

His eyes grew big, perhaps from the shock that those were the only words I had to offer him. We put a pin in the depressing conversation and went out for a family dinner, determined to enjoy our short family visit. Neither one of us mentioned the subject of his enlistment for the rest of his visit. Even before he left, he didn't speak of it, and I was confident my speech had changed his mind.

We had this conversation just weeks shy of walking into that courtroom and witnessing Gordon's trial, all I'd ever known about raising a man was about to change.

"Mom, I signed my papers," my heart sank, listening to him say the words less than a month later.

"I'll be leaving for boot camp here in a couple of months," he sounded so excited.

"Did you think about what I said?" My voice cracked for one last plea.

"Yes, and I decided to go still. I know it isn't what you want, but I have to go for me." His words were confident and bold.

"I understand. Come see me before you leave." What else could I say? It was his life. No one could tell me not to suit up either.

When we were off the phone, I remembered back to when he was twelve, and I worked with a woman whose brother deployed.

* * * *

We were having lunch, and her mother came by to eat with us. As she explained her fear for her son and her resentment for the politics involved, it was an election year, and I made an insensitive joke about one of the presidential candidates.

I was still a self-righteous Christian at the time and felt mighty superior in my beliefs. The mother chimed in for the opposing side, and somehow the topic of homosexuality came up.

"I'd rather my son die at war than worry about him being gay and the troubles he'd face," I said to her in my evangelical voice.

> The attractive older white woman with the prettiest head of silver hair I'd ever seen leaned over the table, looked at me square in my face, and said, "Wait until it's your son. You won't think that way. I'd rather my son die loved than for the ignorance of men who won't remember his name," tears quickly filled her eyes. Pleased with the curse she just bestowed upon me, she leaned back in her seat.

She couldn't have been more right. At that moment, I'd rather he fell in love with a man before enlisting to become an unemotional killing machine like his grandfather and great grandfathers before him.

My comment didn't make me anti-gay. I had many gay and lesbian friends, but as I explained earlier, while seeking spiritual guidance and forgiveness, I made many ignorant and judgmental decisions.

He proudly graduated from boot camp, and for a moment, while taking pictures of him interact with his battle buddies, I felt sorry my dad wasn't around to witness his grandson follow in his footsteps. They were practically strangers, and my stubborn ass didn't bother to call to announce the news he'd joined the military.

We spent the weekend eating junk food and shopping, just he and I.

When I left for the airport and hugged him goodbye, it felt different.

For the first time, I panicked that it could be my last time to see or hug him ever again.

Odd that I never felt this emotion leaving him or my daughter to go battle evil myself, but now that it was his turn, I felt tempted to be a big hypocrite.

Just a week before I sat in that courtroom to listen to Gordon's trial, my son called to tell me he received orders for deployment but wasn't sure where to yet.

I couldn't have been more wrong. This would be the hardest conversation I'd ever have with my son. It was earth-shattering to hear him ask for my information to name me as the beneficiary on his life insurance policy.

If I could've kidnapped him and taken him to Mexico, I would have, and that's pretty desperate for a diluted Latina who doesn't habla.

To know he'd designated me to decide whether he lived or died if tragically put on life support changed everything.

I worked so hard to keep him out of prison that I never

gave one thought to the possibility that I could lose him to war or red-taped politics.

I'd hoped dad not being around would avoid him the bite of the military bug, but here he was infected.

For weeks, I debated whether to call my dad and get his advice. At the very least, ask him to call his grandson and advise what to expect as a soldier, but I was too prideful.

We'd gone four years with successful silence, and I refused to risk more rejection by him. But, it never crossed my mind that the consequence in our cold game of stonewalling would be to run out of time.

In death, it's game over, and your points don't count for shit.

TIMES UP!

My decision to call for a truce and make peace came too late. My father stuck to his stubborn guns and died a couple of months later, with our ties still severed. And honestly, it didn't matter where his soul went. What mattered was that he was gone, and I'd never see him again.

The image of disgust on dad's face, while the disrespectful words proudly ran off my tongue at him, forever stained in my memory. Him deserving of every bit of it was beside the point.

My stepsister put the phone to my dad's ear the first night he was in the hospital, and I was able to tell him how much I loved him. His garbled words ended with a distinctive 'I love you' sound. It was the last time I'd ever hear his voice. Almost a week later, he went home and died.

The many stages of grief deceitfully imply there's an end

to it somewhere, but I'll be cursed with uncontrollable-waves of emotions over his death until I fucking die. Agitation, disbelief, shock, apathy, numbness, sadness, powerlessness, lots of shame, and guilt with a heaping spoonful of betrayal. Anger was my most displaced emotion. I couldn't differentiate who I was angrier at; God or him.

It was hard for me to believe he'd die without making things right between us. How could God allow him to die after all my acts of service without fulfilling the promise of restoration? What about all the time, sacrifice, tithes, and offerings? None of it won me any favor in those final moments with the man I'd given so much loyalty and forgiveness to in the name of Jesus.

Even if I had the extra money to make the trip to be by his side and for his funeral, I couldn't go. I knew there was a small risk that his final words could be cruel and haunt me for the rest of my life. Some people die just as disgraceful as they lived their lives.

He'd already ordered me almost a decade prior, that once he passed, I was to stand down and stay that way.

"When I die, I don't want you bothering Mary. Whatever is left of mine when I die belongs to her, and you don't contact her for anything." Dad's words were stern, and I promised to honor his request at all costs. I did what he ordered like a good soldier and stayed away, even from his burial.

It wasn't easy, but I knew had I disobeyed and went anyways I'd start a fist-fight in the cemetery with an old cripple woman while she sat and mourned in her wheelchair, sucking on oxygen.

For years I yearned for his approval, and now, I'd never get it. But who was I if I wasn't that girl trying to get her dad to approve of her? Or his disapproval?

* * * *

After his death, I learned that his mother, my biological grandmother, was very cruel to him as a child, and their relationship was known to be very toxic all his life. There were rumors of sexual abuse by his parents.

His misogynistic comments may have been just a bitter cry for help and that he too was an abuser for his own set of dysfunctional reasons.

Not long after my seventeenth birthday, while watching an old VHS movie, a porn movie started to play. Dad labeled his porn because he recorded them on the same tapes as non-porn videos, and I'd forgotten this particular tape had one.

It was trans-sexual porn. If that wasn't confusing enough for my prudish upbringing, the trans-sexual star of this film was a black transgender woman, and the other woman was white.

Like any other horny and curious teenager, I watched the adult movie to the end. It was evident at that moment that dad was hiding something, or someone, deep inside him, I had no idea existed. And he wasn't a real racist.

That porn movie awakened many emotions in me as a young girl, I was both afraid and aroused by the man with lady parts who seemed to have the best of both worlds. I wondered for years why my dad had such a movie.

Months later, he popped a question that took me until his death to figure out.

"What would you do if I wanted to be gay?" he asked me after I got home from school one afternoon. He was sitting in his chair watching Geraldo.

Just weeks prior, he pierced one of his ears and started to grow out his beard. I assumed retiring from the military brought out a rebel in him. But none of these prepared me for that question.

"I don't think I would care—I think. Why?" I answered curiously and unsure of what else to say.

"I'm watching this show, and this man decided to be with a man. It's interesting. Just wondered what you thought," dad chuckled to pass off his question as just casual conversation with me.

It haunts me to think that he suppressed his desire to avoid my judgment.

DAD THE CALABAI

Seven months before his death, I heard through the grapevine dad was less than two hours from me visiting relatives. He didn't contact me the entire visit.

I felt tempted to drive to my cousin's house, kick in her door and make him talk to me, but couldn't risk being escorted away in handcuffs only to be still rejected by him. Though, I also could've swallowed my dam pride, knocked, and allowed the rejection to live with knowing that I tried. And because I couldn't give him, my only dad, the man who selflessly risked his life to provide for mine, more gratitude than a stranger on the street, I get to live with not making peace with him for the rest of my life.

Months after he died, I grew obsessed with what happened to him in those final moments and called the military base for his medical records. The gentleman on the phone read me the notes from a few months prior.

Dad had been to the hospital several times in the few years

before his death. Several health problems were listed but nothing out of the ordinary for a man his age with lung damage from years of smoking. But, when he got to the notes of the last hospital admittance, his tone changed.

"He was picked up at five o'clock a.m. by the ambulance and taken to a local hospital," he paused like the notes were illegible.

"He was in distress and couldn't breathe," he paused again before listing all the signs dad's body was failing.

"That sounds like he was almost dead," I gasped, but not at all shocked.

"Yes, he was in severe distress from what the notes state. There's also a note from the doctor written forty-five minutes after admittance that 'no family was present.'"

We couldn't see each other, but he knew what I did, my father's death was suspicious, and the only one who cared was the doctor who wrote the note.

"Thank you for clearing that up for me. Just confirmed what I already knew." I said to him before he offered his condolences, and we hung up the phone.

Dad couldn't accept that he wasn't going out in a blaze of glory with his battle buddies while engaged in a heated scrimmage or war. And possibly why he allowed himself such suffering until the end.

I'll never know whether his bitterness towards me was his disapproval of my life or his own. Perhaps his fear, and the shame, to explore his bisexuality, or homosexuality, or trans-gender desires, made him regret fatherhood in the first place.

* * * *

One afternoon working at the prison, I sat on a stump near a dorm with some co-workers. A petite Latin man, no more than five feet and four inches, weighing one-hundred and twenty pounds, approached speaking Spanish specifically at me. My co-workers laughed at me, staring back at him, confused because I wasn't bilingual, and a couple of them were.

"Yo hablo un paquito" was all I could say to him.

"He's asking if you'd show him where his bunk is," Hanson said, showing off. She responded to him in Spanish with what I could only assume was the assurance I'd assist him. He smiled relieved.

I noticed after opening the door to his dorm that there was a prison-issued bag already sitting on the bunk assigned to him. Strange. Why would he ask if he already knew?

I pointed to his bed and told him, "Aqui," then smiled at him before leaving. He smiled back at me and gave me a most gracious "Gracias."

When I got back outside the dorm and noticed there were an unusual amount of men grouped around but dismissed it because a group of prisoners played volleyball on the other side of the building.

I went back to my co-workers, who immediately started to laugh at me again.

> "Faciane, you didn't notice? The guy had boobs!" one of Hanson's buddies blurted out. He was from another shift and never worked with him before. We weren't allowed to acknowledge transgender women as feminine or 'girls.' If they had a penis, we were to refer to them as men.

"What?" I asked, confused with no clue what was so dammed funny. Then it hit me like a ton of bricks. The guys were grouped around the dorm to get some action from the new transgender woman, and she was right to be nervous about the crowd. And why she came to get me to create a diversion. She must've been taking hormones before her incarceration because she had a visible set of size B breasts that somehow I missed.

I hurried back to the dorm to watch everyone until the game was over but kept my eye on her until I went home. As long as I was in her sights, she was confident to talk with the other prisoners. Within weeks she became the lady of the yard. She earned extra money providing prisoners housekeeping services, ironed their clothes, cleaned their living spaces, and cooked their spreads. She was happy every time that I saw her.

One of the other female guards had to confiscate her homemade thong, and we both felt terrible having to throw it away. It was quite impressive. The prison was the one place she could be herself with no judgment, and once dad died, I wondered if the military provided him with the same refuge.

* * * *

In Bugis society, they recognize five genders, and their culture requires all coexist harmoniously. Gender assignment at birth isn't a defined or required gender role in society. For example, the Calabai gender is generally assigned male at birth but takes on the role of heterosexual females. Their fashions and gender expression are distinctly feminine but do not match that of "typical" cisgender women. Calabai embraces their femininity and live as women, but do not think of themselves as female, nor wish to be female or feel trapped in a female's body, and still respected by society. Family supports them, and men accept them as males, living in the feminine embodiment.

After discovering this beautiful society of people, my dad's secret finally made sense, and I couldn't help but wonder if I was a real feminist or just a pissed off abandoned daddy's girl plagued with a dysfunctional dose of penis envy.

8.

Ceasefire-My Encore

CEASEFIRE – MY ENCORE

FOR RAYMOND

"Marvin Wolgang and Franco Ferracuti (1967), in their now-classic 'The Subculture of Violence,' refers to the "culture within a culture" that exists among some ethnic and lower-class groups and demonstrates favorable attitudes toward the use of violence as a means of resolving interpersonal grievances. In such subcultures, violence is viewed as a necessary means of upholding one's masculinity: "Quick resort to physical combat as a measure of daring, courage, or defense of status appears to be a cultural expectation, especially for lower socioeconomic class males of both races" (Wolfgang & Ferracuti, 1967, p. 189). The Southern United States has traditionally had higher rates of homicide than other regions of the country. This has led some to view the region as imbued with a subculture of violence. Not coincidentally, the South also has the highest rates of firearm ownership. A rival explanation for the higher murder rates in the South may relate to the fact that poorer emergency medical services exist there than in other regions of the county (Doerner, 1988; Doerner & Spier, 1986—Hagan, Introduction to Criminology, Theories, Methods, and Criminal Behavior page 232-233

In 2012, to carry a firearm as a bounty hunter, we had

to qualify through the Sheriff's department Firearms training course, which required an applicant to fire something like one-hundred rounds of live ammunition within so many minutes, so much distance, etc. That's a lot of fucking shooting.

So much, that after one practice session with a fellow bounty hunter and firing numerous rounds from three separate firearms, a 9mm and .45 semi-automatic and a .38 special, that carrying a firearm had lost its shine.

It didn't take long to see less than lethal weapons were also effective to deter an attack while doing my job. But the most effective weapon we ever used was a video camera because most of the people we encountered didn't want to engage in violence. Even more so, there'd be video evidence of them carrying any out.

* * * *

In the 1990s, kids killed their classmates, before, during, and after school, but I don't recall our parents, the schools, or the media, making it a topic for discussion.

Until 1991 I had no clue what it was like to mourn the death of anyone, let alone a classmate who died from a fatal gunshot wound. Raymond Avila's death would mold and shape my life forever, as well as the lives of all who knew and loved him.

It was the end of the school year, about a week from prom night, and Raymond Avila, a Latin boy, and his long-term girlfriend, voted the senior class king and queen.

He was a popular star athlete with a promising career in any sport of his choice, supported by a loving family, adored by everyone, and a model honor roll student.

When I arrived at school that morning, it felt like I stepped into the twilight zone. The entire senior class and a mixture of all the other grades were gathered in the main quad area, sobbing and hugging one another. Even the hardcore football jocks cradled themselves, sitting on the benches while weeping. Raymond had been found dead just hours before in a car with a fatal gunshot wound. We were all devastated.

The bell had rung, but none of us moved. The voice over the speaker that always greeted us with cheer every morning sounded heartbroken. He asked that we all start towards our respective classrooms, but still, no one moved.

Raymond was a close relative to my good friend Lena, and after a few minutes, I walked towards the lockers to find her to give her my condolences. My friend Kari spotted me and ran over with a look of horror on her face.

"Do you know what happened to Raymond?" she screeched, trying to control herself.

"N-n-noo," I heard myself stuttering.

"It was Bobby. Remember that party we went to and the guy you kissed? It was him. He and Raymond got in an argument, and Bobby shot him last night."

My stomach started to churn, and that's when I began to cry.

Bobby was a cute boy who had light-skin and green eyes and already graduated from high school. Bobby had been released from juvenile just weeks before the party Kari, and I snuck out of her house to attend. He and I made out in the back room of the house for about an hour until he realized he wasn't going to get sex from me. He left the party shortly after.

I only saw him one other time at the high school visiting friends, but when I tried to say hello, he ignored me. Kari informed me later that Bobby told the guys he didn't have sex with me because I was on my period. Jerk. Disgusted and embarrassed, I vowed never to mention it again to anyone.

Kari and I stood there for a moment to share a brief silence before separating to our classes. I'm still not sure if my guilt was from associating with a killer or that I wasn't a victim of Bobby's too. Petrified to admit to anyone that I knew him, including Lena, whom I never found that day. At such a young age, I had no way, or resources, to process what an impact this tragic event made on my life or the displaced guilt I felt because of it.

It still feels like a dirty secret. Less than a month later, I met Giovanni.

In time, I grew to accept that most of us are only six degrees of separation from a cold-blooded killer. After my dad's death, I couldn't go on without answers to my questions, and less than a year later, I decided to write Steve Gordon.

DISCLAIMER:

This next section has sensitive content. I don't intend to be insensitive, offensive, or provoke any further emotional distress onto the families and loved ones of the victims, Kianna Jackson, Josephine Vargas, Martha Anaya, Jarrae Estepp, and Sable Pickett. I share this part of my story with compassion and empathy for everyone involved.

These conversations are research with no intention to exploit either side of this tragic coin further. I chose to seek out these conversations to better understand one's evil acts with hope, at the very least, of finding ways to stunt its growth.

I have the utmost respect for these women. To keep them, and others like them, from being forgotten, I volunteered to expose myself to further trauma.

This next section includes excerpts of my corresponding letters with Steve Gordon, who has permitted me to share our conversations. I do so with the respect that this his truth because I, we, cannot learn from him any other way.

They are edited for content.

If this makes you, the reader, uncomfortable, I ask that you close this book now, and thank you for your time.

"The problem of evil is a very big mystery, indeed. It does not submit itself easily to reductionism. We shall, however, find that some questions about human evil can be reduced to a size manageable for proper scientific investigation. Nonetheless, the pieces of the puzzle are so interlocking, it is both difficult and distorting to pry them apart. Moreover, the size of the puzzle is so grand, we cannot truly hope to obtain more than glimmerings of the big picture. In common with any early attempt at scientific exploration, we shall end up with more questions than answers"—M. Scott Peck, M.D. 'People of the Lie,' pg.

LOST IN A MIRROR

I understand the emotional roller-coaster and the devastating impact as parents we can make on our children; our unforgivable mistakes never to be forgotten. Not one of us makes it out of our childhood unwounded or as a parent, without the battle scars of guilt.

But how a man, father, and husband could one day snap and use his hands to snuff out the lives of five girls, most old enough to be his daughters, reflected too much of my family history not to have questions.

Lowering my guard and building a level of friendship with Steve would require me to unlearn all that I held in high regard to being a productive member of society. Starting with my judgment.

A challenge for me, but only Steve, and others like him, had the insight to what provokes that kind of monstrosity and how to, possibly, keep someone else from repeating it.

12-26-17 Me

Dear Mr. Gordon,

I hope this letter finds you well. My name is Roni Faciane, and I was a bounty hunter assigned to locate and arrest Kianna Jackson when she became a fugitive on her last bail bond. Long story short, I built a rapport with her mother and watched your case from the sidelines.

I would like to build a rapport with you to understand better what men (and women) in your position would have done had they more options and better resources.

The points you built your case, one being how parole agents monitor sex offenders, should be expanded upon with more diligent research and effective solutions.

I'd like to pursue changes in legislation that will better monitor transient offenders as well as implement better rehabilitation programs that educate both men and women on sex addiction and offenders.

If this sounds like something you'd like to be included in awesome, if not, I respect your decision and won't bother you again.

1-23-18 Steve

"I had mixed emotions to answer back. For one, trusting people is very hard for me. So I need some confirmation from you, as to you being a bounty hunter and investigator. I would love to help you with the efforts you mentioned. All I want is the truth to be

known and not called a liar, like the interviewer of 'Dateline' did to me.".

"The Silence of the Lambs (Demme & Utt-et al, 1991)" was the only movie to frighten me with nightmares, though Steve was no Hannibal, communicating with him was intimidating all the same.

There was no way I could convince people that conversing with a killer for personal research was reasonable or necessary. Very few want to hear what men like Steve have to say, and trying to convince them otherwise is pointless.

I respected Steve's caution. It let me know the odds of him playing mind games with me were much slimmer than I had predicted.

As he requested, I sent him a couple of news articles from the Blass incident to confirm my identity.

2-5-18 Me

Thanks for the response. I totally understand about trust issues; I have them as well.

As you will read in the articles (my proof of identity), I'm a former corrections officer who worked for a CCF Men's Institution many moons ago. I understand that putting things to paper may be difficult for many reasons, personal and legal, but at some point, and not just for me and my cause, you should.

Your story should be told, if not so much about your crimes, but how you got there.

2-21-18 Steve

"I will try to answer all of your questions. All I ask is you don't

call me a liar. When I tell someone the truth, and they throw it back in my face, that's what angers me the most. Nobody knows why I represented myself, but an ex-girlfriend of mine said something to me back in 1997. When I was arrested for this, I asked my Attorney at the time to see something in evidence, and she refused.

It was then that I decided to represent myself.

Before I end, I just wanted to say one thing, you may or may not have heard my, how do I say it, displeasure for the police? But I find it absolutely crazy that the courts pay bounty hunters to go and find fugitives. Now what I mean is you said you were the bounty hunter to track down Kianna. If it was for prostitution or a small drug case, that's crazy.

That's the problem with the U.S. Get everybody in the system, and they don't care for what just get them into the system."

Because I chose to pursue this research as a student of criminology and not a branch of the law, I gave him the respect he asked for and the trust of his truth.

In my world, any man who puts himself on death row is worthy of my listening ear. That doesn't mean there aren't other traits we could pick apart within his character, but I don't know anyone who doesn't get upset when falsely accused.

I, myself, don't appreciate being called a liar either and have lashed out violently to prove so. (See Bullet 6)

Coping with the consequences of a false accusation, especially many times over, would make any sane person hostile.

3-10-18 Me

I will respect your request and not call you a liar. Not that

there should be a problem with questioning your honesty here, your truth is what I am looking for. As a student of criminology/science and not as the law or the media.

You mentioned in 1997 a girlfriend made a statement that encouraged you to represent yourself 20 years later? Was she someone you respected?

I only ask because you connected this person to such a huge decision in determining the fate of your trail. I'm curious about what you saw in evidence but understand the sensitivity of that information.

Let me first say that I'm a military brat. My dad was in the Army for almost twenty years, law enforcement more than likely was inevitable for me and probably a lot of others raised in a home-like mine.

I agree that its bullshit to criminalize prostitutes, and it's not the courts that hire bounty hunters but the bail bondsman.

Bounty hunters are private citizens exercising their rights stated in Penal Code 837.

4-8-18 Steve

"You asked about a girlfriend I had, that said something to me in 1997, that encouraged me to represent myself 20 yrs later, you asked if I respected her. Not only did I respect her, but she was also the only girl I truly loved, and because of 1992 were taken from each other.

You said at one point I'll need to talk about what I saw in evidence, to help change certain injustices within the system. The injustices of the system are public defenders and paid attorneys who only care about money. I have so much info in my head, to help the families to all this corruption crap, attorney's parole, and probation and the thing with what happened to me and Cano in Nevada."

I hoped assuring Steve I was only interested in his side of the story would avoid any misunderstandings in my intentions writing to him.

And, by giving him some insight about myself, he might trust I wasn't looking to exploit him. I wasn't afraid to divulge a few intimate details to my life because, in my experience, that's how to establish trust.

If I wanted him to give a little, I had to be willing to give a lot more.

Steve, like most prisoners, wasn't a threat to my psyche. I've associated with men a lot more dangerous than him. His co-defendant Frank Cano, on the other hand, is another kind of evil. It glares out at you through his eyes.

But I do know because prison infects people then grid-locks all the good they can do, sometimes being bad is all they left. I've personally seen this happen too many times.

If I had my way, former felons would be allowed in law enforcement. If we can turn cops to felons, why not felons to cops? I'm pretty sure things couldn't get much worse. Just sayin'.

Better yet, how many cold cases would be solved if we gave them to prisoners to investigate? Most cases are unsolved due to a lack of evil imagination and not unreliable information. Like it or not, only a real criminal mastermind can think enough steps ahead to catch another criminal mastermind.

5-9-18 Me

I understand that public defenders have a bad reputation, and people without money for court costs have their own horror stories to share.

People, including myself at one point, always accuse the system of being "broken," and it's not. It's designed that way. That's why I suggested you write about your experiences in the system as well as your life.

You may spark a change in the future.

You mentioned Nevada and the Feds with Cano, is this a separate case? I don't want to overstep my bounds with any information for the current case either, but I remember in court you saying something about Nevada.

I only attended a couple of days and don't recall all the details. I wasn't aware the Feds were involved at all.

You may not like cops or the system, but you believe in justice, and took big steps to try and dispense some. At least in my opinion.

I've spent enough time in those courtrooms as an observer and haven't seen anyone push so hard to make their wrongs right in a courtroom.

I saw someone who felt remorse and wanted others held responsible for their actions too.

I could be wrong, but until proven otherwise (or you tell me I'm wrong), that's what I'm going with.

I do have a few questions, and again if they are too personal, disregard them. I'm pretty open to some questions also if you have them.

Do you think mothers more than fathers affect men who are violent with women?

Have you had experience with violent women?

I know you're attracted to women of other ethnicities, but was that in secret, or did you always openly date outside of your race?

Do you think if society was more open about sex addiction and saw it as a disease more so than an evil possession, most offenders could be rehabilitated?

And if you had had a place to live, a job, and someone to love you when you got out of prison, do you think you would have committed those crimes?

8-9-18 Steve

"I went pro-per for a lot of reasons, one, she (the public defender) wanted to use the girls' profession, as part of my case because of the risk they are taking.

Two, blame my co-defendant for everything, and I wasn't having any part of that.

Franc and I got arrested in Las Vegas for failing to register, and that's how we got a federal case.

I could never find a girl outside my race to go out with me! Before this case happened, I used to go get my boss's lunch, and I was at a Chipotle and met a Hispanic girl, which I tried to set up with Franc, but she was more interested in me. I didn't pursue her because one, she was in her early twenties, and I was forty-five, and two, my parole situation at the time. In my opinion, most offenders can't be rehabilitated.

I have had experience with a violent woman!! I never dated a woman like that.

She came over late one summer night. She was very pissed when I didn't wait for her to come back from 3 weeks in Texas, that she told me about at the last minute when we had been going out for months.

She took the screen off my bedroom window, and came into my room and basically said 'we're having sex.' To make a very long story short, my niece called and wanted a ride, and because she thought it was another girlfriend she grabbed the phone receiver and hit me in the face with it. Well, that was the end of our relationship.

At first, when I got out and parole said to me when I got to the office I would be sleeping on the street, I was pissed beyond belief, but after a while, I was actually more comfortable sleeping on the street.

But Roni, I did have a job at the time of my arrest. It's really hard to answer the last part of your question; I had so much anger flowing through me. From my first true love, my wife and daughter, to my conditions of parole, filing bankruptcy, then having the IRS tell me I owe them more than $1,000 for back taxes. I felt the anger rising, rising, and I just wanted to take what little money I had and leave, but Franc didn't want to go."

But in my opinion, those offender classes you are mandated to attend are worthless. But you are probably correct, had I no contact with other parolees this would not have happened.

Now don't misunderstand me, he's not to be solely blamed for this shit!!!

I was addressing my envelope when I noticed your Scooby-Doo stamp. That was my favorite cartoon as a kid. I'll keep that stamp."

When I started each letter, I had no idea what questions to ask Steve. Not just to avoid wasting his time, but because I worried about moving around in his mind too fast. I'd have to live with whatever his answers were.

Picking the right questions wasn't my only concern, making sure they didn't imply shame or judgmental was. That would be counterproductive. Even if I never shared these conversations with anyone else, I needed to know for myself.

Was it the girl's race? Does he have issues with his mom? Was he sexually humiliated? Is shame linked to why offenders don't seek treatment? Did being homeless as a family man bring out an animal lurking to devour in him?

Being a self-recovering sex addict myself, I understand that the actual act of sex has little to do with the destructive parts of the addiction.

I attended a sex addicts meeting once. The only woman to show up in a group of at least ten men and within minutes, the facilitator, also a man, politely asked me to leave so I wouldn't discourage the men with court-orders from discussing their addictions.

Growing up in an addiction program myself, I already knew that the primary purpose of those meetings was the right to be free from the burden of judgment while sharing one's secrets and struggles. Some of those guys couldn't be honest with themselves with a woman in the room.

When I left, I realized even in my bravery that I wasn't so ready to share mine with them either.

This type of recovery is more personal and complicated and requires raw and uncomfortable discussions that most aren't ready to have.

In my unlicensed opinion, at the heart of some drug and alcohol addicts, there hides a sex, or love, addict. Drugs and alcohol make it much easier to act out sexually.

We may not die from a lack of sexual gratification, but the temptation to lash out violently may emerge. It, too, is a human need.

Being addicted to NOT having sex can also make one a sex addict. For those judging.

* * * *

While out tracking people, I saw a lot of homelessness and also how easily someone could lose sight of their humanity.

Prisoners' outside lives collapse when incarcerated. Jails and prisons provide shelter, food, and water, but when their sentence is complete, they're thrown to the streets to survive and hunt for the basics themselves, even sex, and savagely if they have to.

After reading Steve's story about his girlfriend, who broke in his room and forced sex on him, I must confess that I was relieved. Because women are just as guilty for not obtaining consent before a sexual act as men are, they, too, are left with the perplexed and unexpressed emotions of feeling victimized. I found it interesting that he didn't mention any feelings of anger towards her. The way his words read, he may have allowed that woman even to dominate him.

Of course, I'm not naive. It's also very possible he beat the shit out of her.

Most men who prey on prostitutes to act out violence usually do so because that's the service they're paying for, the freedom to beat a woman who can't call the police for help. Another reason to decriminalize solicitation.

Personally, and by definition, a domestic violence charge should be inclusive with someone who intentionally avoids beating their loved ones only to pay a sex worker to abuse later instead.

Domestic (noun) – a person who is paid to help with menial tasks, such as cleaning.

Many classify sex as a menial task. I'm just sayin'.

WHEN HOES RULED A WORLD

9-29-18 Me

I had believed in the system and that my jobs in law enforcement stood for something, but since this case, I started to question all of it. Reading that a woman attorney actually wanted to blame the victims for being murdered to create a defense for her client is hard to digest as both a woman and a mother.

Do you think they do this with all of these types of cases? Girls that are in these types of professions just get swept under the rug? Or do you think its most prevalent in cases with multiple victims?

So, the violation was because you didn't register in another state, and the charge was an interstate violation, and the feds got involved?

Regarding your story about the Hispanic girl at Chipotle, you said you didn't pursue her because she was younger. Is it safe to say that you were intimidated that she was interested in you? It's understandable, if so.

Young women like to be wooed by older men, and your situation would have made it a challenge, but still possible. Was Franc not interested in her, or were you not willing to break the guy code?

I believe you when you say most can't be rehabilitated, but do you think it's even more so once they have done some jail time or even before that?

Do you think it can be recognized and changed in adolescence or young adulthood? I appreciate your help in understanding all of this.

And your story about the violent ex, so basically she forced you to have sex with her?

She broke in your house, forced sex on you, and then later, assaulted you? The craziest part of that story, Steve, is that she wasn't afraid of you.

And I don't mean that to be negative, but you couldn't have been some crazed monster if this woman felt she could just attack you without consequence.

If you didn't beat the crap out of her after all of that, that speaks volumes. This is a perfect example of why I asked about rehabilitation for some offenders.

I'm curious if, in those situations, if men had the same support and resources as victims, like women, would they still act out violently later?

Thank you for your honesty about your life on the street. I know that shit can't be easy for any of you.

Maybe I have compassion because I've had to provide for a family and understand the insanity it stirs inside you when you can't.

Would you say those offender classes are useless because they don't address real issues? Or is it because they don't create a safe network for men to not only deal with their issues but continue to work through them once they are in real-life situations?

Are they like other forced programs that don't really allow the addict to take the time or do the work to make real changes in their lives?

10-22-18 Steve

"Roni, I'm gonna tell you something that's one hundred percent the honest truth, those parole agents lied on the stand, and we were given permission to;

1. To sleep at the same place

2. To hang out with each other, and

3. I'll admit not to be in the same car together.

You were a bounty hunter, and you must have friends that are top of the line investigators or friends in parole. Parole is behind one of the biggest cover-ups in Orange County.

Do you remember the sex offender in San Diego County who killed a thirteen-year-old girl and seventeen-year-old girl? His parole officer should've violated this guy over a dozen times, before these girls were murdered, but didn't!

Instead, the agent was promoted to supervisor after this, and guess what parole office he eventually landed at? Yep, you got it correct. The same office that Franc and I were assigned to.

He eventually told our agent, 'Yes, they can sleep at the same spot.'

You should check this out. It's really hard to express what I want to say, because who knows how many people read this before you get it.

I wish you were still living in So-Cal, I can promise you parolees are hanging out still.

Listen, if two or more parolees are eating at the same table at a restaurant, let say, they're in violation. If a parolee is contacting another parolee via cell phone or texting, they're in violation.

Here's what really pisses me off, there was five of us sitting on some grass talking in a business district, the cops rolled up, didn't take us in and didn't call our agents.

Another parolee tried to kill us, Franc called the police, we showed them our tent in the bushes and said, 'that's where we sleep,' they didn't take us in. Riding our bikes, they stopped us again, didn't take us in.

Then a fucking asshole Anaheim police officer called our agent and said, 'You got two parolees hanging out,' and that's what really started this spiral of emotions in the downward trend.

Do you know how sex offenders are bucking the system? They register homeless and live with friends and family far away from where they say they're registering!

Blaming the girls for the defense was bullshit! Blaming my codefendant is no defense either, but taking responsibility and blaming parole officers, cops, and female federal judges was what I knew I should do.

What is your position on the death penalty? Did I deserve the death penalty? Be honest and I won't be upset.

As for the Hispanic girl at Chipotle, I was not intimidated by her age, I was pissed at my current parole situation, and never thought I would meet someone and have to explain why I was on parole and for what.

Those offender classes are worthless, think about it, you're putting anywhere between 8-15 people in these classes, talking and meeting on the street. Exchanging phone numbers to text, and what becomes of that??

Whether we like it or not, Steve is on to something. How much danger can we realistically avoid by putting a bunch of homeless sex offending parolees in the same room to discuss something so personal and private?

Especially those who have already gone to such great lengths to avoid their pain. It seems to me that all these classes are doing is providing a place and opportunity for more killer couples to match up with one another.

As much as I wanted to dig further into this first attorney of Steve's and her should be felonious defense, I know of better ways to fight. It wasn't personal, just her job as the public defender to blame the victim and help the jury swiftly convict her client. The only way to fight back and annihilate her defense was to advocate for sex workers myself.

In Reay Tannahill's *Sex in History*, she explains how, in the late 14th century, the Athenian men divided women into three categories. They had concubines for their daily needs, wives for the children and cleaning, and the hetairai for their pleasures.

The hetairai were top-level courtesans (prostitutes) who were beautiful, witty, and known for their knowledge in economics. The men treated these women with greater grandeur than their wives.

What Athenian men liked the most about this group of women, the prostitutes, was that they excelled at the same things they didn't allow their wives to experience. The wives weren't allowed, like the hetairai were, to join in social gatherings where they could learn the same about culture and economics, thus making the life of the wife unsatisfying and undesirable.

Hetairai could find success in a man's world and live a life of power even more than men because they too didn't have to carry the burden of children and domesticated duties. But when the hetairai become too influential, those Athenian men started to criticize that they were also 'money-grubbing.'

Included in this book is a letter between a sailor and his hetairai where he's trying to shame her for taking his money without any regard for his heart:

"Everything was all right when I could give you fine presents," the sailor wrote.

"Why do you bother writing long letters? I want fifty gold pieces, not letters. If you love me, pay up; if you love your money more, then don't bother me anymore. Goodbye!" the hetairai wrote back.

This conversation is more than five-hundred years old and is quite similar to those in modern-day monogamist relationships.

The hetairai eventually were discarded from society, probably to keep them from having the best of both worlds. Branded as outcasts, we continue to punish and exploit them even centuries later.

When Greene first started to harass Staci, Laci, and I, we

reached out to a woman attorney well known for her feminism and advocacy for women's rights.

Personally making the call to her office myself, I spoke with another woman attorney, an associate, or partner of the company who answered the phone.

She took my information and went through some standard questions to assess the viability of our case to keep from wasting their team's time.

After answering all her questions, I began to explain how the harassment had escalated to endangering my home and family. Without even a breath of hesitation, she interrupted me.

"There is nothing we can offer you. These events, unfortunate or not, have taken place during the scope of your duties, you have to expect some backlash, and it sounds like the attorney is legally defending his client. Good luck to you." And she hung up. My interpretation of her statement was, "That's what you get. Don't do the job if you're going to cry like a girl when the boys are mean to you", and I'm sticking to it.

Steve's attorney sounded like the same breed of feminists. Both of the opinions, "That's what women get for doing that kind of job," and "A girl can be whatever she wants except that which gives her real power and independence."

Giving women, and whomever else, the legal right to sell their bodies allows them economic power and influence, as does the right to protect oneself and others in predominantly male careers (i.e., law enforcement military, etc.)

It didn't matter whether Kianna or I fit in the frames of picture-perfect victimology, we were both victims who deserved better from a system allegedly designed to protect us.

Had I been forced to kill Blass or some drug addict in the alley behind my apartment, hired to mess with my family and me, in self-defense because no one would help until after the fact, the police could still charge me with a homicide

If Kianna, or one of the others, had killed Steve and his co-defendant trying to free herself from their murderous grips, she too could've been charged with homicide.

Maybe I'm the one missing something here, but neither of those scenarios sounds like justice or very much progress for women's rights.

With a practical epidemic of human trafficking boldly growing in our midst, I will continue to advocate that solicitation needs to be legal.

* * * *

Young women are the most feared all over the world.

Even in developed countries, a young woman hasn't the right to her sexual desires or the choice to do as she pleases with her own body until shes well out of her baby-making years. By then, society can pity and not envy her.

Just before I moved to Vegas, I worked briefly for a Realtor who had a fifteen-year-old daughter with budding bisexuality.

Her stepmother broke down over lunch one afternoon while explaining to me how out of control this young girl had become. She was trying to take control of her identity and come into her own. Pissing off her parents in the process was priority number one.

What I heard sounded blatantly familiar since I, too, was branded as the same type of girl interrupted.

She was a cute and polite white girl who didn't look the part of a teen witch by any means, but neither had I.

Leaving the office one night, I noticed I hadn't taken one sip of my very large, now watered-down, iced-tea I bought at lunch. It was a shame to have to waste it.

When I went to the kitchen to dump it, I saw her and her three brothers sitting at the table eating some food waiting for their parents. I greeted them all and asked how their day was, they all responded in harmony with a long sighing "fine" as they continued to devour their food.

Only one of them had a drink, so I offered them my tea while assuring them my germs had been nowhere near it.

The young girl jumped up and took the drink gently from my hands, stared stare deeply in my eyes, then stuck her tongue out to lick the straw before she sipped on it, and sat back down smiling.

Almost disturbed, I had just been sex played by a damn teenybopper, I just stood there.

Girlfriend caught me completely off guard, and I wasn't sure whether to be offended or just to pretend I didn't see what I just saw.

I settled on not shaming her while ignoring her felonious invitation. After I told them all good night, I hurried to get the hell out of there. Rarely do I feel nervous when someone flirts with me, but this was a different situation.

It took some time for me to file her bold and suggestive act in its proper place, to avoid unfairly judging her.

Had it been one of her brothers, I would have brushed

it off as normal horny teenage boy behavior. Boys are accepted, even celebrated, when they act this way, but when girls do, they're shamed and labeled, unlovable, promiscuous, mentally-ill, etc.

That young woman just wanted to be my equal sexually and fearlessly tried to express her adolescent crush. It wasn't her job to fit into my image of how she should do so. My job was to treat her like any other under-aged young person I was too old to date.

I got to keep my power, and she didn't have to fight or rebel for hers.

DEATH DOESN'T CURE EVIL

12-20-2018 Me

Was representing yourself worth it?

As far as the parole agent lying about what you were and weren't allowed to do, I believe you. The rules and procedures are all carried out at the discretion of the individual in charge.

By law, you may not have been allowed to do certain things, but the agent or guard, etc., at their discretion, can allow you and then book you if they choose and when they choose.

Now your story about the serial killer in San Diego, I'm not sure which you are speaking of, but that's fucking insane! He could've stopped the guy from killing by violating him and didn't? Now that truly is "the devil in a detail."

Do you think he let you guys stay together because he didn't care about protecting victims or because he doesn't care about making offenders follow the rules? Enabling crimes to get violations and/or new charges?

There must be a motive for someone in that position. Either they're just lazy or have a motive in my experience.

Wait—-what? Sex offenders register homeless and then live with friends? That's how they get away with not being monitored? And no one checks on them?

How do they decide who gets ankle bracelets? I thought that was part of the protocol, for homeless offenders to wear ankle monitors?

Dam, what a cluster fuck!

You know what's scary to me about false imprisonment, and kidnapping charges are how easy you can get one. I don't know how many times I stopped a man from walking away from me or kept them from leaving my house until a fight was finished.

I too could have caught a case; fortunately I never did, but the thought of how easy that could snowball into a sentence is frightening.

Ten years for kidnapping your wife? Do you mind me asking if that is really what happened?

As far as my take on the death penalty, well Steve, honestly that's a complicated one for me.

Before I walked in the courtroom for your trial I was all for you getting the death penalty, but as it unfolded, I started to think differently.

In fact, I had to rethink the punishment in cases like yours in general.

But for you, I think you should be on the front lines of research into minds like your own and others who, for whatever reason, commit those types of crimes. And then help change policies to protect victims.

That should be your punishment. Doing what you did in the courtroom, forever dedicated to stopping the same crimes from happening to someone else.

I recently read a book about Ted Bundy and truly believe for the millions paid to kill him, they could have used him and that money to better research where murderous behaviors come from. Maybe even prevent some from ever developing.

12-23-18

"So you asked was representing myself worth it? The answers are both yes and no.

Yes, because I can dictate how I want the case to go. Whereas having an attorney, they dictate everything, and like I told you in previous letters, the attorney I had mentioned, blaming the girls because of their line of work, blaming my co-defendant for everything and not bringing up parole or Federal probation at all! And I was not in agreement with her way to make a defense and to be honest, there's not a good defense, she just wanted all the credit for helping the D.A. to send me to death row.

Shit, I can do that myself!

I think you missed my point on that San Diego killer killing those two girls.

That parole agent could've violated him numerous times, but didn't, and eventually he killed these two girls. I'm positive that the agent was promoted to supervisor to the parole office on Coronado in Anaheim.

Which he ultimately permitted Agent Johnson to allow us to sleep at the same spot.

I think you might have misunderstood. I'll try and explain better. When a sex offender completes his parole period, they register homeless, but sleep with friends or family! That's how they beat the system.

If I have any anger towards women, as you have asked, it came from my ex and her mom.

I spent 8 1/2 yrs in prison, with no pictures of my daughter, I got out on parole in 2010, and that female parole agent says I gotta where a monitor,

I said 'what for?', She said 'cause of your prior' I said, 'my prior? that was seventeen fucking years ago?' she said. 'Don't matter, it goes on, or you go back to jail.'

At first, I said, 'take me back,' but her supervisor changed my mind. That female agent I had, also kept me from going to Family Court when I told her I wanted to see my daughter. She said, 'not gonna happen!'

I've not seen my daughter since August 17, 2001, or any pictures. And I'm not making excuses but everything that happened with my ex, parole, then that federal shit; shit happened and went bad really really fast.

Just a friendly reminder, I would not send a letter to me after 1/4/19 as I don't know when they are coming for me for court!

Take care. Steve"

When Steve asked my opinion whether I felt he deserved

his death sentence, I admit it took me a couple of days to write an answer. I'm still not stable in my response to him, even now being conflicted between what I know and what I want to believe. I reserve the right to ask myself the same question every few months to continue to evolve.

It's an impossible task for someone like myself with little knowledge of the post-conviction judicial process to start digging into cases looking for errors or corruption by the hands of parole agents.

The failures in the parole system are unfortunately no secret, and a single person won't fix them. Only many people with legislative power who are willing to listen and make changes can.

For now, I'm mostly interested in Steve's side of the story.

He hasn't written back to me since this last letter.

His story about his daughter made me sad for him, as it has for the many other men and women that share that same heart-break. There's no excuse for his evil acts, or is he using one, but it helps to know there were specifics that nurtured them.

I keep a list of all the questions I still have to ask when he's ready. I'm curious about his opinions on whether inbreeding, penis size, and performance, or an oppressed sexual identity, are associated with the behaviors of psychopathy more so than one's race, ethnicity, or culture.

I'm very thankful to Steve and that he took the time to share his story with me. It was brave, and I commend him. I hope that it provides some healing for him too.

UNDERPRIVILEGED BLOODLINES

Like returning to the scene of a crime, after my father died,

I decided to move back to Colorado Springs, Colorado. My goal for chasing his ghost was to understand him better, or at the least, understand me better.

Swapping my wedges for cowboy boots while surround by soldiers in their fatigues was all I needed to lay his spirit to rest and make some peace with his death.

Occasionally, I have to resist the urge to run up to some random five foot four inches soldier in uniform like that little girl waiting for her dad to come home from work.

There was already snow falling on the ground when I met JT.

When we planned to meet for drinks, I asked that he pick me up to avoid having to drive in the snow. No way I was going to cause a five-car pile-up being an inexperienced dumb ass from California.

He didn't mind at all and drove us to a sports bar up the street from my place. I opened his car door to greet him and saw that he was a devilishly cute white man in his forties with a lightly salted five o'clock shadow, and favored a younger Hugh Laurie.

Immediately I was smitten.

His eyes sparkled both green and blue when he smiled, and I couldn't help but blush. When we arrived, he opened the door like a gentleman, and lead me to the table of his choosing, but then sat in the pinche cop seat before I had a chance to. Dammit! It can be a problematic question to ask a man, especially on a date, whether they're qualified to sit in that seat. Trust me—it doesn't go well.

After sitting down, I noticed that the wall next to us had

a glass window that displayed the perfect reflection of the front door. Problem solved.

We ordered drinks and began our date talk.

Mesmerized with how articulate and educated he sounded, he exuded non-privileged confidence I hadn't seen in a man for a long time. But before I could swoon too far over his head, I heard him say, "I'm a Blood."

Wait—what? A Blood? As in a Blood gang member? This guy had to be shittin' me.

I was positive my dad's spirit was floating somewhere in this bar because, in that exact moment, I could hear his voice say, "Only you could move to this state and find the white guy, in a black gang, with a Latin last name!"

"Aww isn't that cute!" I chuckled at the irony. It was cute. In the many places I'd lived, Blood gang members didn't come in his shade of color. It was a surreal revelation of the kind of race culture I was about to experience in my new home state.

JT giggled at my sarcasm but didn't let it interrupt him.

"I've been out of prison for about a year now. I did almost twenty years," he said, then took a drink of his beer.

Twenty years? Did I just sit down with a fucking killer? Good thing, I was close to home and had my knife in my pocket—a dating essential.

"That's a long time," I said, taking a sip of my drink.

"Do you mind me asking for what?" I asked, trying not to sound startled.

"Someone put a gun in my son and his mother's face, and I tried to set him on fire," he said, showing no emotion.

He had no idea how many cool points he'd just earned himself.

"Wow, I think you're my new hero," I smiled. "My daughter's stepmother beat her, but I filed charges." I paused, taking another sip of my drink.

It was the first time in ten years I could compare authentic parental battle scares with someone, and this guy was winning.

He continued with the positive experiences almost two decades in prison gave him. He had experienced a marriage, a few affairs with female cops, and acquired quite the education. Since his release, he purchased a home, two cars, and paid off all his child support. I was in awe to watch him, proudly share his truth.

It was astonishing how humble he was, and his disposition on life was more optimistic than someone who never stepped foot in a jail cell. Prison may have broken him, but what he rebuilt of himself with the pieces left over was deserving of the utmost respect. We ordered our food, waited, and what he said next was unforgettable.

"I was home for about a week, and someone murdered my son. After twenty years inside, and I still lost him." His words were faint under the sounds of football madness on the other side of the bar, but I heard them. I said nothing, giving him ample room to continue.

His son had fallen prey to the same gang violence he had decades prior, and it killed him at only nineteen years old. Though we were strangers, I felt compelled to sit next to him and hold his hand for comfort while he told his story. Instead, I let him speak, knowing all too well myself that listening was the best thing someone can do in moments like these.

JT's story was even more heartbreaking than mine, and as I watched him explain more about his experiences, I wondered how he did twenty years without a murder charge as a white man. Then it dawned on me, he was affiliated with a black gang, and the mother of his child was also black. It's possible living in a predominately white race state a white man of good Aryan stock spreading, and wasting, his seed amongst the local black folk wasn't appreciated. If they could have stuck him under the prison, they probably would have. That long sentence guaranteed he wouldn't raise his bi-racial son.

The timing of his conviction may have also played a significant role. Los Angeles was wrapping up what is historically called the "decade of death" of gang violence.

I know two black men in California who killed someone, and both served less than ten years during the early 2000s.

Not all whites are that kind of privileged.

My mother once told me to be careful that my revenge wasn't big enough to hit my children. JT's story finally proved that I'd done the right thing ten years prior when I wanted to set fire to Toni and Tyrone but instead called the law for help.

It felt like someone released me from a cage of guilt I didn't realize I had locked myself inside. Guilt for allowing Toni and Tyrone to get away with their abuse by only fighting back with my pen and a prayer.

Finally, able to accept that a part of me will always feel like I got punk'd, and there was no changing that.

I envied JT. Not for doing twenty years in prison, but that

he was able to inflict pain on the person who threatened his child, and I didn't get that right. Fathers are honored and respected for protecting their families, even if they commit a crime in doing so. Whereas for me, as a mother, who followed the rules, I didn't get any of that.

He excused himself to use the restroom before our food arrived while I sat and waited in anticipation. Taking another sip of my martini, I smiled.

I couldn't wait to hear more of his story.

9.

The Curse of Willie Lynch

THE CURSE OF WILLIE LYNCH

STRATEGIC PLANNING FOR SLAVERY

There was a psychological strategy for breaking the mind of the human slave indoctrinated into our American culture at its birth that predicted and promised generations of slaves.

I believe they implemented the same strategy in the prison system, on minorities and poverty-stricken immigrants. Poor white people included.

In the letter below, Willie Lynch gives the details of his perfected module, 'Making a Slave,' and how to effectively use it as a slave making machine guaranteed to provide hundreds, maybe even thousands, of years of slavery with only a few humans.

To show, in my opinion, that this tactic still affects all races, ethnicities, and genders, I have replaced "negro, nigger and black" with "savage or slave."

The curse that continues to enslave us, again, in my opinion, was introduced by Willie Lynch. Our only redemption as a society is to, somehow, reverse it.

Willie Lynch letter: The Making of a Slave

By FinalCall.com News | Last updated: May 22, 2009 – 12:45:37 PM

This speech was said to have been delivered by Willie Lynch on the bank of the James River in the colony of Virginia in 1712.

Lynch was a British slave owner in the West Indies.

He was invited to the colony of Virginia in 1712 to teach his methods to slave owners there.

Greetings,

Gentlemen. I greet you here on the bank of the James River in the year of our Lord one thousand seven hundred and twelve.

First, I shall thank you, the gentlemen of the Colony of Virginia, for bringing me here. I am here to help you solve some of your problems with slaves.

Your invitation reached me on my modest plantation in the West Indies, where I have experimented with some of the newest, and still the oldest, methods for control of slaves. Ancient Rome would envy us if my program is implemented. As our boat sailed south on the James River, named for our illustrious King, whose version of the Bible we cherish, I saw enough to know that your problem is not unique. While Rome used cords of wood as crosses for standing human bodies along its highways in great numbers, you are here using the tree and the rope on occasions.

I caught the whiff of a dead slave hanging from a tree, a couple miles back. You are not only losing valuable stock by hangings, you are having uprisings, slaves are running away, your crops are sometimes left

in the fields too long for maximum profit, you suffer occasional fires, your animals are killed.

Gentlemen, you know what your problems are; I do not need to elaborate. I am not here to enumerate your problems, I am here to introduce you to a method of solving them.

In my bag here, I HAVE A FULL PROOF METHOD FOR CONTROLLING YOUR SLAVES.

I guarantee every one of you that, if installed correctly, it will CONTROL THE SLAVES FOR AT LEAST 300 HUNDRED YEARS.

My method is simple. Any member of your family or your overseer can use it. I have outlines a number of differences among the slaves; and I take these differences and make them bigger, I use FEAR, DISTRUST *and* ENVY *for control purposes.*

These methods have worked on my modest plantation in the West Indies and it will work throughout the South. Take this simple little list of differences and think about them.

On top of my list is "AGE," *but it's there only because it starts with an "a." The second is* "COLOR" *or shade.*

There is INTELLIGENCE, SIZE, SEX, SIZES OF PLANTATIONS, STATUS *on plantations,* ATTITUDE *of owners, whether the slaves live in the valley, on a hill, East, West, North, South, have fine hair, course hair, or is tall or short.*

Now that you have a list of differences, I shall give you an outline of action, but before that, I shall assure you that DISTRUST IS STRONGER THAN TRUST AND ENVY STRONGER THAN ADULATION, RESPECT OR ADMIRATION. *The slaves after receiving this indoctrination shall carry on and will become self-refueling and self-generating for hundreds of years, maybe thousands.*

Don't forget, you must pitch the OLD MALE *vs. the* YOUNG MALE, *and the* YOUNG MALE *against the* OLD MALE. *You must use the* DARK SKIN *slaves vs. the* LIGHT SKIN *slaves, and the* LIGHT SKIN *slaves vs. the* DARK SKIN *slaves.*

You must use the FEMALE *vs. the* MALE, *and the* MALE *vs. the* FEMALE.

You must also have ONE RACE OF SERVANTS *and overseers* WHO DISTRUST *all* OTHER RACES.

But it is NECESSARY THAT YOUR SLAVES TRUST AND DEPEND ON US. THEY MUST LOVE, RESPECT AND TRUST ONLY US.

Gentlemen, these kits are your keys to control. Use them. HAVE YOUR WIVES AND CHILDREN USE THEM, *never miss an opportunity.*

IF USED INTENSELY FOR ONE YEAR, THE SLAVES THEMSELVES WILLREMAIN PERPETUALLY DISTRUSTFUL.

Thank you gentlemen."

LET'S MAKE A SLAVE

It was the interest and business of slave holders to study human nature, and the slave nature in particular, with a view to practical results.

I and many of them attained astonishing proficiency in this direction. They had to deal not with earth, wood and stone, but with men and, by every regard, they had for their own safety and prosperity they needed to know the material on which they were to work, conscious of the injustice and wrong they were every hour perpetuating and knowing what they themselves would do.

Were they the victims of such wrongs? They were constantly look-

ing for the first signs of the dreaded retribution. They watched therefore with skilled and practiced eyes, and learned to read with great accuracy, the state of mind and heart of the slave, through his sable face.

Unusual sobriety, apparent abstractions, sullenness and indifference indeed, any mood out of the common was afforded ground for suspicion and inquiry.

Frederick Douglas LET'S MAKE A SLAVE *is a study of the scientific process of man-breaking and slave-making. It describes the rationale and results of the Anglo Saxons' ideas and methods of insuring the master/slave relationship.*

LET'S MAKE A SLAVE *"The Original and Development of a Social Being Called 'The Negro.'" Let us make a slave. What do we need?*

First of all, we need a savage man, a pregnant savage woman and her baby boy.

Second, we will use the same basic principle that we use in breaking a horse, combined with some more sustaining factors.

What we do with horses is that we break them from one form of life to another; that is, we REDUCE THEM FROM THEIR NATURAL STATE IN NATURE.

Whereas nature provides them with the natural capacity to take care of their offspring, we BREAK THAT NATURAL STRING OF INDEPENDENCE FROM THEM AND THEREBY CREATE A DEPENDENCY STATUS, *so that we may be able to get from them useful production for our business and pleasure.*

CARDINAL PRINCIPLES FOR MAKING A SLAVE

For fear that our future generations may not understand the principles of breaking both of the beast together, the slave and the horse.

We understand that short range planning economics results in periodic economic chaos; so that to avoid turmoil in the economy, it requires us to have breadth and depth in long range comprehensive planning, articulating both skill sharp perceptions.

We lay down the following principles for long range comprehensive economic planning. BOTH HORSE AND SLAVE [ARE] NO GOOD TO THE ECONOMY IN THE WILD OR NATURAL STATE.

Both must be BROKEN *and* TIED *together for orderly production.*

For orderly future, special and particular ATTENTIONMUST BE PAID TO THE FEMALE *and the* YOUNGEST OFFSPRING.

Both must be CROSSBRED *to produce a variety and division of labor. Both must be taught to respond to a peculiar new* LANGUAGE. *Psychological and physical instruction of* CONTAINMENT *must be created for both.*

We hold the six cardinal principles as truth to be self-evident, based upon following the discourse concerning the economics of breaking and tying the horse and the slave together, ALL INCLUSIVE OF THE SIX PRINCIPLES *laid down above.*

NOTE: NEITHER PRINCIPLE ALONE WITH SUFFICE FOR GOOD ECONOMICS. *All principles must be employed for orderly good of the nation.*

Accordingly, both a wild horse and A WILD OR NATURAL SAVAGE IS DANGEROUS EVEN IF CAPTURED, *for they will have the tendency to seek their customary freedom and, in doing so, might kill you in your sleep.*

You cannot rest. They sleep while you are awake, and are awake while you are asleep.

They are DANGEROUS *near the family house and it requires too much labor to watch them away from the house. Above all, you cannot get them to work in this natural state.*

Hence, both the horse and the SAVAGE MUST BE BROKEN;THAT IS BREAKING THEM FROM ONE FORM OF MENTAL LIFE TO ANOTHER. KEEP THE BODY, TAKE THE MIND!

In other words, break the will to resist. Now the breaking process is the same for both the horse and the savage, only slightly varying in degrees. But, as we said before, there is an art in long range economic planning.

YOU MUST KEEP YOUR EYE AND THOUGHTS ON THE FEMALE *and the* OFFSPRING *of the horse and the savage. A brief discourse in offspring development will shed light on the key to sound economic principles.*

Pay little attention to the generation of original breaking, but CONCENTRATE ON FUTURE GENERATION.

Therefore, if you BREAK THE FEMALE MOTHER, SHE WILL BREAK THE OFFSPRING *in its early years of development; and when the offspring is old enough to work, she will deliver it up to you, for* HER NORMAL FEMALE PROTECTIVE TENDENCIES WILL HAVE BEEN LOST *in the original breaking process.*

For example, take the case of the wild stud horse, a female horse and an already infant horse and compare the breaking process with two captured savage males in their natural state, a pregnant savage woman with her infant offspring. Take the stud horse, break him for limited containment.

Completely break the female horse until she becomes very gentle, whereas you or anybody can ride her in her comfort. Breed the mare and the stud until you have the desired offspring. Then, you can turn the stud to freedom until you need him again. Train the female horse whereby she will eat out of your hand, and she will in turn train the infant horse to eat out of your hand, also.

When it comes to breaking the uncivilized savage, use the same process, but vary the degree and step up the pressure, so as to do a COMPLETE REVERSAL OF THE MIND.

Take the meanest and most restless savage, strip him of his clothes in front of the remaining male savages, the female, and the savage infant, tar and feather him, tie each leg to a different horse faced in opposite directions, set him afire and beat both horses to pull him apart in front of the remaining savages.

The next step is to take a bullwhip and beat the remaining savage males to the point of death, in front of the female and the infant.

Don't kill him, but PUT THE FEAR OF GOD IN HIM, *for he can be useful for future breeding.*

THE BREAKING PROCESS OF A SAVAGE WOMAN

Take the female and run a series of tests on her to see if she will submit to your desires willingly.

Test her in every way; because SHE IS THE MOST IMPORTANT FACTOR FOR GOOD ECONOMICS.

If she shows any sign of resistance in submitting completely to your will, do not hesitate to use the bullwhip on her to extract that last bit of bitch out of her. Take care not to kill her, for in doing so, you spoil good economics.

When in complete submission, SHE WILL TRAIN HER OFF-

SPRINGS IN THE EARLY YEARS TO SUBMIT *to labor when they become of age. Understanding is the best thing.*

Therefore, we shall go deeper into this area of the subject matter concerning what we have produced here in this breaking process of the female slave.

We have REVERSED THE RELATIONSHIP; *in her natural uncivilized state, she would have a strong dependency on the uncivilized less than privileged male, and she would have a limited protective tendency toward her independent male offspring and would* RAISE MALE OFFSPRINGS TO BE DEPENDENT LIKE HER.

Nature had provided for this type of balance. We reversed nature by burning and pulling a civilized slave apart and bullwhipping the other to the point of death, all in her presence.

By her being left alone, unprotected, with the MALE IMAGE DESTROYED, *the ordeal caused her to move from her psychologically dependent state to a frozen, independent state. In this frozen, psychological state of independence,* SHE WILL RAISE HER MALE AND FEMALE OFFSPRING IN REVERSED ROLES.

For fear of the young male's life, SHE WILL PSYCHOLOGICALLY TRAIN HIM TO BE MENTALLY WEAK *and* DEPENDENT, *but* PHYSICALLY STRONG.

Because she has become psychologically independent, SHE WILL TRAIN HER FEMALE OFFSPRINGS TO BE PSYCHOLOGICALLY INDEPENDENT.

What have you got? You've got the slave WOMAN OUT FRONT *and the slave* MAN BEHIND AND SCARED.

This is a PERFECT SITUATION *of sound sleep and economics. Before the breaking process, we had to be alertly on guard at all times.*

Now, we can sleep soundly, for out of frozen fear his woman stands guard for us.

HE CANNOT GET PAST HER EARLY SLAVE-MOLDING PROCESS.

He is a good tool, now ready to be tied to the horse at a tender age. By the time a salve boy reaches the age of sixteen, he is soundly broken in and ready for a long life of sound and efficient work and the reproduction of a unit of good labor force. Continually through the breaking of uncivilized savage slaves, by throwing the female savage into a frozen psychological state of independence, by killing the protective male image, and by creating a submissive dependent mind of the savage male slave, WE HAVE CREATED AN ORBITING CYCLE THAT TURNS ON ITS OWN AXIS FOREVER; *unless a phenomenon occurs and reshifts the position of the male and female slaves.*

We show what we mean by example. Take the case of the two economic slave units and examine them close.

THE SLAVE MARRIAGE

We breed two savage males with two savage females. Then, we TAKE THE SAVAGE MALE AWAY *from them and keep them moving and working.*

Say one savage female bears a savage female and the other bears a savage male; both savage females—BEING WITHOUT INFLUENCE OF THE MALE IMAGE, *frozen with a* INDEPENDENT PSYCHOLOGY—*will* RAISE THEIR OFFSPRING IN REVERSE POSITIONS.

The one with the female offspring will teach her to be like herself, independent and negotiable (we negotiate with her, through her, by her, negotiates her at will).

The one with the male offspring, she being frozen subconscious fear for his life, will raise him to be mentally dependent and weak, but physically strong; in other words, body over mind.

Now, in a few years when these two offsprings become fertile for early reproduction, we will MATE AND BREED THEM AND CONTINUE THE CYCLE.

That is good, sound and LONG RANGECOMPREHENSIVE PLANNING.

WARNING: POSSIBLE INTERLOPING NEGATIVES

Earlier, we talked about the non-economic good of the horse and the savage in their wild or natural state; we talked out the principle of breaking and tying them together for orderly production.

Furthermore, we talked about paying particular attention to the female savage and her offspring for orderly future planning, then more recently we stated that, by reversing the positions of the male and female savages, we created an orbiting cycle that turns on its own axis forever unless a phenomenon occurred and reshifts positions of the male and female savages.

Our EXPERTS WARNED *us about the possibility of this phenomenon occurring, for they say that* THE MIND HAS A STRONG DRIVE TO CORRECT AND RE-CORRECT ITSELF OVER A PERIOD OF TIME *if it can touch some substantial original historical base; and they advised us that the* BEST WAY TO DEAL WITH THE PHENOMENON IS TO SHAVE OFF THE BRUTE'S MENTAL HISTORY AND CREATE A MULTIPLICITY OF PHENOMENA OF ILLUSIONS, *so that each illusion will twirl in its own orbit, something similar to floating balls in a vacuum.*

This creation of multiplicity of phenomena of illusions entails the principle of crossbreeding the savage and the horse as we stated above, the purpose of which is to create a diversified division of labor;

thereby creating different levels of labor and different values of illusion at each connecting level of labor.

The results of which is the severance of the points of original beginnings for each sphere illusion. Since we feel that the subject matter may get more complicated as we proceed in laying down our economic plan concerning the purpose, reason and effect of crossbreeding horses and slaves, we shall lay down the following definition terms for future generations.

Orbiting cycle means a thing turning in a given path. Axis means upon which or around which a body turns. Phenomenon means something beyond ordinary conception and inspires awe and wonder.

Multiplicity means a great number. Means a globe. Crossbreeding a horse means taking a horse and breeding it with an ass and you get a dumb, backward, ass long-headed mule that is not reproductive nor productive by itself. CROSSBREEDING SLAVES, *mean taking so many drops of good white blood and putting them into as many savage women as possible, varying the drops by the various tone that you want, and then letting them breed with each other until another circle of color appears as you desire.*

What this means is this: Put the savages and the horse in a breeding pot, mix some asses and some good white blood and what do you get?

YOU GOT A MULTIPLICITY OF COLORS OF AS BACKWARD, UNUSUAL SLAVES, RUNNING TIED TO BACKWARD ASS LONG-HEADED MULES, THE ONE PRODUCTIVE OF ITSELF, THE OTHER STERILE. *(The one constant, the other dying, we keep the slave constant for we may replace the mules for another tool) both mule and slave tied to each other, neither knowing where the other came from and neither productive for itself, nor without each other.*

INMATE-AN AMERICAN SLAVE

Prisons in America are the "orbiting cycle that turns on its own axis forever to continue shaving off the brute's mental history and create a multiplicity of phenomena of illusions" just as Willie warned would be necessary at some point.

During the 1980s, the 'war on drugs' epidemic created quite the opportunity for Corporate Prisons when state and federal prisons were busting at the seams. The government allowed businesses to run prisons to save money and space.

The Corrections Corporation of America, or CCA, was birthed with co-founder Tom Beasley known for his quote (in Inc.); "You just sell (prisons) like you were selling cars, real estate, or hamburgers."

During the same time, getting tough on crime created budget cuts in rehabilitation programs for prisoners. Politicians felt that prisoners weren't deserving of anything, and by cutting hundreds of college degree programs, it created the perfect storm for recidivism.

Privates prisons are known to cite more infractions on their prisoners than government prisons creating longer sentences and gaining higher profits. Also known to embed occupancy clauses into their contracts that require states to keep their prisons full basically. A private prison in Arizona didn't make their capacity quota, and the state government had to pay the prison a three-million-dollar fine. A huge incentive for states to keep people in prisons for as long as possible.

Which means prisoners are paying off state debts, not their own.

Currently, over two million people are incarcerated in the U.S. Ten times more than it was just fifty years ago, and more than most states population.

In an NYU School of Law study, it showed as of the year 2000 that mass incarceration of people had zero effect in decreasing our crime rates.

Solitary confinement is a form of cruel punishment and torture that dramatically affects mental health. Delirium, being one condition known to affect prisoners in general.

Designed by the Quakers as a means of punishment to study the Bible and is as old as the 1800's, but even they concluded it was too cruel to continue its use.

The US Supreme court In re Medley, 1890, declared that "prisoners became violently insane, while others committed suicide."

Solitary confinement fell out of the U.S. for a century, but it was brought back at the turn of the 21st century. Not coincidentally, during the same time, private prisons took over. They know it causes severe and permanent brain damage, but still, over 80,000 people per year, statistically, are subject to it. Supermax prisons, mostly sections within prisons, are nothing but solitary confinement cells that hold several people in mini cages designed like for a pet.

Dehumanizing humans for profit provides no justice for us all.

CONTROLLED LANGUAGE

Crossbreeding completed, for further severance from their original beginning, WE MUST COMPLETELY ANNIHILATE THE MOTHER TONGUE *of both the new savage and the new mule, and institute a new language that involves the new life's work of both.*

You know LANGUAGE *is a peculiar institution. It* LEADS TO THE HEART OF A PEOPLE. *The more a foreigner knows about the language of another country the more he is able to move through all levels of that society.*

Therefore, if the foreigner is an enemy of the country, to the extent that he knows the body of the language, to that extent is the country vulnerable to attack or invasion of a foreign culture.

For example, if you take a slave, if you teach him all about your language, he will know all your secrets, and HE IS NO MORE A SLAVE, FOR YOU CAN'T FOOL HIM ANY LONGER, *and* BEING A FOOL IS ONE OF THE BASIC INGREDIENTS OF ANY INCIDENTS TO THE MAINTENANCE OF THESLAVERY SYSTEM.

For example, if you told a slave that he must perform in getting out "our crops" and he knows the language well, he would know that "our crops" didn't mean "our crops" and the slavery system would break down, for he would relate on the basis of what "our crops" really meant.

So you have to be careful in setting up the new language; for the slaves would soon be in your house, talking to you as "man to man" and that is death to our economic system. In addition, the definitions of words or terms are only a minute part of the process. VALUES ARE CREATED AND TRANSPORTED BY COMMUNICATION THROUGH THE BODY OF THE LANGUAGE.

A total society has many interconnected value systems. All the values in the society have bridges of language to connect them for orderly working in the society.

But for these language bridges, these many value systems would sharply clash and cause internal strife or civil war, the degree of the conflict being determined by the magnitude of the issues or relative opposing strength in whatever form.

For example, if you put a slave in a hog pen and train him to live there and incorporate in him to value it as a way of life completely, the biggest problem you would have out of him is that he would worry you about provisions to keep the hog pen clean, or the same hog pen and make a slip and incorporate something in his language whereby he comes to value a house more than he does his hog pen, you got a problem.

He will soon be in your house.

Additional Note: "Henty Berry, speaking in the Virginia House of Delegates in 1832, described the situation as it existed in many parts of the South at this time:

"We have, as far as possible, closed every avenue by which light may enter their the slaves minds. IF WE COULD EXTINGUISH THE CAPACITY TO SEE THE LIGHT, OUR WORK WOULD BE COMPLETE; *they would then be on a level with the beasts of the field and we should be safe. I am not certain that we would not do it, if we could find out the process and that on the plea of necessity." From Brown America, The story of a New Race by Edwin R. Embree. 1931 The Viking Press.*

References

REFERENCES

I, the author am grateful for permission to use excerpts from the following works of art:

Bullet 1:

Arbys Arrest with Lipstick Bounty Hunters – https://ronifaciane.com/videos

Training Day Movie (Fuqua, Silver & Newmyer, 2001

Inside Edition (CBS Television Distribution, 1989)

John Armstrong, *Conditions of Love, 2002.*

Ghostbusters II Movie (Reitman, 1989)

Menace to Society Movie (Scott & Hughes, 1993)

West Side Story (Wise & Robbins, 1961)

Bullet 2:

Dog the Bounty Hunter (Hybrid Films, 2004-2012)

Flesh and Blood (Verhhoeven &Versylus, 1985)

Up in Smoke (Chong-Adler & Lombardo, 1978)

Bullet 3:

Dream to Believe (Lynch & Kramreither, 1986)

Fatal Beauty (Goldwyn, Jr. & Holland, 1987)

Friday (Gray & Charbonnet, 1995)

101 Dalmations movie (Herek, Hughes & Mestres, 1996)

Natalina Molina, *How Race is made in America, 2014*

Alex Haley, *The Autobiography of Malcolm X*, 1964

Howard Zinn, *A People's History of the United States*, 1980

Inside Edition (Lachman, 1988-present)

Christine (Kobritz, Franco & Carpenter, 1983)

Bullet 4:

Inside Edition (Lachman, 1988-present)

Boyz in the Hood (Singleton, 1991)

Airplane! (Zucker & Davison, 1980)

Sherry Argov, *Why Men Love Bitches, 2000*

Natalina Molina, *How Race is made in America, 2014*

The Ku Klux Klan In Washington State, https://depts.washington.edu/civilr/kkk_intro.htm

Frank Hagan, *Introduction to Criminology: Theories, Methods and Criminal Behavior-9th Edition, 2017*

City Attorney San Bern tells residents to bare arms-https://losangeles.cbslocal.com/2012/11/30/city-attorney-tells-san-bernardino-residents-to-lock-their-doors-load-their-guns-because-of-police-downsizing/

Three California Cities Bankrupt-https://finance.yahoo.com/blogs/daily-ticker/three-california-cities-bankrupt-tip-iceberg-says-fmr-155121281.htm

The Assault Weapons Ban of 2013-https://www.congress.gov/bill/113th-congress/senate-bill/150

SoCal police chiefs on A.B. 109, http://www.pasadenastarnews.com/general-news/20130203/socal-police-chiefs-on-ab-109-this-is-dangerous

California Becomes First State To End Cash Bail After 40-Year Fight-https://www.scpr.org/news/2018/08/28/85760/california-becomes-first-state-to-end-cash-bail-af/

Bullet 5:

The Killing Season (Zeman & Gibney, 2016)

I'm Gonna Git You Sucka (Wayans & Craig, et-al, 1988)

Duval arrest for murder – https://ocweekly.com/daniel-lee-Blass-charged-with-murdering-uncle-at-birthday-party-for-accused-accessory-6463890/

Duval gets sentenced 80yrs – https://www.google.com/amp/s/www.ocregister.com/2017/04/14/westminster-man-who-spent-half-of-adult-life-behind-bars-man-gets-80-years-for-killing-uncle-at-birthday-party/amp/

Gordon Cano caught friends – https://www.ocregister.com/2014/04/24/serial-killing-suspects-friends-for-years/

Gordan/Cano arrest timeline – https://www.scpr.org/news/2014/04/14/43470/2-suspected-serial-killers-arrested-for-murders-of/

Jpiexon pepper gun – http://www.jpxteppergun.net/

Bullet 6:

War of the Roses (DeVito & Brooks, 1989)

California Officers Charged in Drug Raid, 1999 – http://www.mapinc.org/drugnews/v99/n037/a02.html?7912

Inmates are moved after Riot Kills 2 – https://www.latimes.com/archives/la-xpm-2003-oct-29-me-riot29-story.html

Laura King, *The Science of Psychology: An Appreciative View, 2016*

Streets of Fire (Hill & Gordon-Silver, 1984)

John Armstrong, *Conditions of Love, 2002.*

Frida (Taymor & Hayek-et al, 2002)

Pretty Woman (Marshall & Goldsten-et al, 1990)

Jacqueline Brookie Jernigan Obituary – https://www.worthingtonfuneralhome.com/obituaries/Jacqueline-Brookie-Jernigan?obId=8461022#/celebrationWall

Lyrical Reference (Aerosmith, *Crazy, 1994)*

Bullet 7:

Frank Hagan, *Introduction to Criminology: Theories, Methods and Criminal Behavior-9th Edition, 2017.*

Seven (Fincher, Kopelson-Carlyle, 1995)

Video News Clip of Gordon's closing speech before sentencing – https://www.youtube.com/watch?v=-Fa_Ee2ULkM&t=26s

The Good Son (Page & Ruben, 1993)

Home Alone Columbus & Hughes, 1990)

Boyz In The Hood (Singleton & Nicolaides, 1991)

Life in Bugis society https://en.wikipedia.org/wiki/Gender_in_Bugis_society

Ceasefire – My Encore

The Silence of the Lambs (Demme & Utt-et al, 1991)

Frank Hagan, *Introduction to Criminology: Theories, Methods and Criminal Behavior-9th Edition, 2017*

Reay Tannahill, *Sex in History, 1980, Revised 1992*

The Curse of Willie Lynch

Adam Ruins Everything, Season 2 Episode 10, with more information and links – adamruinseverthing.com/prison

Willie Lynch Letter – The Making of a Slave –

http://www.finalcall.com/artman/publish/Perspectives_1/Willie_Lynch_letter_The_Making_of_a_Slave.shtml

Tom Beasley co-founder of CCA interview on selling prisons like hamburgers https://www.inc.com/magazine/19880601/803.html

Made in USA - North Chelmsford, MA
1111086_9781734816143
05.20.2020 1149